The West the Railroads Made

"A Romance of Wonderland." Beginning in the 1880s, railroads often used the term "wonder-land" to draw tourists to the West's many natural attractions. *Courtesy of Special Collections, Washington State Historical Society.*

The West the Railroads Made

CARLOS A. SCHWANTES | JAMES P. RONDA

For Don Jensen
May all your signal lights show green
May all your express trains arrive on time
All good wishes,
Jim Ronda

UNIVERSITY OF WASHINGTON PRESS   SEATTLE & LONDON *in association with*
WASHINGTON STATE HISTORICAL SOCIETY   TACOMA, WASHINGTON *and*
THE JOHN W. BARRIGER III NATIONAL RAILROAD LIBRARY *at the*
ST. LOUIS MERCANTILE LIBRARY   UNIVERSITY OF MISSOURI-ST. LOUIS

"Winds of change" as depicted in the early railroad landscape of Laramie, Wyoming Territory. Wind power used to pump water for locomotives is juxtaposed with steam power. Courtesy of Barriger Railroad Library of the St. Louis Mercantile Library.

COPYRIGHT © 2008

by Washington State Historical Society

Printed in China

Designed by Ashley Saleeba

Typeset in Fairfield

15 14 13 12 11 10 09 08   10 9 8 7 6 5 4 3 2 1

University of Washington Press
P.O. Box 50096, Seattle, WA 98145, U.S.A.
www.washington.edu/uwpress

LIBRARY OF CONGRESS

CATALOGING-IN-PUBLICATION DATA

Schwantes, Carlos A., 1945–

The West the railroads made /

Carlos A. Schwantes and James P. Ronda.

p. cm.

Includes bibliographical references and index.

ISBN 978-0-295-98769-9

(cloth : alk. paper)

1. Railroads—West (U.S.)—History.

2. West (U.S.)—History—19th century.

I. Ronda, James P., 1943- II. Title.

HE2771.A17S39 2008

338.978—dc22

2007029363

Frontispiece: An engine of empire. The camera of Hiram F. Wilcox recorded Northern Pacific locomotive #9 in Spokane Falls, Washington Territory, in February 1888. *Courtesy of Haynes Foundation Collection, Montana Historical Society, Helena, Montana, H-1926.*

Dedicated to David Nicandri and John Neal Hoover

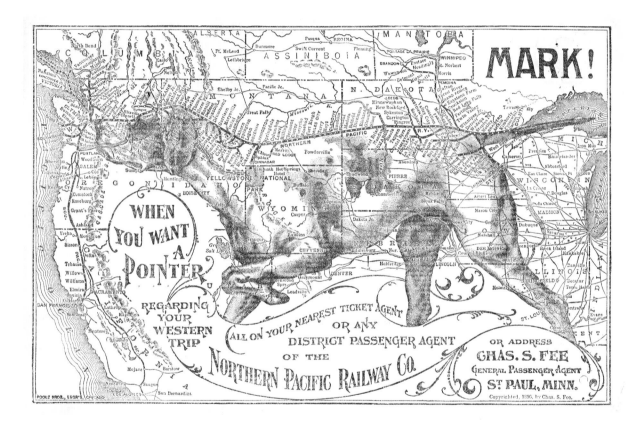

"The Way West," as defined by a cleverly designed Northern Pacific map. *Courtesy of Special Collections, Washington State Historical Society.*

WESTERN
WONDERLANDS

UNION PACIFIC

Contents

Proud employees of the Oregon Railway and Navigation Company personalized their locomotive with lace curtains. *Courtesy of University of Oregon Library.*

A rail road will pass through here, east and west, from the Atlantic to the Pacific: on that road the commerce of Asia will find its channel to our America and to Europe . . . many who are now present will see this road and will ride upon it . . . on to San Francisco.

—THOMAS HART BENTON, "LECTURE ON THE PROGRESS OF THE AGE"

The iron horse is coming, and save for the Savior, the Bible and the Printing Press, he is to do more for man's civilization than any other which has appeared since creation's early dawn . . . thousands of willing hearts and brawny arms are smoothing his pathway from the east . . . Missouri's sons have caught the spirit and are now preparing the iron track, to speed him on his way towards California's Golden Gates, so that ere long he will find an unobstructed pathway from the shores of the Atlantic to those of the Pacific.

—HUDSON E. BRIDGE, ADDRESS AT THE ANNUAL MEETING OF THE
ST. LOUIS MERCANTILE LIBRARY ASSOCIATION

Foreword

SAINT LOUIS AND OTHER CITIES TIED TO THE AMERICAN WEST in the nineteenth century were filled with great dreamers, who dreamed big, planned on a wide scale, and then acted decidedly. These builders of half a continent were impatient. They were full of energy. They possessed strident and boundless vision. For generations thus, the West was imagined as in a dream, and technology and commerce, coming together profoundly in locomotives, was the method by which a dream of commerce, power, and empire would be realized by Americans with diverse plans, agendas, hopes, and broad aspirations to knit up and make over an entire nation. If "America is West," then a huge portion of the American West—geographical, political, and cultural—was forged on tracks of iron and rails of steel.

It is with great pleasure that those of us proudly associated with the Barriger Railroad Library at the University of Missouri's St. Louis Mercantile Library, the home of this great and preeminent collection of railroad history for the past generation, can copublish this important history with our colleagues at the Washington State Historical Society and the University of Washington Press. The collective vision and generous commitment of the Barriger Board of Trustees, the M. J. Murdock Charitable Trust, and co-authors Jim Ronda and Carlos Schwantes has been brought to fruition with a companion exhibition that celebrates the stirring and triumphant story of the ways in which a special chapter of what librarians call "Western Americana" came out of railroad development across the continent.

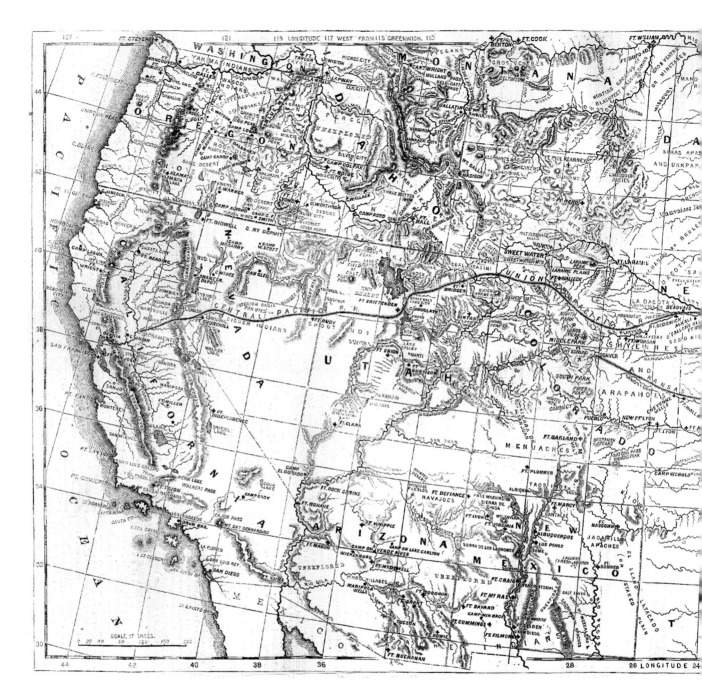

Harper's Weekly provided its readers with a map of the West that showed the "Overland Route" of the transcontinental railroad in mid-1867. Note that the map featured Indian tribes as the region's main inhabitants. *Courtesy of Barriger Railroad Library of the St. Louis Mercantile Library.*

The genesis of this book could be said to have begun in Saint Louis. Long before the last steamboat whistles sonorously blew through its levees and riverfront, and before James Buchanan Eads linked east and west with his great bridge, other track-bound iron monsters, other sounds of whistles and signals and clanging bells, gathered inexorably on the city's east bank. By the 1840s they were clamoring ever more insistently to cross and join the new lines of the "Pacific" railroad already starting to spread across Missouri.

A new, small library in the 1840s, the Mercantile, founded by some of the very first railroad entrepreneurs of the West, would have heard these determined notes. In its chambers (never really as silent as a library was thought should be), excited senators, soldier-explorers, brokers, speculators, travelers, and business leaders met in those years to discuss the latest financial backing, the best grades, the challenges, and the profits by which one city would have its share in making the land over for thousands of miles to the west. The Mercantile holds some of the oldest records and documents, which tell the story of the way the railroads in America succeeded, took shape, forged a national link, and exerted a profound cultural impact on the American nation. This story is the patrimony of a special historical institution.

This early collection, one formed on the doorstep of history itself, was reborn, and tremendously enhanced and enlarged nearly a century and a half later, when some of the Mercantile's own members, the family of John W. Barriger III, first approached the Mercantile with the offer to acquire and develop Barriger's broad collection of railroadiana focusing especially on Barriger's illustrious career. This seminal donation led to an in-depth collection of hundreds of thousands of books, papers, maps, photographs, and art, which in the short span of a generation has reinforced the story of the West the railroads made.

This theme is well reinforced by the broader collecting mission of the Mercantile Library, traditionally an institution that collected the West as part of the heritage of the great metropolis at the confluence of the Missouri and Mississippi rivers. However, this story of a railroad-made West, coursing out of older cities like Saint Louis and Chicago and Omaha, cannot be told by such cities alone, and the Mercantile was indeed very fortunate to have had such an able partner in the Far West itself at the Washington State Historical Society in Tacoma, Washington. Indeed, this book reflects the depth of the collections of these and other institutions that have found the theme of the West so instructive and so mirrored by the growth of a nation.

As to all of our donors and curators mentioned above, I would like to thank the Mercantile's colleagues at the Washington State Historical Society, David Nicandri and Redmond Barnett, and the staff there, as well as the staff at the

Mercantile who brought this work to life. I would also like to thank Thomas S. George, Gloria Leonard, and Robert Mayo of University of Missouri-Saint Louis, our sponsors, and especially the curator of the Barriger Railroad Library, Gregory Ames, who was central and steadfast in his labor to make this work and exhibition possible.

The theme of this exhibition, its protagonist really, is the American West. There are two centuries—and many libraries' worth—of books about the West, and an equal number of books about railroads. There are not many studies of the struggles and triumphs regarding the ways the railroads in America and the West helped shape each other. If this work leads to further inquiry by readers and future scholars, then it succeeds in its original purpose. Through the partnership, collecting vision, and mission of the Washington State Historical Society and the Barriger Railroad Library, the western railroad history, herein offered, is a dramatically accessible story, still evolving and vital to our understanding of a vast, legendary region of our country.

JOHN NEAL HOOVER

St. Louis Mercantile Library

A Great Northern brochure depicted the West as framed by the window of one of its passenger cars. *Courtesy of Barriger Railroad Library of the St. Louis Mercantile Library.*

Various modes of transportation dominate Northern Pacific's art deco postcard image of Seattle in 1930. Conspicuously featured is King Street Station, with its clock tower modeled after the famous campanile in Venice's St. Mark's Square. *Courtesy of Special Collections, Washington State Historical Society.*

One turns towards the east with feelings of regret. This western world is so full of surprises, so full of attractions, so great in its promise and possibilities that one would like to have a hand in the great game of development that he sees going on everywhere about him.

—WILLIAM H. MAHER, *THE GOLDEN WEST: "WHERE MONEY GROWS ON TREES"*

Preface and Acknowledgments

T HE BOOK BEFORE YOU HAS MANY PARENTS. ONE PERSON above all others deserves recognition as its instigator. David Nicandri, director of the Washington State Historical Society, is obviously a serious lover of trains. It is his good fortune that his office in the Washington State History Museum, a magnificent edifice for which he also deserves a generous measure of credit, overlooks the working waterfront of Tacoma and the busy Burlington Northern Santa Fe main line along Puget Sound. The idea for a museum exhibition showcasing "The West the Railroads Made" was David's alone, and it was he who contacted James Ronda and me to suggest that we collaborate as exhibition curators and authors of this book. Ronda, the H. G. Barnard Professor of Western History at the University of Tulsa, had recently curated an exhibition and authored a book called *Beyond Lewis and Clark: The Army Explores the West* (2003) for the Washington State Historical Society.

From my perspective, it was an inspired idea. Though nothing was fixed in concrete when Jim and I began our partnership, as it turned out, after much brainstorming I felt most comfortable writing the three middle chapters that detail the impact of railroads on the Northwest (a region about which I have written for many years), while Jim wrote the two bookend chapters that placed developments in the West in national and international perspective. I have long admired Ronda's work, most notably his numerous contributions to the history of exploration, and to Lewis and Clark in particular. His book *Lewis and Clark Among the Indians* (1984) is a classic text. I also knew that Jim had a passionate behind-the-scenes interest in railroad history. Working with Jim on this book and the exhibition has been both a personal delight and an inspiration. I wanted to list his name first on the title page, but with characteristic modesty he insisted that it be the other way around. Regardless of how our names are listed, this has been a work of collaboration in the fullest sense. I am only glad to play a role in Jim's debut as a historian of railroads, and I thank David Nicandri for being the instigator.

Another project parent deserves to be properly recognized, and that is John Neal Hoover, director of the venerable St. Louis Mercantile Library. While my work with David Nicandri and the Washington State Historical Society extends on several decades, my work with John Hoover, by contrast, covers a relatively brief five years, but it has been no less satisfying. After teaching and writing in the Pacific Northwest for more than thirty years, I relocated to Saint Louis in 2001 to become the St. Louis Mercantile Library Endowed Professor of Transportation and the West at the University of Missouri-St. Louis. In this way I came to recognize John's talents as the builder of the premier center for research on Saint Louis and the American West, and on railroads in particular. As an ambidextrous author,

The Milwaukee Road urged travelers to follow the electrified Trail of the Olympian, the name of its premier transcontinental train in the early twentieth century. *Courtesy of Special Collections, Washington State Historical Society.*

teacher, organizer, fundraiser, and collector, John is without peer, and he has been a vital supporter of the exhibition and book project.

In addition to the enabling skills of David Nicandri and John Hoover, I must hasten to recognize the untiring efforts of curator Edward W. Nolan, head of special collections at the Washington State Historical Society, and Gregory P. Ames, curator of the John W. Barriger III National Railroad Library at the St. Louis Mercantile Library. The illustrations in this book are in large measure a tribute to the incomparable document-finding skills of these two individuals.

Both, by the way, have track records as diligent students of railroad history, and thus they themselves are invaluable sources of information and counsel. Ed is the author of a fascinating book called *Northern Pacific Views: The Railroad Photography of F. Jay Haynes, 1876–1905* (1983) and Gregg's most recent book is *Old Maud: A Life & Times: America's Pioneer Mallet* (2006).

Both Ed and Gregg preside over vast and incredibly valuable collections of railroad ephemera. We historians are fortunate to have these materials preserved and catalogued in public institutions and made readily accessible to researchers. All too often in the past, railroad timetables and promotional pamphlets were treated as little more than throwaway items, but to historians seeking to capture the flavor of times past—and especially to showcase the varied imagery of an era—they are a peerless resource. I only hope that public collections of transportation ephemera continue to grow and multiply.

The purpose of this Southern Pacific tourist brochure from the early 1920s was to transform the "Oregon Outdoors" into a marketable commodity. *Courtesy of Special Collections, Washington State Historical Society.*

At the St. Louis Mercantile Library we also want to recognize the support provided by Charles Brown, Julie Dunn-Morton, Bette Gordon, and Deborah Cribbs. Likewise, at the Washington State Historical Society we are indebted to Elaine Miller, the photo archivist who through her heroic efforts scanned a mountain of transportation ephemera, and Lynette Miller, head of collections. Redmond Barnett, director of exhibits, was an unfailing source of inspiration and good dinner cheer. When at times the track ahead seemed blocked, Redmond could always be counted on to find ways to bypass the obstacle.

Both the museum exhibition and the book illustrations required considerable financial support from both the Washington State Historical Society and the St. Louis Mercantile Library for top-quality reproductions. In addition, we want to

The Denver and Rio Grande
Railroad issued this pamphlet
in 1915 to call attention to the
agricultural wealth of Utah.
*Courtesy of Special Collections,
Washington State Historical
Society.*

thank the following enterprises for help in funding this project: Burlington
Northern Santa Fe Foundation, M. J. Murdock Charitable Trust, the TTX Corporation, and the Union Pacific Foundation. We appreciate the support we
received from start to finish from members of the Barriger Library Board of
Trustees.

Finally, I want to thank several colleagues at the University of Missouri-Saint
Louis for various forms of encouragement. In particular, I cannot conceive of
working on a transportation-related project without the generous support and
abiding good cheer of Dr. Ray Mundy, director of the Center for Transportation Studies, where my campus office is located. History professor Steve Rowan
has shared his expertise on German artists and mapmakers connected with the

Swimmers enjoy the buoyant waters of Utah's Great Salt Lake, one many natural curiosities contributing to the railroad image of the American West as an incomparable tourist wonderland. *Courtesy of Barriger Railroad Library of the St. Louis Mercantile Library.*

The front cover of the *Pacific Coast Official Railway & Steamship Guide* depicts the basic forms of transportation used in the West. *Courtesy of Special Collections, Washington State Historical Society.*

railroad surveys of the 1850s. History chair Louis Gerteis not only provided the support necessary to work on this project, but his knowledge of Saint Louis and Missouri history has saved me from numerous errors of fact and conception. Dean Mark Burkholder continues to be a source of encouragement.

Jim Ronda wishes to thank the staff in the Special Collections Department-McFarlin Library, The University of Tulsa, for unfailing generosity, good cheer, and sound advice. Together we thank Ron Goldfeder and Ben Schwantes, our research assistants, for helping us find many elusive items.

As always, we must state that any errors or omissions from the text are our responsibility alone.

CARLOS A. SCHWANTES
Saint Louis, Missouri

Hiking through Glacier Park in the era of "See America First" in the early twentieth century. High mountains and other natural attractions of the West provided tourists with an American counterpart to the cathedrals and other historic sites in Europe. *Courtesy of Special Collections, Washington State Historical Society.*

With the "MOUNTAINEERS" in GLACIER NATIONAL PARK

"See America First"
GREAT NORTHERN RAILWAY
Glacier National Park

WALKING TOURS BOOK

The Rock Island Lines made the mountain scenery of Colorado easily accessible to residents of Chicago, Saint Louis, Minneapolis, and other major cities served by its sprawling network in the late 1920s, though its tracks never entered the Rockies west of Denver and Colorado Springs. *Courtesy of Barriger Railroad Library of the St. Louis Mercantile Library.*

The West the Railroads Made

Such is the ruling passion of the day for locomotives and rail-roads, that, to doubt of their utility is a serious offense, and to speak agains their success absolute treason.

—JOHN HERAPATH, *THE RAILWAY MAGAZINE AND ANNALS OF SCIENCE*

Whatever constantly enters into the daily life soon becomes an unnoticed part of it, and the infinitely varied influences of the railroad system are so much a part of our everyday acts and thoughts that they have become familiar, and have ceased to be marvelous. The changes have been so gradual that we have failed to notice their completeness.

—CHARLES FRANCIS ADAMS, JR., AND HENRY ADAMS, *CHAPTERS OF ERIE*

We live, as it were, in the dawn and blush of the era of railroads; and it may take centuries to round out the full interpretation of them to the slow intelligence of man.

—ISRAEL E. DWINNELL, *THE HIGHER REACHES OF THE GREAT CONTINENTAL RAILWAY: A HIGHWAY FOR OUR GOD*

1

The Magician's Rod:
Railroads, the West, and Manifest Destiny

O F ALL THE AMERICAN WRITERS, POLITICIANS, AND PROMOTERS who considered the significance of railroads and the future of the West, Henry D. Thoreau appears the least likely to have anything useful to say. The leafy wizard of Walden Pond seemed preoccupied with Nature and with life within the bounds of his beloved Concord. While others boasted of their journeys to distant places, Thoreau proudly reported that he had "traveled a good deal in Concord."[1] But Thoreau the stay-at-home adventurer had read deeply in the literature of western exploration. For him the West was not only geography but a statement about the American character. In his essay "Walking" he captured the widely held view of the West as a place of freedom and new beginnings. "Eastward I go only by force," he wrote, "but westward I go free."[2] Just as he was drawn to this promise of the West, Thoreau could not escape the presence of the railroad. The railroad came to Concord in June 1844, just a year before Thoreau went to the woods at Walden Pond. Like others in his generation, Thoreau quickly understood that the railroad had fundamentally changed the nature and rhythm of American life. No landscape—not even Concord or Walden Pond—would ever be the same again.

In a chapter of *Walden* entitled "Sounds," Thoreau tried in his own sharp and witty way to catalogue those changes and account for them. At first glance Thoreau seemed to demonize the railroad, labeling locomotives as "the devilish Iron Horse" and famously complaining, "We do not ride on the railroad; it rides on us."[3] But Thoreau had a deeper, more nuanced appreciation of the world the railroad made. Standing trackside in a landscape already changed by the presence of tracks and trains, Thoreau watched as a freight train rumbled by. What he saw carried in the cars were pieces of Nature soon to be the products of daily life. There were cranberries on the way to Boston kitchens, cotton bound for textile mills, lumber from the Maine woods soon to become chairs and tables, and cattle destined for cooking pots and evening dinners. Nature transformed was the message in carloads of lime, salt fish, molasses, and Spanish hides. This procession on the right-of-way prompted Thoreau to describe himself as a "citizen of the world."[4]

But Thoreau knew that the railroad meant more than new products and expanding markets. Watching how Concord's citizens responded to the railroad, he quickly grasped the relationship between the locomotive and time. Once, time had been seasonal, something experienced and measured by the motions of the sun and the unchanging cycles of planting, tending, and harvesting. But "railroad fashion," as Thoreau called it, changed all that. In one of the most perceptive passages in *Walden*, Thoreau wrote that "the startings and arrivals of the cars are now the epochs in the village day. They go and come with such regularity and precision, and their whistle can be heard so far, that farmers set their clocks by it, and thus one well conducted institution regulates a whole country." Thoreau saw the railroad quickening the pace of daily life. Half joking, he wondered if his neighbors had not "improved somewhat" since the coming of the railroad; grasping the profound difference between movement by muscle power and by mechanized power, Thoreau pointedly asked, "Do they not talk and think faster in the depot than they did in the stage-office?"[5]

Thoreau was not the only one in Concord watching as trains rattled through the New England countryside, bringing change wherever tracks were laid. Ralph Waldo Emerson, well on his way to becoming one of the most widely known American thinkers, could not ignore the railroad revolution. Thoreau had felt what he called the "electrifying" atmosphere of the railroad station. Emerson went one step further in trying to understand the possible meanings and potential consequences of the railroad in America. He did so in the middle of a growing public debate about railroads in American life—a debate that already included proposals for a transcontinental railway.

In 1844 Emerson delivered a compelling lecture in Boston entitled "The Young American." It was Emerson's hymn of praise to all the political, economic, mechanical, and cultural changes that were on the loose in what would soon be called the era of Manifest Destiny. In one memorable phrase, Emerson captured what his and subsequent generations believed about the transforming power of the railroad: "Railroad iron is a magician's rod, in its power to evoke the sleeping energies of land and water."[6] In this single sentence Emerson asked his listeners and readers to think past their visual fascination with the locomotive as a machine and consider what the Iron Horse could accomplish. As he saw it, America's nature—both its character and its physical Nature—was asleep. The magic of the railroad could rouse the nation from its sleep. The iron rod would transform the potential into the actual. No other human invention, so Emerson believed, had that enormous power.

By the time Thoreau and Emerson witnessed railroad magic, writers on both sides of the Atlantic were busy exploring the new world locomotives had made. Nearly everyone recognized that the railroad was not just an extension or refinement of the wagon or the stagecoach. It was something profoundly—even sometimes disturbingly—new and different. Railroad tracks seemed to mark a line between the old and the new, the past and the future. Recalling the moment the railroad came to Boston in 1844, historian and philosopher Henry Adams insisted that "the old universe was thrown into the ash-heap and a new one created."[7] But what was the shape of the future, the character of the new? Years earlier Thomas Jefferson had commanded Lewis and Clark to describe "the face of the country." Just a year before the completion of the first transcontinental railroad in 1869, journalist I. Edwards Clarke announced, "Now a new era

A Union Pacific train at the 100th Meridian, returning from the West. *Courtesy of New York Public Library. Photograph by John Carbutt.*

begins."[8] What would that western country look like once the iron road spanned the continent?

"Change" was the word virtually every writer used when talking about the world the railroad made. As Emerson said, it was as if the very presence of flanged wheels on iron rails prompted astounding changes. Just as Thoreau paused to catalogue lumber and cattle on the Fitchburg Railroad, we might stop for a moment to consider the kinds of transformations that railroad visionaries sought and that railroad observers experienced.

LOOKING AT THE FUTURE RIGHT-OF-way for the Kendal and Windermere Railway, the English poet William Wordsworth was onto something when he complained, "Is there no nook of English ground secure / From rash assault?"[9] Perhaps more than any other form of transportation before the Interstate Highway System, the railroad changed the physical landscape. The railroad line itself—its right-of-way with bridges, cuts, and tunnels—chewed up the land. Railroad buildings—stations, roundhouses, and freight yards—gave the landscape a different look. This was the transformation John Stilgoe describes in his book *Metropolitan Corridor*, the "built environment" that reached out from urban America to remake rural America and

The Union Pacific's "Empire of the West" as imagined on the front cover of a promotional brochure issued in the late 1860s. *Courtesy of Barriger Railroad Library of the St. Louis Mercantile Library*

in the process blur the distinction between the two. What the railroad fashioned was the architectural shape of the future, the constructed face of modern America.

But when advocates of a railroad across the West such as Connecticut Senator John Niles spoke about "the creative power of the railroad," they meant more than tracks or stations.[10] What they had in mind was a sweeping "second creation" of the West itself. If the West was the Great American Desert, as some said, then the railroad would make it the Garden of the World. Or, if the West was already the garden, as others thought, then the presence of the railroad iron could make the garden bloom. Asa Whitney, one of the Pacific Railroad's most vocal proponents, promised that a line across the West would "change the wil-

KANSAS.

VIEW FROM MT. PROSPECT, NEAR MANHATTAN.

THE GOLDEN BELT LANDS

——— ALONG THE LINE OF THE ———

KANSAS DIVISION OF THE U. P. R'Y.

·······················

B. McALLASTER, Land Commissioner,

Kansas City, Mo.

The second creation: Union Pacific tracks delineate a "Golden Belt" of highly productive agricultural land as they extend across Kansas. *Courtesy of Barriger Railroad Library of the St. Louis Mercantile Library.*

derness waste to cities, villages, and richly cultivated fields."[11] So it seemed when Sidney Dillon, one of the principal contractors for the Union Pacific Railroad, revisited the scene of the last-spike ceremony some twenty years later. "The whole aspect of the country," he wrote, "from the Missouri River to Salt Lake, has marvelously changed. Where there were once only tents, there are now well-built, substantial, and prosperous towns, and instead of the great desert wastes . . . one may now see an almost unbroken stretch of corn-fields and cultivated lands."[12] Dillon probably had a touch of the real-estate promoter about him, but at the deepest level he was right. Several generations of Americans believed that railroads could awaken and then transform the West. And in the eyes of many that is just what happened as prairie grass gave way to wheat and corn, as bison retreated in the face of sheep and cattle, and as fences marked the lines between American farms and ranches and Indian reservations.

A decade after completion of the first transcontinental rail line, the influential *North American Review* published an article by Henry Varnum Poor simply titled "The Pacific Railroad." Poor was the longtime editor of the *American Railroad Journal.* What he wrote bore the stamp of extensive experience and carried considerable weight. Poor sought to measure how the West had changed since 1869. He had no doubt that those changes were beneficial. Poor offered the predictable list: miles of railroad track laid, income from gold and silver mines, growing population in western states, and the rewards reaped by railroad companies riding on a wave of western prosperity.

But it was the matter of time and distance that most intrigued Poor. By the 1870s it was commonplace to say that railroads had "annihilated time and space." As *Niles' Weekly Register* put it in 1835, "Distances will not be measured by miles but by hours and minutes."[13] It was one thing to consider how the railroad had changed perceptions of time and distance between Boston and Concord, and quite another to confront the vast space between Sacramento and Omaha. But Poor was convinced that the mere touch of railroad iron had collapsed such

ACROSS THE CONTINENT,
"WESTWARD THE COURSE OF EMPIRE TAKES ITS WAY."

space. As a way to dramatize a West reduced to "hours and minutes," Poor drew the reader's attention to the Lewis and Clark Expedition. It took Jefferson's travelers two and a half years to make the circuit from Saint Louis to the Pacific and back. This was time and distance as experienced in the Age of Muscle. Now it was the Age of Steam. Poor reported that earlier in the year, Pennsylvania Railroad president Thomas Scott had chartered an excursion train for a grand tour from New York City to San Francisco. It was, so Poor noted, a distance of 3,322 miles. Scott's excursion made its transcontinental crossing in eighty-three hours, or a mere three and a half days. As Poor exclaimed, "With the railroad, a day will now accomplish, in the transmission of persons and merchandise between them, that for which, within the memory of man, a year would hardly suffice." The limitless plains and those tremendous mountains had been reduced to numbers on the face of a railway clock.

When empire rode the rails: Frances Palmer's *Across the Continent: "Westward the Course of Empire Makes Its Way"* by Currier & Ives, 1868. *Courtesy of Library of Congress.*

Among the many transportation treasures of the St. Louis Mercantile Library that date from the era of Henry David Thoreau is a lengthy run of the influential *American Rail-Road Journal*, among the oldest such publications in the world. Its first issue appeared in early 1832, not 1831 as a printer's error suggests. *Courtesy of Barriger Railroad Library of the St. Louis Mercantile Library.*

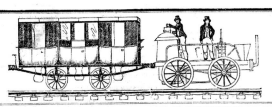

WHEN HENRY D. THOREAU STOOD TRACKSIDE TO watch the Fitchburg Railroad cars carry loads of Spanish hides and West Indian molasses, he was prompted to call himself "a citizen of the world." However remotely, Thoreau understood that railroads were changing the pace of commerce if not the very nature of economic relationships. Local economies were becoming regional ones; regional markets expanded to become national in scope; and a century before the word "globalization" became part of the vocabulary, national economies had entered a worldwide marketplace. Railroads were not the first global enterprise to enter the West. Pride of place belongs to the fur trade. But railroads extended the reach and expanded the influence of that marketplace.

For the early Pacific Railroad promoters, economic transformation was tied to a new version of an old dream. No geographic illusion was more persistent than that of the ever-elusive Northwest Passage. From the Age of Columbus, generations of explorers had gone in search of a water route across North America to the riches of India and China. Thomas Jefferson was just one more in that long line of exploration patrons when he sent Lewis and Clark to find the plain path to the Pacific. The railroad dreamers imagined that path as an iron road. This was the new Northwest Passage, one running on rails and powered by the tireless energies of steam. An anonymous writer for *Putnam's Monthly Magazine* made the connection between the Pacific Railroad and the wealth of Asia unmistakable: "The primary object of a road to the Pacific is to facilitate access to the opulent commerce of the East, which has been the golden vision of all ages and nations."[15]

Thanks to the Pacific Railroad, the United States would surpass its European rivals—especially Great Britain—

and become the economic master of the world. Always the confident prophet, Whitney was sure that his iron passage would give "the entire control of the commerce of the world" to the American republic.[16] This was Manifest Destiny on the grandest scale, all made possible by railroad iron.

For all the promising talk about the transforming power of the iron passage to India, the real economic changes took place throughout the interior West. "None of us dreamed," recalled Sidney Dillon, "that the future of the Pacific roads depended on the business that would grow out of peopling the deserts it traversed."[17] Dillon's analysis was accurate, but his memory misled him. At the end of the 1860s, others were already envisioning the Pacific Railroad as not only a passage through the garden but a route into it as well. Well before the events at Promontory in 1869, railroad advocates insisted that "the development of American commercial power as against the world is secondary to the internal development of our own resources."[18] No one made that argument more persuasively than Saint Louis attorney John Loughborough. In an eighty-page pamphlet titled "The Pacific Telegraph and Railway" published in 1849, Loughborough spelled out the ways railroads would transform the economy of the West. Like Dillon, Loughborough appreciated the fundamental economic difference between East Coast railroads and the line crossing the West. Eastern railroads could exploit producers and markets already in existence. Western railroads first had to build into the region and then develop those markets and centers of production. As Loughborough saw it, the Pacific Railroad could serve as a conduit for investment capital flowing into the West. The railroad would carry settlers into what seemed empty land ready for the plow while employing a substantial company workforce. In Loughborough's mind, the railroad was not a line but rather a "broad belt of civilization." With visionary passion he predicted, "This belt will go on widening and building, until the vast pastoral region spread out between the line of the States and the base of the Rocky Mountains will be brought into cultivation, and herds, and flocks, and rural beauty, and domestic happiness will diffuse themselves

The Union Pacific advertised five million acres of farmland in Kansas and Colorado to prospective German immigrants in the early 1880s. *Courtesy of Barriger Railroad Library of the St. Louis Mercantile Library.*

over the whole land."[19] The locomotive was not simply metal and wood with fire in its belly. It was a veritable force of nature with boundless potential.

British historian Harold Perkin once wrote, "The men who made the railways were not merely creating a revolutionary means of transport. They were helping to create a new society and a new world."[20] Isaac I. Stevens, the congressional delegate from Washington Territory, caught that sense of expectancy and expansion in 1858 when he exclaimed, "The imagination of man can scarcely set bounds to the future grandeur of our Pacific empire."[21] As leader of a major expedition to chart a northern route for the Pacific Railroad, Stevens knew that steam and empire rode the rails together. Within the expanding boundaries of American empire, the transformations produced by railroad iron seemed to be everywhere, particularly in the social fabric of the nation's life.

Pacific Railroad visionaries—and many of their fellow citizens—believed that the railroad could domesticate the Wild West and make it part of the "civilized world." And how would that "civilized" West look? Two years before the completion of the first transcontinental railroad, the influential *Atlantic Monthly* confidently predicted that the railroad would "populate the West in a few years; and along its lines will spring up a hundred cities."[22] The Wild West would vanish, and in its place might come a region more urban and eastern—something the magazine thought more suited to an American future than a West of fur trappers, cowboys, and Indians.

Those cities and the surrounding countryside would bear all the marks of a modern, capitalist society. By its very presence, the railroad had the power to make possible farms, ranches, and factories. What the West produced from farms, ranches, and mines would be carried to an ever-expanding marketplace.

And its citizens might enjoy the benefits of modern life as the railroad brought books, ready-made clothing, and agricultural implements. Those westerners, whatever their occupations, would become a disciplined workforce wedded to precision in everything, from grading wheat and breeding cattle to assaying precious metals and measuring out yards of cloth. In a marketplace increasingly pointed toward mass production and mass consumption, the railroad West quickly became part of a standardized world. The railroad shaped a West where everything from time zones to the uniform size of nuts and bolts was predictable and reliable. The "Old West" was full of surprises; the "New West" sought to smooth out the rough edges. Yesterday's West promised adventure; tomorrow's railroad West offered the settled satisfactions of home and family.

CHANGE IN ONE DEGREE OR ANOTHER is present in all human societies. What the railroad West experienced in the decades from the 1850s to the 1870s was sweeping change at a remarkable speed. Where one week there was seemingly empty prairie, the next week there was a town with a depot, grain elevator, and bank. In less than a year, the presence of the Union Pacific Railroad made Cheyenne, Wyoming, a western metropolis boasting hotels, grocery markets, dry goods stores, and even a diamond dealer. This was transformation at the speed of a locomotive. A writer for *World's Work* magazine at the beginning of the twentieth century put it best: "We are going fast upon our way."[23] Few dared consider that what grew so rapidly might vanish as quickly.

In Willa Cather's novel *A Lost Lady,* the retired railroad contractor Captain Daniel Forrester proudly says, "We dreamed the railroads across the mountains."[24] Forrester knew that building a railroad demanded backbreaking labor as well as healthy measures of hard cash. A successful railroad enterprise seemed no place for dreamers. But Forrester also recognized that before a share of stock was sold or a mile of track laid, there had to be a compelling idea and someone passionate enough to convince others of that idea. A railroad to the

A contract for the purchase of Northern Pacific lands in eastern Washington. *Courtesy of Special Collections, Washington State Historical Society.*

Pacific and eventually the entire West bound to the nation by bands of iron was such an idea. It joined together a remarkable new technology and the appeal of a western empire. That idea captured the imagination and energy of two generations of Americans at the very time of the nation's most dramatic territorial expansion. This company of railroad dreamers included entrepreneurs, missionaries, journalists, politicians, and the occasional eccentric. In the expansive age of Manifest Destiny, some thought that the scream of the American eagle was in fact the shrill cry of a locomotive whistle. Railroad visionaries were convinced that the Iron Horse could span the plains, leap the mountains, touch the Pacific, and shape the life of the nation. It was an ambitious dream

fit for a nation confident of its future yet anxious about its ability to accomplish such dreams.

ASA WHITNEY IS OFTEN CALLED "THE FATHER OF THE Pacific Railroad." His 1845 memorial to Congress advocating a railroad from Lake Michigan to Puget Sound is frequently cited as the beginning of the long and often contentious debate about building a transcontinental railroad. Whitney was an indefatigable promoter of the Pacific Railroad dream. His tireless efforts surely gave visibility to that grand idea—but in many ways Whitney stands not at the beginning of the story but several chapters into it.

Well more than a decade before Whitney came on the scene, a small and unlikely group of Americans began to promote—or at least consider—building a railroad linking the Atlantic states to the Pacific shore. Never mind that such a line would inevitably pass through lands claimed by the Republic of Mexico or held under joint occupation with Great Britain. And never mind that there was a substantial gap between the idea and existing railroad technology. Anything seemed possible in an age increasingly fascinated with machines of all sorts. Drawing on the age-old search for the Northwest Passage, these dreamers conjured up a railway where Lewis and Clark had once hoped to find a waterway. They saw with the eyes of hope and desire. For them, imagination and passion could remake any landscape and shape any future.

Perhaps it was nothing short of inevitable that many Americans began to make a connection between railroads and the West. As French traveler Guillaume Poussin wrote in the early 1840s, the locomotive "appears to be the personification of the American."[25] At first the idea of a railroad to the Pacific was present only by implication. In 1820, when architect Robert Mills advanced plans for a proposed system of steamboat lines, roads, and canals across the country, he flirted with the notion that steam carriages moving on "rail roads" might cross the mountains at the remarkable rate of eighty miles a day. Some ten years later, with advances in steam technology, a line to the Pacific seemed even more imaginable. William C. Redfield, author of *Sketch of the Geographical Rout of a Great Railway*, was perfectly at home urging construction of "a Railway . . . *across the Continent to the Pacific Ocean*."[26] In 1831, a year after Redfield's remarks, the editor of *Niles' Weekly Register* reported that "a railroad across the Rocky Mountains may soon enter into the speculations of some enterprising people of the 'Far West.'" Bursting with enthusiasm, editor Hezekiah Niles predicted that "a journey of a couple of thousand miles in our country is reducing down to a mere excursion."[27] Writing in the Ann Arbor, Michigan,

MILLS'
MAP
of the several Routes
Proposed
to the PACIFIC OCEAN from the
HEAD WATERS OF THE MISSOURI,
to the Isthmus of Darien

Western Emigrant, editor Samuel Dexter insisted, "It is in our power to build up an immense city at the mouth of the Oregon [the Columbia River] . . . in fact to unite New York and the Oregon by a railway by which the traveler leaving the city of New York shall, at the moderate rate of ten miles an hour, place himself in a port right on the shores of the Pacific."[28]

By the late 1830s a growing number of Americans were at the junction between amazing steam-powered motion and an exuberant expansionism. If the West was a garden, there would surely be an easy locomotive passage through it.

Railroad dreaming: The Mills map of the early 1840s illustrated Whitney's proposed route from Lake Michigan to the Columbia River. *Courtesy of Special Collections, Washington State Historical Society.*

So it seemed to the Reverend Henry Harmon Spalding, missionary to the native peoples of the Oregon Country. At the Hudson's Bay Company's Fort Vancouver, Spalding wrote a letter in 1836 that would be widely reprinted in East Coast newspapers and magazines, predicting that the day was near when a railroad would connect "the waters of the Columbia with those of the Missouri."[29] This was exactly Jefferson's dream, now modernized by the power of steam.

Spalding's letter caught the attention of two more Pacific Railroad advocates—John Plumbe, Jr., and Samuel Parker. In 1838 Plumbe was an enterprising businessman eagerly promoting all sorts of schemes in and around Dubuque, Iowa. He may have addressed local citizens about a railroad to the Pacific as early as 1836. What is certain is that by 1838—after publication of Spalding's letter—Plumbe offered a series of resolutions advancing the notion of a railroad to the Columbia River. In their comprehensive study of early Pacific Railroad visionaries, historians Richard V. Francaviglia and Jimmy L. Bryan, Jr., observe that, while Spalding may have been "the most influential early advocate," Parker "deserves special mention for his spreading the gospel of the Pacific railroad."[30] Parker traveled to the Oregon Country in 1835–36 and published his *Journal of an Exploring Tour* in 1838. In a prophetic declaration that defied geography but revealed the optimism of the age, Parker contended that "there would be no difficulty in the way of constructing a rail road from the Atlantic to the Pacific ocean; and probably the time may not be far distant, when trips will be made across the continent, as they have been made to the Niagara falls."[31] It was not the originality of Parker's thought that counted; it was how popular his book proved to be. Parker's *Journal* went through five editions, selling perhaps as many as 20,000 copies.

By the end of the 1830s the idea of a railroad to the Pacific was in the air. Newspapers like the influential *New Orleans Bee* promoted it; Texas entrepreneurs dreamed about it; and some derided it as pure fantasy. But the dream had become part of a larger public conversation about the West and a nation determined to be an empire. By the time Asa Whitney delivered his first Pacific Railroad memorial to Congress in late January 1845, two things were settled in the public mind: the locomotive represented the future, and the future of the American nation lay in the West. Whitney inherited ideas about technology and nationalism, refined them, and did all in his power to spread them.

Like Thoreau, Asa Whitney seems an unlikely advocate for the Pacific Railroad. A New York businessman who made substantial profit in the China trade, Whitney is an example of someone captured by an idea and obsessed with making it reality. His biographer believes that Whitney formulated his own Pacific Railroad plan on the way back from China in 1844. He certainly knew about the growing sophistication of railroad technology. His potent nationalism was especially focused on weakening British commercial power. Whitney may have also been prompted by a recent treaty allowing Americans equal status with the British in the China trade. Now there was real reason to pursue a passage to the Orient.

Although Whitney expanded and refined his plan several times after 1845, its fundamentals remained much the same. He proposed a transcontinental route from Lake Michigan (at a point just south of present-day Milwaukee) to Puget Sound by a northerly track that would take trains through the present-day states of Iowa, Nebraska, Colorado, Utah, Idaho, and Oregon. Whitney's Pacific terminal shifted a bit over the years, but by the end of the 1840s he increasingly had Puget Sound in mind as the great entrepôt for the China trade. Building the line would surely be a vast and vastly expensive undertaking. Financing always seemed to be the sticking point in so many Pacific Railroad schemes. Whitney's plan was simplicity itself: Congress would set aside a strip of land sixty miles wide, from Lake Michigan to the Pacific Coast. Prospective settlers would buy the land and farm it while also helping build the railroad. The proceeds from the land sales would finance railroad construction. Land not sold by the time the railroad reached the Pacific would be given to Whitney or his heirs to sell for their profit. Whitney admitted that the railroad might take twenty years to finish, but foresaw that it would be built in a logical, gradual fashion, without expense to the federal treasury. That the Pacific Railroad "should" be built was beyond debate for Whitney. How it "would" be built was another question.

The five year "war" that Whitney waged to gain congressional approval—a struggle that ended in personal failure by 1850—is an often-told story. Whitney knew that the Pacific Railroad was more than a matter of engineering. It was all about the future shape of the republic. His importance to the history of the West and the railroads lies in what he thought would be the consequences of building a Pacific Railroad—an understanding that evolved over the years. In 1845 the interior West did not loom large in his mind. The Iron Road to India was his passion; China was the object of his desire. The West was an empty space at

The Union Pacific's land department issued a special brochure to promote sale of the railroad's extensive landholdings across Nebraska. *Courtesy of Barriger Railroad Library of the St. Louis Mercantile Library.*

Bold and multicolored type, not unlike that used to promote circus daredevils and exotic displays of lions and tigers, proclaimed the countless attractions of the Northern Pacific's landed empire, the largest ever held by a single company in the United States. *Courtesy of Special Collections, Washington State Historical Society.*

best, and a dangerous wilderness at worst. Just as creators of the first Northwest Passage saw America as a barrier to penetrate, so Whitney initially considered the West an unpleasant geographic annoyance.

But in the years after 1845, and certainly after the territorial conquests of the Mexican War, Whitney reconsidered his notions about the West. If it was not Jefferson's Garden of the World, perhaps railroad iron could make it so. On the most metaphysical level, Whitney came to believe that the very presence of the railroad could change the physical character of the land. "I propose, by this work itself," he wrote in 1848, "to change the wilderness waste to cities, villages, and richly cultivated fields."[32] Emerson and Whitney shared this common faith in the power of the magician's rod.

The great railroad builder James J. Hill is reputed to have said, "If you put a railroad in the Garden of Eden and had none but Adam and Eve to patronize the road, it would be a failure."[33] Like Hill, Whitney thought that a significant part of the transformation brought by the railroad would come from passengers who became settlers. The garden needed many Adams and Eves. While some of those prospective westerners left homes in Ohio or Pennsylvania, Whitney linked the Pacific Railroad to immigration from Europe. By the end of the nineteenth century, railroads had made the West a place of ethnic and cultural diversity. For all his interest in immigration, Whitney made it clear that those future westerners should be English-speaking Western European Protestants. As he once explained, his railroad West would be filled with people of "the same manners, habits, thought, tastes, actions, and interests; and yes, the same religion" as most of white America.[34] In an early version of what historian Frederick Jackson Turner later called "the safety valve theory," Whitney suggested that the promise

Deer hunting in Oregon:
Nature pays the price of
change. *Courtesy of Barriger
Railroad Library of the St.
Louis Mercantile Library*

of western land might alleviate Europe's overcrowding and political oppression. But, even more important, the railroad would ensure that newly arrived immigrants would not be caught in eastern cities. The railroad, so Whitney imagined, might allow immigrants to "escape the tempting vices of our cities."[35] Railroads could not only change the face of the country but act as a force for moral and political reform as well.

Whitney's railroad might populate a West he once considered an empty space. It would also bind that western space to the nation. Fears of disunion and separatism went back to the earliest years of the republic. Those anxieties had never gone away. In the 1840s—by war and diplomacy—California, Texas, the Southwest, and the Pacific Northwest had become part of the American empire. In the face of that imperial expansion, all the old and unresolved questions about the tensions between a small republic and an expansive empire resurfaced. What would it mean for the future of the United States if California became an independent republic? What if what is now Washington and Oregon were to become a sovereign nation with close ties to neighboring Canada and the British Empire? Could a nation reach from ocean to ocean and still maintain a politically stable union? Whitney and many other railroad visionaries were convinced that a transcontinental line might be "the iron band" holding the nation together. Thinking particularly about the Pacific Coast after the Mexican War, Whitney was persuaded that a railroad was "the only safe avenue by which they [Americans in California and the Pacific Northwest] can participate in our prosperity and glory."[36] That iron band could never be broken. In the face of dramatic territorial expansion and mounting arguments over slavery and secession, the railroad promised national salvation.

But in all of this there was a price to pay—a price Whitney did not consider too high. Some would gain by transformation, while others might lose. Writing in 1846, Whitney predicted that the Pacific Railroad "would produce a revolution in the situation of the red as well as the white man."[37] Employing a divide-and-conquer strategy, Whitney believed that the railroad line would separate one tribe from another. This might lessen the possibility of intertribal warfare and eventually weaken the native nations. Two years later, in an address to the Pennsylvania assembly, Whitney linked the future of native people with what he was sure would be the inevitable decline of game animals. "The Indian disappears with the game, and it cannot be supposed that game, such as Buffalo and Elk, the dependence of the Indian, would remain long in the vicinity of a railroad constantly in use, as this must be."[38] Falling victim to the fantasy of "the vanishing Indian," Whitney counted the cost of the Pacific Railroad in terms of Indians and wildlife. Finding decline inevitable, Whitney judged the price negligible.

Like so many other nineteenth century prophets and dreamers, Whitney spoke in nearly millennial terms. The railroad would usher in the final transformation, the creation of a world without war. "It is our destiny," he confidently wrote, "to accomplish this vast revolution for all mankind."[39] The revolution was a renewal of simplicity and rural virtue. Conflict would cease, prosperity would end poverty, and the promise of "domestic tranquility" might at last come true. It was as if the locomotive had become the emblem of the Peaceable Kingdom, the motive power bringing the American dream. This was the machine in the garden. Somehow the Machine Age and the Peaceable Kingdom would live in harmony.

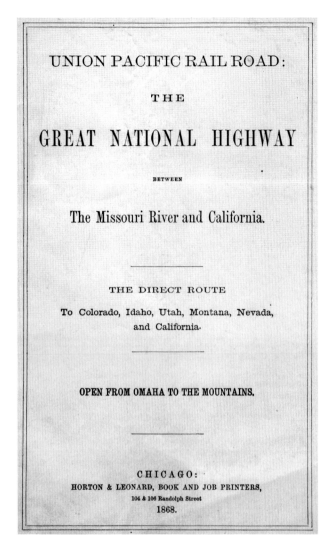

UNION PACIFIC RAIL ROAD:

THE

GREAT NATIONAL HIGHWAY

BETWEEN

The Missouri River and California.

THE DIRECT ROUTE

To Colorado, Idaho, Utah, Montana, Nevada, and California.

OPEN FROM OMAHA TO THE MOUNTAINS.

CHICAGO:

HORTON & LEONARD, BOOK AND JOB PRINTERS,
104 & 106 Randolph Street
1868.

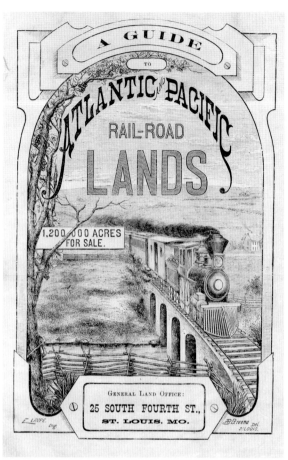

WHILE CONGRESS ALTERNATELY DEBATED AND ignored not only Whitney's proposal but others as well, popular support for the Pacific Railroad rode on the rising tide of Manifest Destiny. Whitney proved to be a master of public relations. Newspapers carried editorials championing his and other plans, local politicians sought support for one city or another as the eastern terminal for the line, and railroad conventions kept the idea before the public. But it was not until the Mexican War made the United States a truly continental nation in 1846–1848 that the Pacific Railroad idea gained what seemed irresistible momentum. As a writer for the *American Whig Review* explained, "It has become evident that the addition of California and New Mexico . . . has made it *necessary* that some means of speedy communication should be established between ourselves and the new territories. Our mighty empire on the western side of the continent" would be secure only if that "iron band" tied East to West.[40]

The Mexican War and the Oregon Treaty of 1846 between the United States and Great Britain convinced many railroad doubters—including Missouri's influential Senator Thomas Hart Benton—that a Pacific Railroad was essential for national prosperity, if not survival. From 1848 to 1853 Congress was locked in endless debates about routes and terminals. At the time, it seemed obvious that only one line would be built. Cost seemed to dictate that decision. But what route would it take? What city would reap the rewards of being the eastern terminal? The congressional arguments not only pitted section against section but city against city. Memphis, New Orleans, Louisville, and Saint Louis all claimed pride of place as the ideal eastern terminal. Construction of only one line meant that the chosen city need not share its victory with another. What should have been an engineering decision became a partisan political one. By the time the 32nd Congress met for its second session in 1852–53, there appeared no way the deadlock could be broken. In the face of growing sectional tensions, the future of the Pacific Railroad looked bleak.

If this was the Railroad Age, it was also a time when many looked to science as a source for objective truth about the physical world. Faced with a political stalemate, Senators William Gwin of California and Richard Brodhead of Pennsylvania proposed asking science to do what politics could not. On March 2, 1853, Congress ordered Secretary of War Jefferson Davis and the army to undertake a survey of available transcontinental routes and select the one "most practical and economical."[41] The army's Corps of Topographical Engineers, who had an enviable reputation as the premier scientific explorers of the West, was given the assignment to complete the survey in ten months.

One way around the political stalemate was for Congress to commission the Pacific Railroad Surveys. Soldier-explorers and civilian scientists not only surveyed five principal east-west routes but also studied western plants, animals, terrain, and native cultures. The findings of the army surveys were published in thirteen lavishly illustrated volumes. While science was well served by the railroad expeditions, they proved a political failure. For a number of reasons (sectional bias and personal preference being just two) Davis selected only one northern route to be surveyed; the others were further to the south and southwest. (Ironically, the tracks of the first transcontinental railroad followed a route not explored by any of the surveys. Isaac I. Stevens, leader of the northern expedition, and perhaps imagining himself following in the footsteps of Lewis and Clark, developed elaborate arguments to support that route. Jefferson Davis did

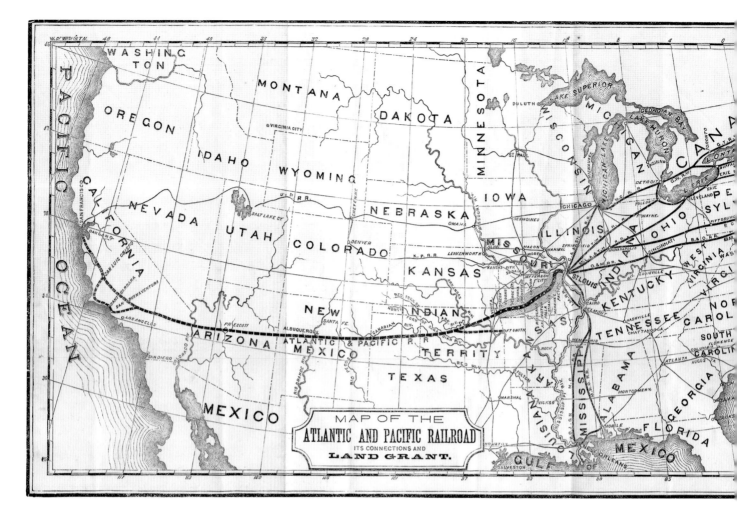

not fancy himself a Thomas Jefferson. There would be no Northwest Passage for him.)

For those paying attention, the route Davis chose and announced at the end of February 1855 should not have come as a surprise. An earlier report drafted by senior army officers had made it plain that they believed that railroad iron could neither transform the wasteland of the Great Plains nor penetrate the snows of the Rocky Mountains. Davis's report to Congress was uncompromisingly blunt. There was only one practical and economical route, and that was along the 32nd parallel, from a point on the Mississippi River to San Francisco. Davis had chosen a southern route; congressmen who read the survey reports preferred other routes, based on their own opinions and prejudices. Congress rejected Davis's recommendation, much to the embarrassment of the Corps of Topographical Engineers. Agreement now seemed further away than before.

The Atlantic & Pacific line across Missouri became part of the Frisco, now a component of modern Burlington Northern Santa Fe. *Courtesy of Barriger Railroad Library of the St. Louis Mercantile Library.*

*I*N THE FIVE YEARS PRECEDING THE CIVIL WAR, CONGRESS AND the nation were increasingly occupied with sectional controversies and the debate over the extension of slavery into the new western territories. The Pacific Railroad did not die as a source for argument, but it did take second place to issues of greater import. Disappointed by his failure to win congressional support for his scheme, Asa Whitney quietly left the railroad struggle in 1850, but others kept the dream alive. It was not until 1862 that a Northern-dominated Congress, goaded by another visionary, passed the Pacific Railroad Act. That visionary was Theodore Judah, a clear-eyed, single-minded engineer who represented California railroad interests. Judah was every bit as determined as Whitney. His great advantages were two: timing, and the financial support of four ambitious Sacramento businessmen—Collis P. Huntington, Mark Hopkins, Charles Crocker, and Leland Stanford. Known as the Big Four, they provided the cash to fuel Judah's transcontinental dream. That money and Judah's persistence carried the day.

Railroads and the future of the West. *Courtesy of Barriger Railroad Library of the St. Louis Mercantile Library.*

Despite all the controversies, personal feuds, and ugly frauds that swirled around the building of the first transcontinental railroad, expectations for what the line might accomplish remained sky-high. Some twenty years before the Promontory moment, a writer in the *American Whig Review* confidently predicted that "the instant of the completion of the road would be the epochal moment of a grand movement in the commerce of the world."[42] Less than a year before locomotives from the Central Pacific Railroad and the Union Pacific Railroad touched pilots, journalist I. Edwards Clarke painted an even more dramatic picture: "Now a new era begins. The locomotive, pushing into the new country, bears with it all the essentials of civilization; and towns and cities rise up in a day; states spring forth full panoplied!"[43] What Clarke described on paper artist Francis Palmer put in a Currier and Ives lithograph. In that now-famous print *Across the Continent: Westward the Course of Empire Takes Its Way,* a train rushes across an endless prairie, leaving in its wake schools, shops, and well-manicured farms. All these trappings of American civilization fill the plains while a buffalo herd and Indian hunters fade into the background. In her novel *O Pioneers!* Willa Cather pronounced the land as "the great fact." Charles Nordhoff, writing in *Harper's Monthly* in 1872, insisted that the railroad was "the one great fact."[44]

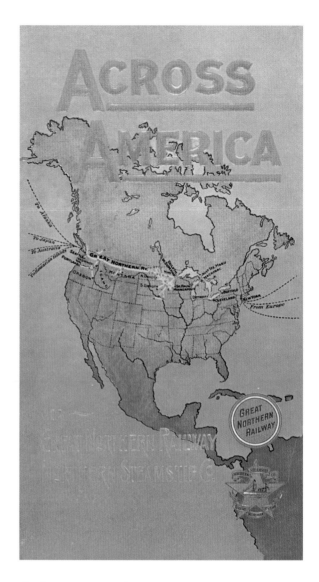

Across America: Railroads of the West were early promoters of a global economy. *Courtesy of Special Collections, Washington State Historical Society.*

After 1865, war weariness slowly gave way to a revival of optimism and national pride. A renewed sense of Manifest Destiny filled the air, this time using the Pacific Railroad as a metaphor for what many thought would be the final conquest of the West. Charles Nordhoff's "one great fact" had many faces. One of those was the American brand of nineteenth-century civilization. Speaking to a group of tourists traveling on the eastern division of the Union Pacific Railroad, General Winfield S. Hancock claimed, "This great railroad brings civilization with it, so that when the Rocky Mountains are reached, the wild Indian and the buffalo will have passed away."[45] But it was Secretary of the Interior J. D. Cox who most fully expressed the connection many made between the Pacific Railroad and civilization. Writing in the Department of Interior annual report for 1869, Cox claimed that "every station upon the railway has become a nucleus

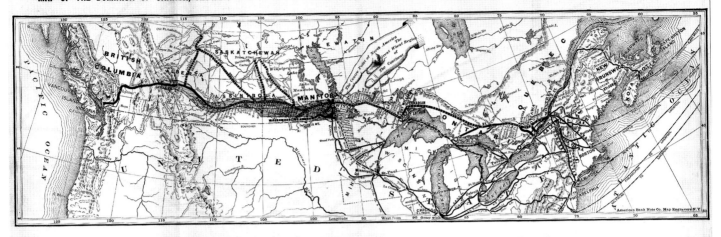

Around the world: Various railroads of the United States claimed the title "transcontinental," but during the nineteenth century the tracks of only one company actually spanned North America, and that railroad was located in Canada. After the Canadian Pacific completed its new transcontinental line between Montreal and Vancouver in 1885, it proclaimed itself a vital link in the globe-spanning British Empire. *Courtesy of Barriger Railroad Library of the St. Louis Mercantile Library.*

for a civilized settlement and a base from which lines of exploitation for both mineral and agricultural wealth are pushed in every direction."[46] The buffalo and the Indian represented the savage West. The train carried civilization in its cars. To anyone looking closely, the civilized West was supposed to look much like Ohio or Virginia.

In the troubled years after the Mexican War, as sectional rivalries and fears of separatism grew, many proponents of the Pacific Railroad saw the enterprise in terms of preserving the national union. After the Civil War, that language was employed in the service of triumphant nationalism. Samuel Bowles, a Connecticut newspaper man who had traveled widely in what was now called the "New West," captured the feeling of political and cultural unity that the railroad made possible. In a remarkable passage worth quoting in full, Bowles portrayed the Pacific Railroad as the single force that made a transcontinental United States both possible and real: "The Railroad is the Chord along whose quick lines move this food [the life of the mind] for the early settlers of our New West. It brings them home; more, it carries home to them. Though they may never see its rails, or ride on its trains, they will feel its influence, and be more content and richer in their lives. It puts the great sections of the Nation into sympathy and

unity; it marries the Atlantic and Pacific; it destroys disunion where it was ever most threatening; it brings into harmony the heretofore jarring discords of a continent of separated peoples; it determines the future of America."[47]

In many ways, the high-flown rhetoric about civilization and national unity belonged to the world of journalism and chamber-of-commerce boosterism. That talk was an abstraction often far from the concerns of potential westerners looking for future homes and farms. For them it was a certainty that the railroad had already transformed the West from wasteland to farmland. They took as gospel what Samuel Bowles wrote from the security of his Hartford, Connecticut office: "The Pacific Railroad unlocks the mysteries of Our New West. It opens a new world of wealth, and a new world of natural beauty."[48] The railroad seemed to have the power to change the very physical character of the landscape. Something so powerful as a locomotive might even be able to alter the climate of the West and enhance the fertility of its lands. Great Plains promoter J. H. Noteware put it this way: "The present fertile State of Nebraska was known only a few score years ago as the Great American Desert." Now, in the early 1870s, the desert had "vanished into the air."[49] If rain followed the plow, as many hoped, then the railroad would bring the plow and the plowboy to the West. The Rock Island Railroad boldly described western Kansas as "the garden spot of the world. Because it will grow anything that any other country will grow and with

Thomas Jefferson's imagined garden in reality: a cattle ranch near North Platte, Nebraska. *Courtesy of Barriger Railroad Library of the St. Louis Mercantile Library.*

less work. Because it rains here more than in any other place, and just at the right time."[50]

Perhaps no one caught the post-Civil War optimism about the railroad West better than journalist Charles Nordhoff: "The 'Great American Desert' which we school-boys of a century ago saw on the map of North America has disappeared at the snort of the iron horse." With just a hint of irony, Nordhoff reported that "coal and iron are found to abound on the plains as soon as the railroad kings have need of them; the very desert becomes fruitful, . . . in the midst of alkali country you will see corn, wheat, potatoes, and fruits of different kinds growing luxuriantly."[51] Thomas Jefferson's Garden West had come true, so Nordhoff believed, with a little help from the magician's rod.

FOR DECADES AFTER THE 1830S, RAILROAD PROPHETS AND promoters filled the American marketplace with an endless stream of promises and fantasies, all driven by a new technology and the unruly energies of Manifest Destiny. Few voices urged caution; even fewer suggested that the Pacific Railroad might transform the West into something less than paradise on earth. Henry George was one of those willing to ask difficult questions and face unsettling answers. Born in Boston in 1839, George went to sea as a young man and, like many, drifted to California, lured by promises of adventure and wealth in the gold fields. After a failed attempt as a miner, George became a printer and newspaper publisher. By the end of the 1860s, he was part of San Francisco's colorful literary scene. There he rubbed shoulders and shared ideas with the likes of Bret Harte and Mark Twain. In 1868, on the eve of the completion of the first transcontinental railroad, George wrote one the most perceptive essays on railroads and the West. Entitled "What the Railroad Will Bring Us" and published in Harte's *Overland Monthly*, the article asked the West what Thoreau had asked the individual: "What is the railroad to me?"[52]

George was quick to acknowledge that the railroad would bring wealth and prosperity to the West in general and to California in particular. The Pacific Railroad had the power to transform the western wilderness into a vast empire. George imagined precious metals pouring into the national treasury while immigrants peopled the West. And looking deeper into the future, he envisioned an era when the political and economic center of the nation would shift from New York and the East Coast to San Francisco and the West. This would be a future marked by "steady, rapid, and substantial growth." If prosperity meant "more people, more houses, more farms and mines, more factories and ships," then Emerson's rod was about to work its magic in California.[53]

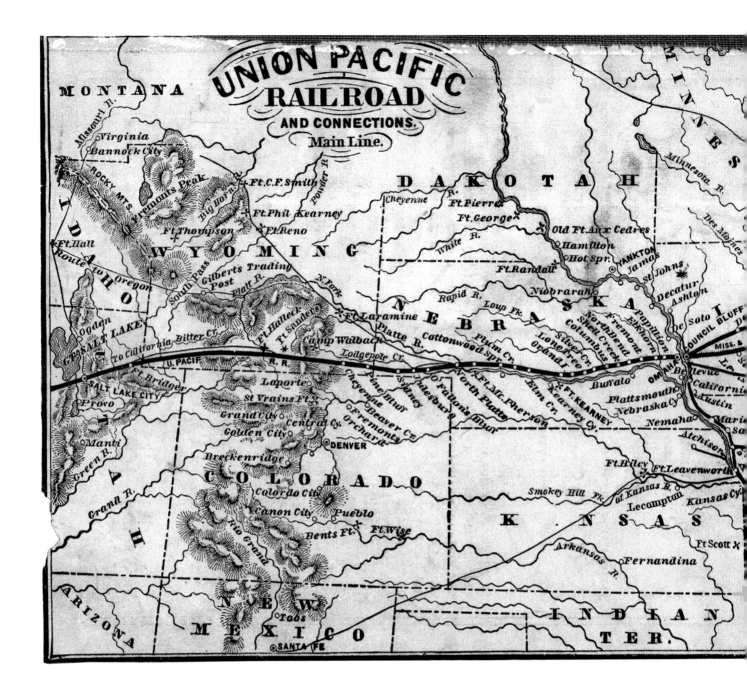

Union Pacific tracks were not yet completed across Wyoming Territory when this map appeared in 1868. *Courtesy of Barriger Railroad Library of the St. Louis Mercantile Library.*

But, in all of this, George was haunted by the inevitability of what he called "The Law of Compensation." For every gain there must be loss; for every victory there must be a defeat. Each blessing brings its own curse. California would be the richer once the Pacific Railroad was finished, but a price had to be paid. Not all transformations are welcome ones. California might experience a tidal wave of newcomers, but what kind of people would these be? There would be wealth, but how would it be distributed? Might that wealth widen the gap between rich and poor? Might "Old California" be swept away by the relentless power of speculation and materialism?

George's often prophetic answers flew in the face of decades of enthusiastic rhetoric. He dared to suggest that all might not be well in a West the railroads were about to make. Rising land values meant that working families could not afford to become home or land owners. Pushed out of the real-estate market, working-class families were bound to become renters of the least desirable housing. Slums, squalor, and crime of all sorts might become part of California's human landscape. In one of his most powerful lines, George predicted, "The locomotive is a great centralizer." He was convinced that the railroad would inevitably concentrate wealth and power in the hands of corporate elites answerable to no one. Like the muckraking journalists of a later time, George saw a railroad enterprise that "kills little towns and builds up great cities, and in the same way kills little businesses and builds up great ones."[54]

What troubled George most was what we now call "quality of life." As something of a romantic, he imagined "Old California" as a gentle, charming place with few social distinctions and a slow pace of life. George was sure that would be lost once the Iron Road linked West to East. The spirit of speculation would be everywhere; the pace of life would overwhelm old traditions and values. Most worrisome was the inevitable loss of personal independence in a world ruled by competition and the clock. George's essay was not a jeremiad from a Puritan pulpit, but it did conclude with a grim biblical warning. "The future of our State, of our Nation, of our race, looks bright and fair." Modern civilization, embodied in the locomotive, promised a new age. But, recalling Babylon and the builders of the Tower of Babel, George reminded his readers that "so did the tower which men once built almost to heaven."[55] What befell Babylon might come to pass in California and the West.

Henry George's warnings about the possible shape of the future in a railroad West were either ignored or discounted. Far more in tune with the times were the reassuring words of Robert P. Porter, a prominent official with the government's Bureau of the Census. In a remarkable book entitled *The West from the Census of 1880*, Porter offered a near-perfect summary of all the great expectations

A map of Henry George's California, 1868. *Courtesy of Barriger Railroad Library of the St. Louis Mercantile Library*

Opposite, above: Perhaps it was unintended irony, but in this illustration from *Harper's Weekly*, May 29, 1869, the tracks of the "Great Link" connecting the United States from east to west appear to divide its Native American population on the right from everyone else on the left. *Courtesy of Barriger Railroad Library of the St. Louis Mercantile Library.*

Opposite, below: "The locomotive is the great centralizer." The last spike at Promontory, Utah, linked California by rail to the rest of the United States. This image appeared in *Harper's Weekly*, June 5, 1869. *Courtesy of Barriger Railroad Library of the St. Louis Mercantile Library.*

COMMERCE

California Limited was one of the Santa Fe's premier trains in the early twentieth century, though to anyone who recalled Henry George's prophetic words of 1869, the name may suggest an ominous irony. *Courtesy of Barriger Railroad Library of the St. Louis Mercantile Library.*

and glowing promises the Pacific Railroad seemed to embody. The locomotive was not the destructive centralizer; it was "the burden bearer for the pioneer to new lands."[56] The railroad enterprise would not bring wealth for a few and poverty for many. Rather it promised "cheap lands, pioneer farming, and gross products." The West would not be the new Babylon. "We shall have skilled labor, high farming, perishable products, and the railroad will equalize the advantages of them all, so that the laborer in the factory will have cheap food, the plowman in the Red River country or herdsman on the Colorado ranges, will have comfortable clothing and shelter."[57] All those who were part of Asa Whitney's prophetic band could not have agreed more. Whatever the outcome—and Whitney's band was sure it would be for the good—the magician's rod was about to touch the West.

A brochure cover for Pathway to the Setting Sun. *But for whom is the sun really setting?* Courtesy of Special Collections, Washington State Historical Society.

We feel that we cannot too powerfully or earnestly appeal to every citizen of St. Louis in regard to this important subject [connecting the city to the transcontinental railroad]. We feel that it is almost a life and death struggle; and if St. Louis shall fail in it, that Chicago will have gained an advantage that St. Louis may never be able to reclaim."

—REPORT OF THE ST. LOUIS DELEGATION TO OMAHA AND TERMINUS OF THE UNION PACIFIC RAILROAD

The busy waterfront of Saint Louis in 1854, two years before a railroad bridged the Mississippi at Rock Island and diverted an increasing amount of upriver commerce to Chicago. *Courtesy of A. G. Edwards & Sons Inc., Saint Louis, Missouri.*

2

Space Race; or, A Tale of Rival Cities

*I*T WAS NOT A PARTICULARLY ATTRACTIVE BRIDGE, AND UNLIKE the Brooklyn Bridge or the Golden Gate Bridge it never became a popular icon. Structurally, it did not test the limits of engineering know-how in the mid 1850s and thus serve as a landmark along the road to more impressive technological feats. But neither was it an ordinary bridge. The five wooden spans of what some people called the "mammoth" railroad bridge carried the first tracks across the broad Mississippi River, and this feat alone made the bridge a potent symbol of a fast-approaching revolution in transportation—a truly magnificent symbol to believers in the power of railroads to transform the American West, and a frightening one to observers comfortable with older and simpler technologies that had well served the transportation needs of the region for more than thirty years.

All revolutions have winners and losers. Veteran boatmen worried about losing valuable business to the Chicago and Rock Island Rail Road Company after it completed its bridge across the Mississippi River in April 1856.[1] For some time the steamboatmen and the ports they served had feared that rails would divert river commerce to Chicago, the upstart city on Lake Michigan, instead of allowing it to follow its accustomed channel downriver to the time-honored cities of Saint Louis and New Orleans. The Saint Louis *Republican* fumed in April 1854, "Chicago will soon stretch her iron arms across Illinois and Iowa, down to the

37

Illinois River, and to the upper Mississippi, controlling the travel and business of a vast territory, naturally tributary to St. Louis."[2]

The simmering anger of boatmen apparently boiled over a few weeks later on the night of May 6, when the *Effie Afton*, one of the swiftest boats on the Mississippi River, crashed into a support of the new bridge. Fire from an upended cookstove aboard the steamboat consumed the *Effie Afton* and one of the bridge's wooden spans. To some observers, the crash had been a deliberate attempt by boatmen to topple the object of their anxiety. Deliberate or not, they were overjoyed to learn that the hated hazard to navigation, as boatmen viewed the bridge, had been reduced to ashes that floated lazily toward the Gulf of Mexico. Up and down the Mississippi, jubilant captains repeatedly sounded their deep-voiced steam whistles to celebrate the news.

John Hurd, owner of the *Effie Afton*, sued the bridge's owner for fifty thousand dollars in damages. The Chicago and Rock Island Rail Road defended itself by hiring a forty-six-year-old Illinois trial lawyer named Abraham Lincoln. Meanwhile, the railroad hastily repaired and reopened its long bridge only four months after the incident. No steamboat whistles celebrated the occasion.

Like all commercially minded Americans in the 1850s, veteran steamboatmen understood clearly that trade flowed like water—that is, it invariably followed the paths of least resistance. Human ingenuity could divert trade into innovative channels that offered speedier, safer, and more convenient access to markets. Only a quarter century earlier, New York City visionaries had successfully used this argument to enlist state support for an "artificial river" that linked the Hudson Valley with rich farmland in the Ohio Country beyond the Appalachian Mountains. After its completion in 1825, the Erie Canal's fast-growing and lucrative stream of trade brought unprecedented prosperity to New York and bolstered the trade-as-water analogy. Merchants in Philadelphia, Boston, Baltimore, and other rival East Coast cities envisioned constructing canals of their own to tap Ohio's agricultural cornucopia—and if not canals, they would employ the new technology of railroads to fashion the innovative channels of commerce needed to protect and extend their home city's imperial reach.

Chicago and Rock Island broadside from 1857. Courtesy of Barriger Railroad Library of the St. Louis Mercantile Library.

In the Midwest of the 1850s, steamboatmen opposed all bridges across the Mississippi not just because the bridges were hazards to navigation but because they reasoned (correctly) that the lucrative commerce of Minnesota, Wisconsin, and Iowa would flow by train through Chicago instead of continuing by boat to the well-known wharves and warehouses in Saint Louis. After that there would be no end of trouble for boatmen familiar with the great river corridors that radiated out from the Missouri metropolis. Together, the Mississippi, Missouri, Illinois, Ohio, and their tributary rivers formed a lengthy and time-tested water highway of incalculable commercial importance.

Saint Louis in 1855, just before Rock Island rails first bridged the Mississippi, recorded nearly seven thousand arrivals and departures of steamboats." Scarcely an hour during that period," boasted a respected local newspaper, the *Missouri Republican*, "but some gallant steamer ploughed the waves of the Mississippi, bringing the products of the richest and most extensively improved country in the world. The levee was stored from day to day with the staples of each section. Perhaps in no other mart of the Union are the genius, enterprise and diversified interests of the nation better represented." As exciting and comforting as such claims were to smug Saint Louisans, the historical geographer D. W. Meinig noted 150 years later (with the considerable advantage hindsight confers) that railroads, not steamboats, emerged "as a space-conquering instrument of revolutionary possibilities."[3]

Technology as represented by railroad lines—and not geographical advantage, as represented by river connections—would henceforth be paramount in determining the growth and influence of cities in the American West. "The Railroad will do most of the business now done by steamboats on the upper Missouri and its tributaries," predicted advocates of the Minnesota-based Northern Pacific Railroad in 1873. "That business is of long standing and very considerable amount."[4]

During the 1850s, in fact, the nation's midsection had witnessed a fundamental reorientation of the flow of commerce, from the north-south orientation of steamboat traffic linking Pittsburgh, Cincinnati, Louisville, Saint Louis, and New Orleans, to an east-west orientation of rail traffic that benefited Chicago, Indianapolis, Columbus, and other upstart cities. For this reason, rail commerce spanning the Father of Waters in 1856 would assuredly not originate or terminate on the Mississippi's western bank. Rock Island tracks could easily extend the reach of Chicago well beyond the borders of Illinois and far across the fertile farmland of Iowa. "Chicago is an argus-eyed competitor for the carrying trade from East to West," the *Missouri Republican* warned in early 1859.

Just how far west Chicago's reach might extend, no one knew: probably to

To provide readers of *Harper's Weekly* with an accurate picture of the mammoth amount of steamboat traffic that still served Saint Louis in 1871, the magazine's artists, photographers, and engravers must have tested the limits of their illustrative skills. *Courtesy of the St. Louis Mercantile Library.*

San Francisco Bay, and perhaps even to the distant Pacific Northwest. Significantly, in mid-1866 the railroad changed its name to the Chicago, Rock Island, and Pacific. It aspired, in other words, to link Lake Michigan and the Mississippi Valley with the distant Pacific Coast. For more than two decades, dreamers from many different backgrounds had promoted a railroad to the Pacific shore of the United States. At first most Americans thought that they were crazy, because seemingly insurmountable financial, geographical, and technological obstacles blocked the tracks. With the passage of time and improvements in technology, the Pacific Railroad idea won increased respectability and a growing legion of supporters. Initially this seemed like good news for Saint Louis, long acclaimed as the primary gateway to the West.

The American West was imperial space Saint Louis merchants had long claimed for themselves by using specially constructed "mountain steamboats" and economical water highways to extend their reach across Missouri and the High Plains. Beginning in 1819, two generations of steamboatmen had bucked muddy currents and forced shallow-draft vessels around deadly snags and across sandbars to probe ever farther up the Missouri River until, in the early 1860s, they reached the fur-trade outpost of Fort Benton, Montana Territory, beyond which steamboat travel was impractical. In this way the steamboatmen functioned as the advance guard of an expanding commercial empire based in Saint Louis.

A map of the Chicago and North Western Railway in 1877. This was one of many railroads that linked Chicago with an expansive hinterland rich in the products of mines, forests, and fields. *Courtesy of Barriger Railroad Library of the St. Louis Mercantile Library.*

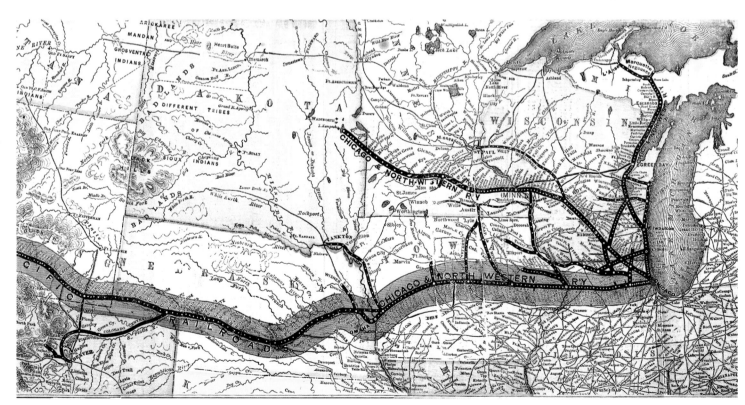

HO FOR THE YELLOW STONE
AND THE
GOLD MINES
OF IDAHO!

A NEW AND VERY LIGHT DRAUGHT STEAMER WILL LEAVE
SAINT LOUIS FOR BIGHORN CITY!
THE JUNCTION OF BIGHORN AND YELLOW STONE RIVERS,
SATURDAY, APRIL 2D, AT 12 O'CLOCK M.

Parties taking this route save 400 miles river transportation and over 100 miles land transportation. Bighorn City being by a good wagon road from Virginia City 200 and from Bannack City 265 miles.

I WILL ALSO SEND TWO LIGHT DRAUGHT SIDE-WHEEL STEAMERS
TO FORT BENTON
One leaving at the same time, and the second about fifteen days later. I am prepared to contract for Freight and Passage either to Bighorn City or Fort Benton.
I refer to W. B. DANCE, JAS. STEWART and N. WALL, Virginia City, or to M. MANDEVILLE, Bannack City.

For Freight or Passage apply to JOHN G. COPELIN,
Care JOHN J. ROE & CO., St. Louis, M

Missouri River steamboats once linked Saint Louis with the gold mines of Idaho (actually Montana Territory, which separated from Idaho Territory in 1864). *Courtesy of Montana Historical Society, Helena, Montana, P-157.*

The first serious fight between steamboatmen and railroaders, the case of *Hurd vs. Rock Island Railroad Company,* ended in a deadlocked jury. When a federal judge in Chicago dismissed the case, it was nonetheless clear which side had prevailed: John Hurd and the steamboatmen he represented were the past; the Rock Island and all other railroads were the future. The real winner in the informal race to control and dominate western space was Chicago, the fast-growing city on Lake Michigan. During the 1850s Chicago entrepreneurs and their Boston financiers wove a network of iron and steel across the Midwest that fundamentally reoriented the flow of commerce. However, when tracks hurdled the Mississippi River at Rock Island in the mid-1850s and bounded across Iowa toward the sunset side of the continent, Chicago's commercial aspirations collided with those of Saint Louis, a city much older than Chicago and dependent on steamboats, overland trails, freight wagons, stagecoaches, and telegraph lines to extend and maintain its commercial dominance of the West. Its mercantile interest in the Great Plains and the Rocky Mountains dated back at least to 1804, when the Lewis and Clark Expedition proceeded up the Missouri River bound for the Pacific Coast, and possibly to an earlier generation of fur traders based in Saint Louis.

SINCE THE EARLY NINETEENTH CENTURY, WHEN PRESIDENT Thomas Jefferson dispatched an expedition headed by Meriwether Lewis and William Clark to seek a viable corridor to the Pacific using mainly the waters of the Missouri and Columbia rivers, Saint Louis had served as the nation's launching pad for the exploration of seemingly boundless western space. The City of Saint Louis, it can be observed without excessive exaggeration, was to American exploration of western space in the first half of the nineteenth century what the Kennedy Space Center became to American exploration of space beyond the surly bonds of the earth's gravitational pull. Each form of space exploration required a base or a launching pad.

Following closely on the heels of the Saint Louis-based explorers of western space were merchants and other entrepreneurs who sought to commercialize it. "Saint Louis is the great central outfitting point for miners and western emigrants," emphasized the *Illustrated Miner's Hand-Book and Guide to Pike's Peak.* "The miner and emigrant will find in St. Louis a greater variety and better stock of outfitting articles, more competition and better goods at lower prices than anywhere else west of New York."[5]

After Lewis and Clark, and for the next fifty years, Saint Louis and the Pacific Northwest carried on a long-distance love affair. Saint Louisans equated the resources of the far Northwest (a vast region held jointly by the United States and Great Britain until 1846) with their city's prosperity and wealth. Even before Lewis and Clark launched their exploratory journey from Saint Louis to the mouth of the Columbia River in 1804, the city's fur merchants discovered that the compass of opportunity pointed northwest up the Missouri River. For several more decades, they competed with their counterparts in Montreal and London for the "soft gold" of beaver and other pelts coming from distant Rocky Mountain valleys. Saint Louis steamboats pushed steadily up the Missouri River in search of trade until in the early 1860s they at last reached the foothills of the Rockies at Fort Benton, just in time to profit from a decade of gold rushes in Montana and Idaho.

In the Pacific Northwest the list of early movers and shakers who first headed west from Saint Louis, or who maintained ties with the Missouri metropolis, reads like a regional *Who's Who*. The names include the Catholic missionary Pierre Jean DeSmet, the Protestant missionaries Marcus and Narcissa Whitman, and the ubiquitous explorer John C. Frémont, who did so much to map and popularize the route known as the Oregon Trail. Missourians came to make up a preponderance of first settlers in Oregon's fertile Willamette Valley. When pioneer residents of the Pacific Northwest received the latest news from the East, it usually arrived by way of Saint Louis.

Over the course of several decades the Missouri city naturally anticipated the present and future prosperity made possible by its position as America's gateway to the Pacific (and all western space in between). But in the mid-1850s, Chicago's new rail bridge represented the opening shot in a spatial rivalry that upset previous assumptions about the development of the American West. As the new railroad technology rapidly extended Chicago's reach west, it threatened the commercial aspirations of Saint Louis merchants as well as the livelihoods of the city's sizeable community of boat captains, pilots, mates, deckhands, and roustabouts.

Ever since the days of Lewis and Clark, two generations of explorers and fur traders had extended the reach of Saint Louis up the waterways of the West and along dusty trails overland into new regions where navigable rivers did not flow. Merchants pioneered a

Missouri was the jumping-off point for the Pike's Peak gold regions in the late 1850s. *Courtesy of Barriger Railroad Library of the St. Louis Mercantile Library*

trail to Santa Fe, in northern Mexico in the 1820s, and then joined a swelling
stream of missionaries and home seekers in the 1830s and 1840s as they headed
west to Oregon and California. Most of them launched the trans-Mississippi
portion of their journeys from Saint Louis.

Even before Lewis and Clark, the first families of Saint Louis had profited
from the fur trade of the West. Building on geographical knowledge amassed by
fur traders and explorers, missionaries from various denominations crossed the
Great Plains and the Rocky Mountains to convert Indians of the far Northwest
to Christianity. In the vanguard were Marcus Whitman and Samuel Parker,
who in 1835 headed west from Saint Louis by steamboat. Parker continued overland from Council Bluffs to the Columbia River.

When Parker later published a book about his six-month overland ordeal—
and it was truly an ordeal to surmount range after range of high mountains
across the future state of Idaho on his way west—his popular 1838 recounting

contained a short but prophetic passage about how easy it would be to extend a Pacific Railroad over the Rocky Mountain divide in central Wyoming. At the time, a Pacific boundary of the United States had not yet been determined, but at best it seemed likely to extend only along the shores of future Oregon (which included Washington). California remained part of the new Republic of Mexico, and no one imagined the gold bonanza waiting to be unearthed in the foothills of the Sierra Nevada in the late 1840s.

Parker, as already noted, was not the first prophet to envision a rail line to the Pacific, but he was among the first to do so after surveying the mountainous terrain with his own eyes. The missionary was no armchair theorist. He was a dreamer nonetheless, because railroad technology of the mid-1830s was so primitive that even the finest locomotives imported from Great Britain proved woefully underpowered to meet the challenges posed by the complex terrain of

Jolly flatboatmen of the Missouri River, as immortalized in the 1840s by George Caleb Bingham. *Courtesy of the St. Louis Mercantile Library* the United States. Many observers were skeptical about the pulling power of iron drive wheels on iron rails on all but the gentlest inclines.

Rail advocates at the time conceded they would probably have to use canal locks and incline planes to lift rail cargoes up and down steep grades, such as would be needed to cross the crest of the Appalachian Mountains west of Philadelphia and Baltimore. The high point on the Pennsylvania state-funded rail-and-canal corridor that opened between Philadelphia and Pittsburgh in 1834 was slightly more than two thousand four hundred feet. The elevation of South Pass, the Rocky Mountain gateway where Parker foresaw the tracks of a transcontinental railroad, was 7,546 feet, or more than three times as high. Ten incline planes powered by twenty stationary steam engines used rope and wire cables to hoist rail cars and canal boats over Pennsylvania's Appalachian Mountains. Could Americans at that time even imagine the kind of technological marvels required to haul trains over the high passes of the Rocky Mountains?

Perhaps even more remarkable, in the mid-1830s when Parker first dared to dream of a railroad to the Pacific, the future cities of Portland, Tacoma, and Seattle did not exist. Nor did the future states of Oregon, Washington, and California. In fact, not a single state lay west of Missouri. At the time, the population centers of the far Northwest consisted of a handful of fur trading posts of the Hudson's Bay Company, a London-based enterprise, and numerous but scattered Indian villages. The non-Indian population of the entire region numbered

The Golden West, as delineated in terms of proposed routes across the continent in 1863 or 1864. Idaho Territory at the time covered an area larger than the present state of Texas. *Courtesy of Montana Historical Society, Helena, Montana, C-61.*

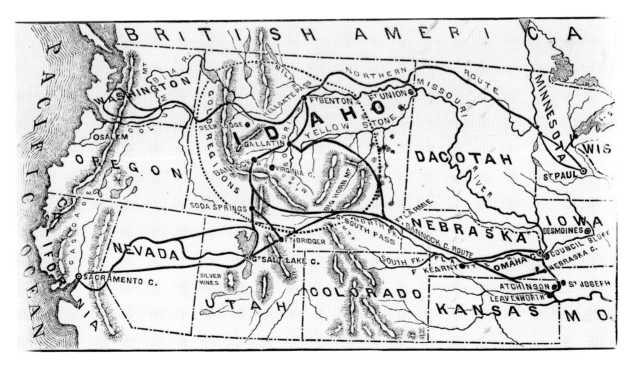

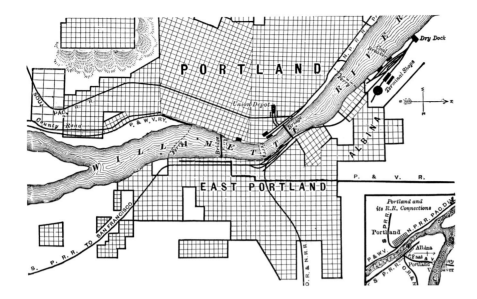

A map of Portland, Oregon, in 1889, showing the location of the Willamette River, which historically had provided steamboat commerce with easy access to the Columbia River and the rich gold diggings and expansive grain fields of eastern Oregon, Washington, and Idaho. *Courtesy of Barriger Railroad Library of the St. Louis Mercantile Library.*

far less than that of the city of Saint Louis alone, which in 1840 counted 16,469 residents.

The first steamboat on the entire West Coast of North and South America was the Hudson's Bay Company's *Beaver*, which commenced regular service at Fort Vancouver on the lower Columbia River in 1836. Among the invited guests on its inaugural excursion run was the missionary Samuel Parker, for whom the novelty of steamboat travel on the Pacific Coast "awakened a train of prospective reflections upon the probable changes, which would take place in these remote regions, in a very few years."[6]

T HE SIGHT OF STEAM PROPULSION ON WILDERNESS WATERWAYS no doubt encouraged Parker's published speculation about a railroad extending to the Pacific. However, apart from a Pacific Railroad inspiring a young nation to flex its growing technological muscle to claim the promise of Manifest Destiny, the question remains: Why should an investor of sound judgment risk even a dollar to build such a line? From a financial standpoint it made absolutely no sense. What passengers would a Pacific Railroad serve? What freight would it carry? Unlike Pennsylvania and New York, or even South Carolina or Indiana, which numbered among the several states that eagerly underwrote the cost of internal improvements in the 1830s, the far Northwest had no functioning governments of any type (apart from Indian tribes and the Hudson's Bay Company) and no sources of investment money.

The village of Portland did not appear on a map of Oregon until 1845, and the villages of Seattle and Tacoma did not appear on a map of Washington Territory until 1854 and 1865, respectively. Seattle and Tacoma could both be characterized as frontier outposts until the 1860s and 1870s. For several more decades the most populous and commercially vigorous of the three isolated settlements was the river city of Portland, which recorded 2,874 residents in 1860 and a mere 8,293 as late as 1870. Given these unimpressive population statistics, the question remains: Even if it were technologically feasible, why should investors spend their dollars to construct a railroad from Saint Louis to the Northwest? Until the discovery of California gold in the late 1840s, the only possibility that made commercial sense was a transcontinental railroad that somehow profited from the wealth of Asian nations, but starting in 1846 the majestic and speedy Clipper ships around Cape Horn proved that they could provide a passage to India and China for far less money. Nonetheless, the vision of lucrative trade with Asia remained topmost in the minds of advocates of a transcontinental railroad.

In the days of Lewis and Clark, Jefferson had dreamed of using the Missouri and Columbia rivers to forge a commercial highway across the West, and the two explorers did suggest that to be a possibility, though only as far as the waterways extended—and that was not nearly far enough. A vast and precipitous emptiness lay between navigable parts of the two great river highways and posed seemingly insurmountable challenges. This was the mountainous terrain that Parker found such an ordeal to cross.

It is easy to dismiss Parker as another of the harmless cranks that enlivened public discourse in the 1820s and 1830s, not unlike the Saint Louisan John Cleaves Symmes, a retired army captain who advanced the theory that the earth was hollow, and that just beyond the icy barrier at its two poles lay the entrance to a mild and enticing interior landscape. Strange as Symmes' "holes in the poles" theory seems today, it attracted a popular following that resulted in the United States Exploring Expedition of 1838–1842. Charles Wilkes commanded the navy equivalent to the Lewis and Clark Expedition, clearly proving that ideas do have consequences, even if Symmes was dead wrong.[7]

While Samuel Parker only speculated that a railroad to the Pacific was possible, Asa Whitney in the mid-1840s committed himself and his financial resources to promoting and launching a project that in many minds must have originally ranked alongside Symmes' "holes in the poles" chimera. Made independently wealthy by business dealings in the Far East, Whitney spent much of his later life lobbying Congress for a transcontinental railroad. In many ways, Whitney, like Jefferson and Parker before him, was a dreamer, though he persisted to promote his grand dream even when faced with Congressional skepticism.

Another dreamer of considerable note in the pre-railroad era was Thomas Hart Benton, a contemporary of Whitney and a United States senator from Missouri after its admission to the Union in 1821. Benton became a good friend of the explorer William Clark, who established his permanent home in Saint Louis not long after returning from his epochal journey to the Pacific. Benton no doubt enjoyed listening to Clark's tales of adventure, and so, too, did his vivacious daughter Jessie Benton, who in 1841 married a noted explorer of her own, John C. Frémont, whose expeditions across the West in the 1840s and early 1850s would inspire Frémont's contemporaries far more than the great odyssey of Lewis and Clark had done in the previous generation.

Benton originally dreamed of using a combination of waterways and wagon roads to connect Saint Louis with the Columbia River region, which offered the best water highway to the imagined wealth of Asia. As early as 1825, Benton urged fellow lawmakers to fund a line of "communication for commercial purposes" between the Missouri River and the north Pacific Ocean. He firmly believed that the compass of opportunity for Saint Louis and the young United States pointed in a northwesterly direction.

Later, after failing to secure support from Senate colleagues to underwrite the cost of an expedition by Frémont to establish the practicality of a passage to the Pacific along the 38th parallel (which happened to run conveniently close to both Saint Louis and San Francisco), Benton arranged for several prominent Saint Louis businessmen, notably Robert Campbell, to bankroll Frémont's fourth exploratory expedition in 1848. Frémont was unsuccessful in locating a workable rail route through the Rocky Mountains along Benton's cherished 38th parallel, but this did not stop the Missouri senator from continuing to champion a national transportation corridor—first a highway and later a railway—extending west to the Pacific from Saint Louis. Political will, he apparently believed, would ultimately triumph over perverse geography.

When an elderly Thomas Hart Benton departed the Senate in 1850 after an unsuccessful bid to serve a sixth term, it still seemed likely that Saint Louis would form the principal commercial gateway to the Pacific, but by that year, significant changes had taken place, upending long-held convictions by Ameri-

Thomas H Benton

Portrait of Thomas Hart Benton (1782–1858), U.S. senator from Missouri from 1821 to 1851. *Courtesy of the St. Louis Mercantile Library.*

cans everywhere. An expansion-minded United States acquired California and other western land in 1848 after a brief war with Mexico. In this way, the nation extended its Pacific coastline another 840 miles south from Oregon to the redrawn border with Mexico. Discovery of gold in newly acquired California and the promise of instant wealth to anyone fortunate enough to find the elusive yellow metal changed how Americans perceived the West. In 1850 Golden California leaped far ahead of the more economically sedate Oregon Country to become the first state west of the Rocky Mountains—the first west of Missouri, in fact. It is no wonder that booming California was thought of as an "island on the land," isolated from the rest of the United States by distance and enclosed by formidable ocean, desert, and high mountain barriers.

A year before California joined the Union, Benton introduced a bill calling for his Congressional colleagues to support a transcontinental railroad west from Saint Louis. That same year, 1849, a Pacific Railroad convention assembled in Saint Louis. It was actually one of several such gatherings in the late 1840s to show popular support for cities aspiring to be the nation's railroad gateway to the Pacific: Memphis held a railroad convention in 1845, and Chicago held another in 1847.

For the Saint Louis convention in October 1849, nearly nine hundred members from ten states assembled in the rotunda of the city's federal courthouse.

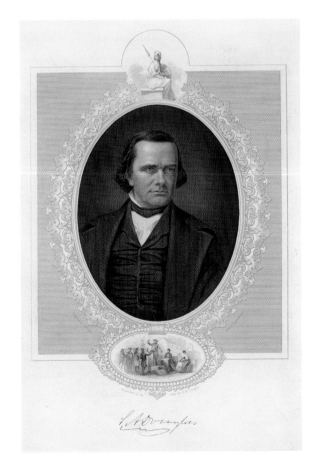

This portrait of Stephen A. Douglas (1813–1861), U.S. senator from Illinois from 1847 to 1861, appeared in *Harper's Weekly*, June 15, 1861, shortly after his untimely death from typhoid fever. *Courtesy of the St. Louis Mercantile Library.*

As might be expected, the two largest delegations came from Missouri and Illinois. Also present were two United States senators representing states on opposite sides of the Mississippi: Thomas Hart Benton, the aging, familiar, and bombastic spokesman for Missouri, and Stephen Arnold Douglas, a fast-rising young Illinoisan elected to the Senate just two years earlier and always a vigorous promoter of the rapidly rising city on Lake Michigan.

The two men vied to chair the gathering. However, after the delegates selected the Illinois senator, Douglas quickly came to believe that the majority had made him chair only to "muzzle" him as an advocate for Chicago. Benton, who had once proclaimed that the western boundary of the United States ought to stop at the crest of the Rocky Mountains, now told delegates that he would like to see a statue of Columbus overlook the proposed corridor through the peaks—"pointing with outstretched arm to the western horizon and saying to the flying passengers, there is the East, there is India."[8] After four days of wrangling, the convention formally supported a railroad route extending

from Saint Louis to San Francisco, with major branch lines running to Chicago
and Memphis. The several railroad conventions of the 1840s illustrated how
important marshaling widespread political support was to bolster a city's territorial ambitions.

At that time, the location of the Pacific Railroad's western terminus was also
a matter of conjecture. Popular excitement caused by the gold bonanza in California in 1848 and 1849 redirected national attention from the Pacific Northwest to booming San Francisco Bay. Already by 1850 the instant metropolis of
San Francisco could claim a population of 34,776, while much older Saint Louis
recorded a population of 77,860, and Chicago, a population of 29,963. Portland,
Oregon Territory, fast becoming the population center and economic hub of the
Pacific Northwest, recorded in 1850 a population of 821 (on a good day).

T HE DECADE OF THE 1850S PROVED CRUCIAL IN THE HISTORY
of a railroad to the Pacific. The dream that Parker, Whitney, and
others first dared commit to paper in the 1830s and 1840s took a
more concrete shape in 1853 when Congress authorized the United
States Army Corps of Topographical Engineers to survey the principal routes for
a Pacific Railroad. Back in 1848, Benton had advised his colleagues regarding
Whitney's proposal that first "we must have surveys, examinations, and explorations made, and not go blindfolded, haphazard into such a scheme."[9]

Secretary of War Jefferson Davis, who oversaw the 1850s surveys, publicly envisioned how a transcontinental railroad would unite a nation prone to division and sectionalism. Such a corridor (noted the future president of the secessionist Confederate States of America) would inspire in Americans living "on opposite sides of snow-covered mountains a common interest, a common feeling, " and Davis looked forward to seeing freight cars loaded with Pennsylvania iron "creeping in a long serpentine track to the slopes of the Pacific" to further the nation's trade with Asia. He also regarded a railroad across the continent as essential to the defense of America's West Coast.[10]

Throughout the 1850s, Saint Louis remained a favored gateway for commerce and travelers to and from the trans-Mississippi West. When John Butterfield launched a transcontinental stage line in 1858—the first commercial transportation across the continent—he promised to provide twice-weekly mail and passenger service across 2,800 miles of open country between the Mississippi Valley and California. On average, twenty-five days of arduous traveling by coach separated the end cities of San Francisco and Saint Louis. A branch line extended across Arkansas to Memphis, a city that benefited from the fact that the nation's postmaster general, who approved federal mail contracts needed to underwrite the overland stage line, hailed from Tennessee. As this example illustrates, federal and state politics played inordinately large roles in determining where the early transportation corridors should run and what cities they should serve, though Missouri in the 1850s still benefited from favorable geography and its location at the center of the United States.

The Pony Express offered still speedier communication across the West, starting on April 3, 1860. In just eleven days, its team of brave riders sped messages from the western end of telegraph and rail lines in Saint Joseph, Missouri, to Sacramento. In all, they sped some thirty-four thousand pieces of mail across the continent until October 26, 1861, the day the nation's first transcontinental telegraph line opened for business. The wire linked Saint Louis and San Francisco by way of Salt Lake City. Communication by Pony Express was exciting and romantic, even to contemporary observers, but the fastest horse could not compete with messages sent coast to coast at the speed of lightning. Thus the Pony Express ceased business after only eighteen months.

At this time, the levee in downtown Saint Louis was still lined with steamboats, and, in fact, steamboats based in Saint Louis pushed ever farther up the Missouri River until they reached the fur outpost of Fort Benton in 1861—ascending more than two-thousand feet to Montana Territory without the aid of locks or any other type of support structures along the river. From Fort Benton, named for Senator Thomas Hart Benton and indicative of how the High Plains

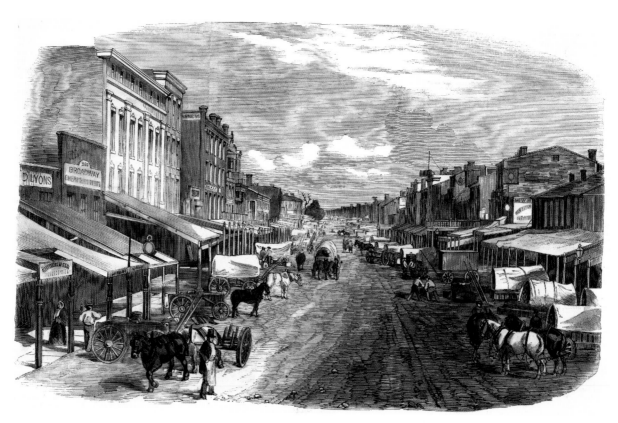

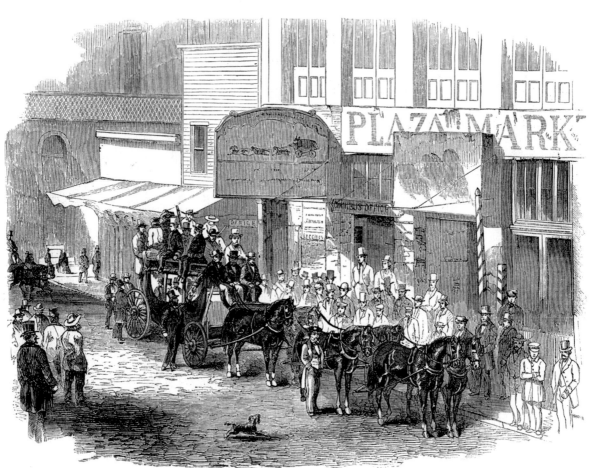

. THE OVERLAND PONY EXPRESS.—[Photographed by Savage, Salt Lake City, from a Painting by George M. Ottinger.]

remained for all practical purposes a satellite of Saint Louis, Congress authorized construction of a military road extending 624 miles west across the Rocky Mountains to Fort Walla Walla, in Washington Territory, where steamboats reached up the Columbia River from Portland. Intended to be part of an army plan for wagon roads in the West, the new corridor seemed certain to benefit both Saint Louis and Portland, the two cities that most effectively controlled the commerce of the Missouri and Columbia rivers. But that was not to be. Captain John Mullan, who had earlier traveled west with Isaac I. Stevens' railroad survey party, launched the project at Fort Walla Walla in the spring of 1859, and he and his 230–member crew completed the road to Fort Benton on August 1, 1862.

A troop of soldiers steamed upriver from Saint Louis and marched from Fort Benton to Fort Walla Walla in fifty-seven days, but the Mullan Road, as the

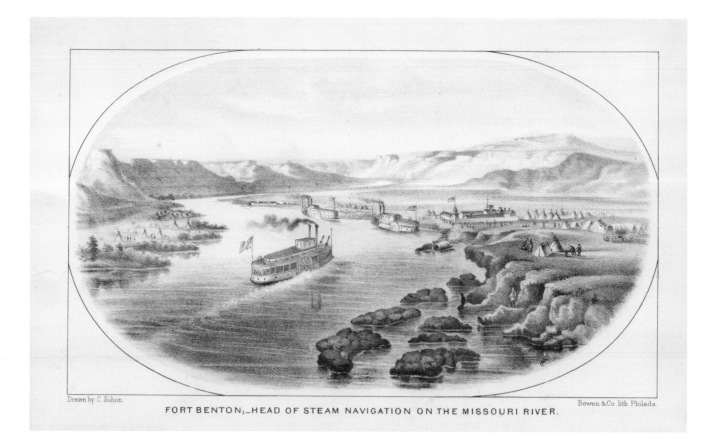

FORT BENTON;—HEAD OF STEAM NAVIGATION ON THE MISSOURI RIVER.

modest trail came to be called, never lived up to its promotion as a new North-west Passage. Despite Congressional expenditures of $230,000 for its construc-tion, its precipitous sections proved impassible in wet or snowy weather, and across the high Rocky Mountains the Mullan Road deteriorated to little more than a horse path unusable by wheeled vehicles. Soon much of the route fell into ruin. It became increasingly obvious in the early 1860s that the passage to the Pacific was to be a railroad line, not a military trace hacked through hundreds of miles of mountain wilderness separating two great waterways. But where should a transcontinental railway begin? That nagging question continued to provoke debate on Capitol Hill and elsewhere.

Only in 1830, when the Baltimore and Ohio completed thirteen miles of track to Ellicott Mills, Maryland, did the first "real" railroad begin operating in the United States. The goal of the railroad was to provide Baltimore and the Chesa-peake Bay region a way to compete successfully for the agricultural wealth of the Ohio Country, which seemed destined to flow through the Erie Canal almost exclusively to the benefit of New York City. By end of the 1850s, railroads from the East Coast had reached the Mississippi River and Lake Michigan, and the

Arriving at Fort Benton in the 1860s, the limit of navigation for Missouri River steamboats from Saint Louis. *Courtesy of Special Collections, Washington State Historical Society.*

Rock Island pushed beyond the Mississippi to give Chicago its first edge over Saint Louis. That was one of many advantages Chicago gained during the crucial 1850s in the contest to define basic spatial relationships in the nation's western hinterland.

T HE COST OF BUILDING A RAILROAD RANGED FROM EXPENSIVE to exceedingly expensive, depending on the nature of the terrain. One estimate is that every mile of track that extended west across the Illinois prairies from Chicago cost an average of $30,000. By contrast, the estimated cost of laying rails west from Saint Louis averaged $50,000 per mile, the increase over Illinois attributed to the hilly terrain of the Ozark Mountains that extend to the south bank of the Missouri River. Barely twenty miles west of the Saint Louis levee, ridges of the Ozark Mountains rose high enough to require the financially struggling Pacific Railroad of Missouri to dig a tunnel six hundred feet long, followed almost immediately by a second tunnel four hundred feet long. That was only the beginning. Missouri's mountain landscape, one Saint Louis enthusiast observed, grew "bolder and grander" and extended "as far as the eye can follow this magnificent scenery."[11] To put the railroad's construction costs in perspective, the money needed to extend a single mile of track west from Saint Louis would purchase a high-quality steamboat or as many as forty elegant Concord stagecoaches. Building a railroad to the Pacific

Route profiles depict the rugged Ozark country that made railroad building west from Saint Louis more expensive than across the relatively flat prairies west of Chicago. *Courtesy of Barriger Railroad Library of the St. Louis Mercantile Library*

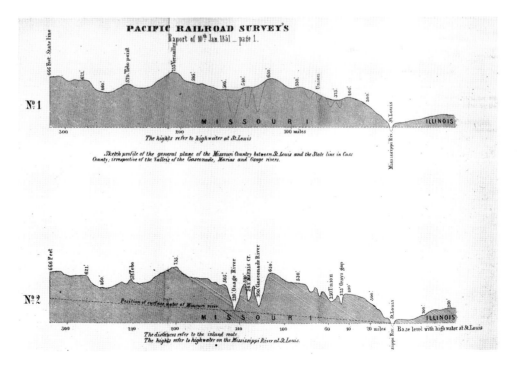

in the 1840s and 1850s, in sum, was expensive beyond the imagination of all but the boldest financial adventurers.

The dollars required to build a railroad line west from Saint Louis or Chicago came in large measure from New England money lenders, all of whom were certain that slavery was wrong. Here the railroad history of the Midwest takes a curious twist as the result of the intermingling of dollars and conscience. When in 1854 Congress passed the Kansas-Nebraska Act sponsored by Senator Douglas, one of the senator's intentions was to open a way for tracks headed to the Pacific from Chicago. What the feisty Illinois lawmaker apparently did not foresee was the political firestorm his legislation would ignite in Kansas, the heat from which reached all the way back east to outrage abolitionist New England.

Pro- and anti-slavery bloodshed in Kansas after 1854 heightened the abolitionists' abhorrence of the "slave power." In Boston and similar communities in the 1850s, many prominent families possessed the tender consciences and fat pocketbooks needed to bankroll an antislavery fight on the plains of Kansas. Many of the same affluent families had provided money to build early railroads across the Midwest, but after the Kansas-Nebraska firestorm in 1854, they redirected their investments from slaveholding Missouri and metropolitan Saint Louis to Chicago in the slavery-free state of Illinois.

During the middle to late 1850s, the flow of New England investment dollars dramatically changed course. As historian William Cronon noted in his classic study, *Nature's Metropolis*, as late as 1850, Saint Louis still handled twice as much wheat and flour as Chicago. But within five years, Chicago had surpassed Saint Louis. The trend only accelerated in the following years, much to the dismay of Saint Louisans.

One Saint Louisan who clearly anticipated the consequences of what Chicago (and to a lesser extent, Memphis) might accomplish with rail lines was Thomas Allen, first president of the Pacific Railroad. The Missouri company (chartered in 1849) was perhaps the first railroad in the United States to declare the distant Pacific Coast as its stated objective, and among the first of dozens of railroads with the name "Pacific" as part of its corporate title.

When President Allen addressed the first meeting of its board of directors in early 1850, the Pacific Railroad existed entirely on paper. That bothered him, and he spared no words to rouse Saint Louisans from what he believed was a type of lethargy fostered by overconfidence. "Nature has done much for us; and it is precisely because she had done so much, that we have not felt the necessity of doing anything for ourselves, while neighbors, at the north and at the south of us, are making much greater exertions to triumph over nature, and to obtain by [industrial] art those advantages with nature left them unprovided." It would be

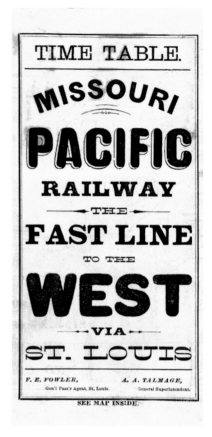

The word "Pacific" still figures prominently on the cover of an 1879 timetable issued by the Missouri Pacific, successor to the Pacific Railroad chartered in 1849. *Courtesy of Barriger Railroad Library of the St. Louis Mercantile Library.*

difficult for Allen or anyone else to immediately reorient the thinking of leading merchants of Saint Louis or to rouse a city made prosperous and too smug and technologically complacent by its growing stream of river commerce. Allen nonetheless counseled his directors, most of whom were the leading merchants of Saint Louis, that if "enemies" succeeded in diverting "the trade of the Upper Mississippi and the Illinois" rivers away from Saint Louis, "the consequences would be felt to be of serious weight." Warming to his subject and dropping the stilted language of his day, Allen went on to warn that Saint Louis "is doing nothing, and proposing to do nothing" but "reposes confidently" on her past growth and prosperity.[12]

During the Pacific Railroad's formal groundbreaking ceremonies in Saint Louis on July 4, 1851, a crowd of as many as twenty thousand residents listened as Allen boasted that within two years his company would receive and deliver more freight and passengers than the entire fleet of Missouri River steamers serving Saint Louis. The day's featured speaker, Edward Bates (a future attorney general in President Lincoln's cabinet), sounded a familiar theme when he boldly predicted that the railroad would run west to California and Oregon and unlock an "immeasurable store of mineral treasures."[13] However, before that could happen, many serious challenges lay ahead, and Allen's worst fears were

Alexander Gardner photographed the modest Pacific Railroad depot in Saint Louis in the 1860s. The palatial Saint Louis Union Station, which once claimed to be the busiest passenger terminal in the world, replaced earlier structures in 1894. *Courtesy of Barriger Railroad Library of the St. Louis Mercantile Library.*

soon realized when Rock Island tracks crossed the Mississippi and diverted river commerce by rail to Chicago, as he had forewarned.

Though the Pacific Railroad received a generous grant of federal land in 1852 to accelerate construction, the pace of track laying remained so agonizingly slow that it made a plodding Missouri mule seem fast by comparison. At one point in 1854 the company received a gift of $1.2 million from Saint Louisans hoping to spur construction of the railroad. But Saint Louisans found it increasingly difficult to raise investment capital from outside the state at a time when rails extended less than halfway across Missouri.

The situation was made still worse by the events of November 1, 1855, the day a celebratory excursion train commenced an inaugural trip from Saint Louis to the end of the track at Jefferson City, the Missouri capital some 125 miles distant. The train, which was composed of eleven cars filled with five-hundred Saint Louis dignitaries (and included a baggage car overflowing with liquor and fine foods), met with unexpected trouble when it started across a temporary trestle spanning the Gasconade River. The nine-hundred-foot wooden structure collapsed without warning and hurled the locomotive and the first three cars into the river. A total of thirty-one passengers died in the Gasconade disaster, including the mayor of Saint Louis, a United States congressman, several state legislators, some prominent merchants, and the railroad's chief of construction. The accident severely injured another seventy people. The blow to the prestige and prospects of the Pacific Railroad was incalculable.

Saint Louis's political and economic fortunes sank to a new low, but as bad as the Gasconade bridge disaster was, things only got worse for the city after the creation of the Confederate States of America and the outbreak of the American Civil War in 1861 dried up the city's lucrative steamboat commerce along the lower Mississippi River. Only in 1865, following the war's end, and after having suffered considerable property damage and loss of life at the hands of guerilla bands sympathetic to the North or South, did the Pacific Railroad of Missouri spike into place the last of 283 miles of track to link Saint Louis and Kansas City. It was a case of too little, too late. Already, by 1860 fully one-third of the thirty-thousand miles of railroad lines in the United States were located in the Old Northwest, with Chicago emerging as the hub of tracks radiating out to Indianapolis, Detroit, Saint Louis, and numerous other points.

I N CONTRAST TO THE RIVALRY BETWEEN SAINT LOUIS AND Chicago to serve as the rail gateway to the American West, events in the Pacific Northwest moved far more slowly during the 1850s. That region's first railroad had no grand aspiration to reach east to Lake Superior, Chi-

Overleaf: A map of the Missouri Pacific and affiliated companies in 1912. The Saint Louis–based railroad reached the Pacific Ocean after a fashion three years earlier, when the Western Pacific Railroad completed a line between Salt Lake City and San Francisco Bay. *Courtesy of Barriger Railroad Library of the St. Louis Mercantile Library.*

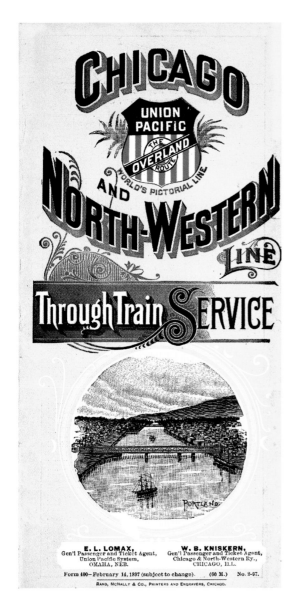

cago, or Saint Louis. It dated from 1850 or 1851 and consisted of a six-mile-long wooden tram that employed a mule and a flat car to portage passengers and freight around a turbulent stretch of the Columbia River that blocked through steamboat travel between Portland and its upriver hinterland. Periodic flooding required rebuilding the portage line several times during the 1850s. By the early 1860s, the pioneer carrier was physically the equal of East Coast railroads of the 1830s, which used wooden rails topped with a bearing surface of iron—though by this time all but the most impoverished eastern railroads had switched to the familiar T-shaped rails fashioned from iron (and later steel).

The Pacific Northwest's earliest rail line (located at the site of present Bonneville Dam) may have been primitive by technological standards of the day, but it served well the needs of a transportation frontier that had little spare capital to invest in expensive projects. The first steam locomotive in the Pacific Northwest was the Oregon Pony, which the Vulcan Iron Works of San Francisco finished in 1861 for the Oregon Portage Railway. The diminutive engine shuttled freight and passengers between steamboats on the lower and middle stretches of the Columbia River for several years.

It is noteworthy that the first railroad in the Pacific Northwest was intended to improve steamboat service on the region's great waterways and thus benefit the fortunes of Portland, where investors in the Oregon Steam Navigation Company became some of the city's first millionaires. Indeed, until the late 1880s it appeared that the region's rail lines were destined to serve mainly as handmaidens of waterways, notably the Columbia and Willamette rivers and majestic Puget Sound in western Washington. All early rail lines threaded their way along river valleys, or linked inland centers like Walla Walla—the former mine supply outpost that became capital of a grain-rich agricultural hinterland, and the most populous settlement in Washington Territory during the 1870s (boasting 2,394 residents)— to a busy steamboat landing on the Columbia River, thirty-two miles away.

The Walla Walla and Columbia River Railroad was a bootstrap operation, a "rawhide railroad" in the derisive lingo of the day, because its track and cars had been constructed

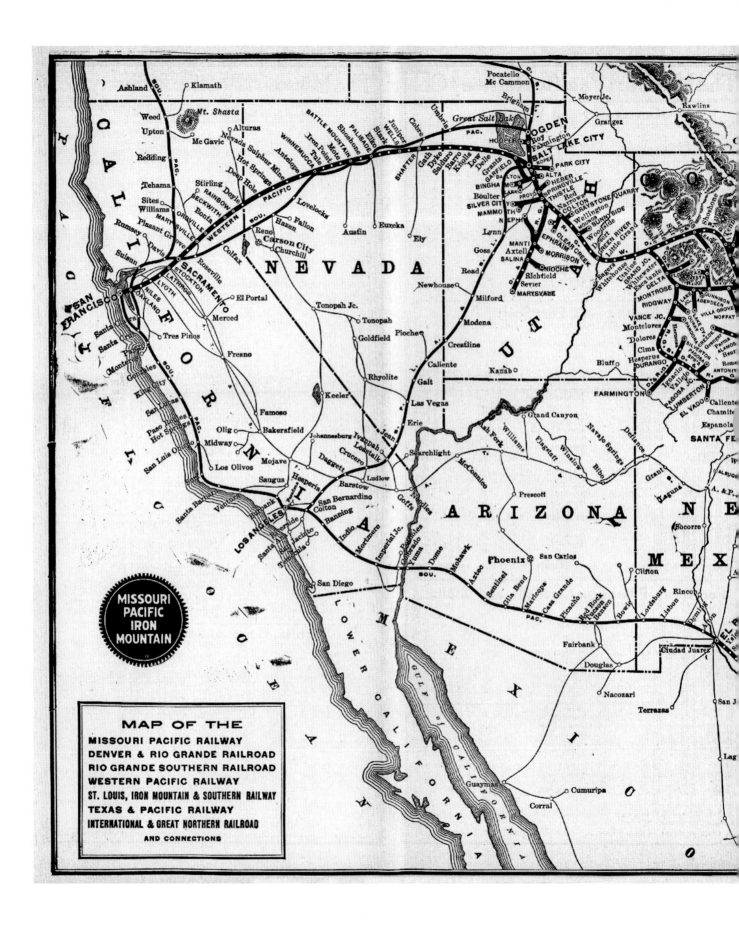

MAP OF THE
MISSOURI PACIFIC RAILWAY
DENVER & RIO GRANDE RAILROAD
RIO GRANDE SOUTHERN RAILROAD
WESTERN PACIFIC RAILWAY
ST. LOUIS, IRON MOUNTAIN & SOUTHERN RAILWAY
TEXAS & PACIFIC RAILWAY
INTERNATIONAL & GREAT NORTHERN RAILROAD
AND CONNECTIONS

MISSOURI
PACIFIC
IRON
MOUNTAIN

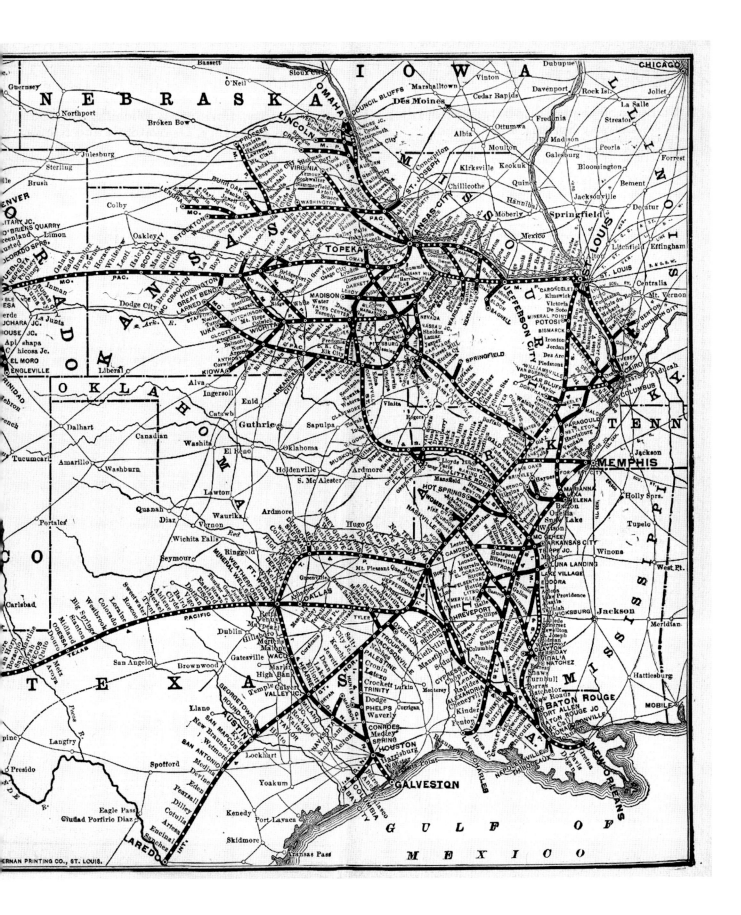

largely from homespun materials. Though an object of general "ridicule and contempt" at the time of its construction in the early 1870s, only fools were still laughing when W. Milnor Roberts, chief engineer for the Northern Pacific Railroad, visited Walla Walla in 1878. As Roberts observed, "it is a perfect gold mine now." He learned from Dr. Dorsey Baker, the local entrepreneur who spearheaded the project, that the railroad had paid off all its debts and was earning "not less than $1,000 per day clear profit—perhaps considerably more."[14]

No wonder the Oregon Steam Navigation Company eagerly added Baker's lucrative railroad to its expanding transportation holdings in the late 1870s. Further, in recognition of the growing railroad contribution to the corporation's bottom line, the Oregon Steam Navigation Company changed its name to the Oregon Railway and Navigation Company in 1879, though the carrier, by whatever name, remained a financial powerhouse. To maintain its monopoly of freight and passenger traffic through much of Oregon and Washington, the pioneer moneymaking machine relied on a large fleet of steamboats in addition to its expanding network of rail feeder lines.

I N THE 1860S, WHEN THE DREAM OF A RAILROAD TO THE PACIFIC dated back at least thirty years, a transcontinental railroad finally took shape. Even as a bloody Civil War threatened to rip apart the United States in 1862, Congress approved legislation to underwrite the cost of a transcontinental railroad. Given the challenges of building such an enterprise across the sparsely populated West, it can be said that Congress's measured response was entirely appropriate to the capabilities of the evolving technology and the slow pace of settlement of the High Plains and Rocky Mountains, though lawmakers were also reacting to sobering new political realities, notably the secessionist menace posed by the South and its rumored appearance on the West Coast.

With Southern states temporarily out of the Union, the partisan debate over which rail corridor was best was effectively resolved in favor of the North—and Chicago in particular. The proposed route embodied a corridor between Omaha and San Francisco Bay that had long been favored by the Pony Express, stagecoaches transporting the United States mail, and the transcontinental telegraph. When completed with appropriate fanfare in the Utah desert in May 1869, the tracks of the nation's newest overland route directly linked Chicago and San Francisco and reduced travel time between them to five days. Meanwhile, Saint Louis struggled to build a Pacific Railroad of its own, though its tracks did not yet extend beyond the boundaries of Missouri. As for the overland stagecoaches that linked Saint Louis and the far West and were operated in

Opposite: A map of Union Pacific tracks across the Pacific Northwest in the early twentieth century. *Courtesy of Special Collections, Washington State Historical Society.*

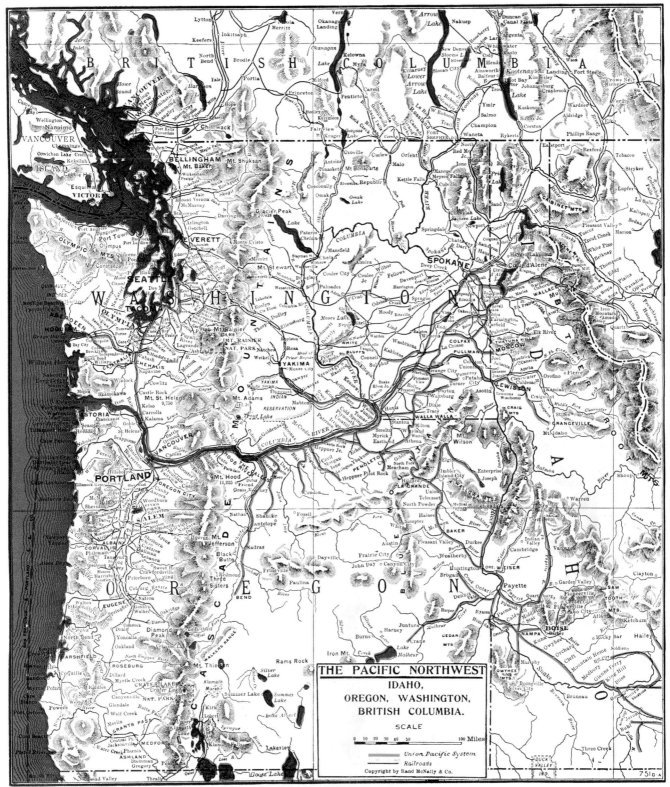

THE PACIFIC NORTHWEST

IDAHO,
OREGON, WASHINGTON,
BRITISH COLUMBIA.

SCALE

0 10 20 30 40 50   100 Miles

———— Union Pacific System

———— Railroads

Copyright by Rand McNally & Co.

JAMES, KERNS & ABBOTT CO. PORTLAND

751o A

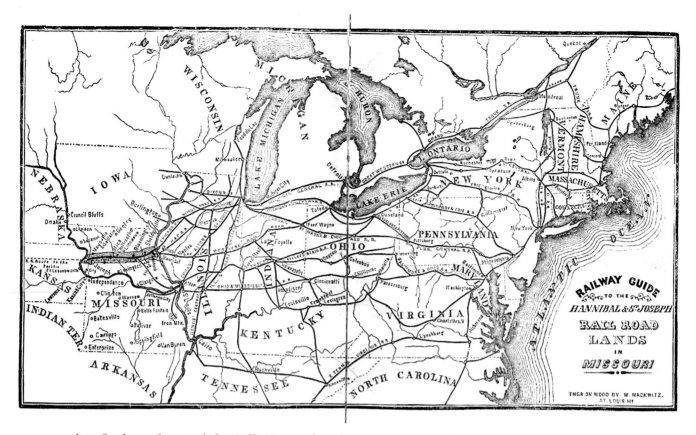

their final months mainly by Wells Fargo, a last short segment ceased running the day after a golden spike joined Union Pacific and Central Pacific tracks at Promontory.

As if to further flabbergast true believers who insisted that Saint Louis was still the nation's gateway to the West, Chicago financial interests acquired the Hannibal and Saint Joseph Railroad, a pioneer Missouri carrier that was without doubt the state's most prosperous early rail link. Chartered by the Missouri Legislature in 1847, the Hannibal and Saint Joseph was initially promoted as likely to benefit Saint Louis by offering easy access to the rich agricultural prairies of northern Missouri and a shortcut for steamboat commerce along the Missouri River above Saint Joseph. However, the railroad, when joined to the prosperous and expanding Chicago, Burlington and Quincy system (funded with New England money), enabled commerce to flow smoothly between Chicago and Kansas City, the metropolis in western Missouri that was fast emerging as the primary commercial nexus for the Great Plains cattle and grain trade, without having to pass even close to Saint Louis.

The cattle trade that made the Chicago stockyards famous could have just as easily gone to Saint Louis, according to the account of cattle pioneer Joseph McCoy. He recalled making a trip to Saint Louis in the 1860s to propose that

The Hannibal and St. Joseph in the late 1850s and early 1860s pictured itself as the most important railroad link between East and West, bypassing Saint Louis to serve a Chicago-oriented hinterland. *Courtesy of Barriger Railroad Library of the St. Louis Mercantile Library.*

CHICAGO AND ALTON RAILROAD.

NO CHANGE OF CARS OF ANY CLASS, And Two Trains a Day Each Way between

CHICAGO AND KANSAS CITY, CHICAGO AND ST. LOUIS, and ST. LOUIS AND KANSAS CITY.

An 1880s map of the Chicago and Alton Railroad illustrates how trains linking Kansas City and Chicago could bypass Saint Louis. *Courtesy of Barriger Railroad Library of the St. Louis Mercantile Library.*

the Pacific Railroad of Missouri invest in the infrastructure needed to transport tens of thousands of Great Plains cattle to Saint Louis slaughterhouses. According to McCoy, the railroad president kicked him out of his office, after which McCoy approached another Missouri railroad, the Hannibal and St. Joseph, which was wholly receptive to his novel idea. Livestock carried by this railroad bypassed Saint Louis by traveling from cattle towns of Kansas straight to Chicago.

During the decades from the 1850s through the 1870s, Chicago's railroads built bridges over both the Mississippi and Missouri rivers to lengthen the city's commercial reach. Ironically, the Mississippi River that had brought prosperity to Saint Louis during the era of the steamboat created nearly insurmountable problems for the city during the early railroad era. What Saint Louis once celebrated as the greatest of water highways increasingly came to be regarded as a moat stifling the flow of commerce. As early as 1857, through rail service com-

menced between Atlantic coast cities and Illinoistown (East Saint Louis) on the bank of the Mississippi River opposite Saint Louis, yet for seventeen more years, all passengers and every box and barrel of freight had to be ferried across the Father of Waters. This cumbersome system proved another impediment to the rapid commercial growth of Saint Louis.

By contrast, Chicago's earliest railroad opened in 1848, and by 1856, only eight years later, it had become the goal of no fewer than ten trunk lines heading its way from cities of the East. Not one of those railroads needed to cross a barrier comparable to the Mississippi River or the Ozark Plateau in its final push to reach its destination. Chicago, not Saint Louis, became the nation's new meeting place between East and West.

The first trans-Mississippi bridge opened at Saint Louis only in 1874, nearly two decades later than Chicago's Rock Island bridge farther north. As with its majestic Gateway Arch completed in 1965, Saint Louis sought a truly monumental

As portrayed in the nation's
centennial year of 1876, the new
"Eads Bridge" connected the
rail yards of East Saint Louis,
Illinois, with metropolitan Saint
Louis, Missouri, on the opposite
bank of the Mississippi River.
Today a light-rail passenger system called Metrolink uses the
lower deck of the historic bridge
to connect Saint Louis with its
suburbs in both states. *Courtesy
of the St. Louis Mercantile
Library.*

structure. The bridge made the boldest possible engineering statement about the
future intentions of the Missouri metropolis, as well as provided it with through
rail connections to markets east of the Mississippi River. In other words, an
impressive new bridge would "symbolize its aspirations of reestablishing economic
dominance in the Middle West, in the face of Chicago's explosive growth."[15]

At Saint Louis, the Mississippi River Bridge (popularly known as the Eads
Bridge after it opened in 1874) was revolutionary in design because its chief
engineer James Buchanan Eads, made extensive use of a strong new construction material called steel. But once again, as had happened so often in its rivalry
with Chicago, it was a case of too little, too late. Curiously, the imposing hori-
zontal steel framework of the Eads Bridge was supposed to have inspired Chicago architect Louis Sullivan to erect a ten-story vertical steel framework that
became the basis for one of America's early skyscrapers, the Wainwright Building, completed in Saint Louis in 1891. But it was in Chicago and New York that

the skyscraper flourished, and in Chicago today stands the tallest building in America, the Sears Tower.

Northern Pacific tracks bridged the Missouri River at Bismarck, Dakota Territory, going west by land where explorers Lewis and Clark had gone by water nearly a century earlier. F. Jay Haynes recorded one of Henry Villard's excursion trains on its way to the final spike ceremony in Montana in September 1883. *Courtesy of Haynes Foundation Collection, Montana Historical Society, Helena, Montana, H-981.*

D URING THE DARK DAYS OF THE CIVIL WAR, IN 1864, Congress authorized federal support for a second transcontinental railroad to be built along the corridor Isaac I. Stevens originally surveyed from Minnesota to Puget Sound in the mid-1850s. The Northern Pacific line was not completed until 1883 because it proved exceedingly difficult to raise the investment dollars needed to build a railroad across what was popularly, if mistakenly, regarded as some of the least desirable land in the United States. Significantly, the first two segments of the Northern Pacific to be completed were overland links between waterways. Tracks at the western end joined Puget Sound with the lower Columbia River and formed a hundred-mile-long rail portage between Portland and Tacoma and Seattle. Tracks at the eastern end joined Lake Superior near Duluth with the Missouri River at Bismarck, a distance of 450 miles.

The onset of hard times in 1873 dried up capital, halted construction, and left a gap of more than a thousand miles between the two segments of the Northern Pacific. Work did not commence again until almost the end of the 1870s. When it did, one achievement of great practical as well as symbolic importance was the completion of an impressive rail bridge over the Missouri River at Bismarck. Lewis and Clark had passed that way almost eighty years earlier, and the Northern Pacific later liked to brag in advertisements that it had completed what Lewis and Clark began.

Significantly, when the Northern Pacific reached the Columbia Valley near Pasco, Washington Territory, its trains switched to the tracks of the Oregon Railway and Navigation Company to reach Portland before returning to its own tracks from there to Puget Sound, the Northern Pacific's intended terminus. The roundabout course benefited Portland and continued to utilize the banks of the Columbia River for a railroad right-of-way.

However, thirty-two years after Rock Island tracks bridged the Mississippi River, to the lasting benefit of Chicago and the consternation of steamboatmen, Northern Pacific tracks bridged the Columbia River at Pasco in 1888. From there they threaded their way along the fertile Yakima Valley and through a

Northern Pacific tracks bridged the Columbia River between Kennewick and Pasco in the mid-1880s on their way west to Puget Sound. *Courtesy of Special Collections, Washington State Historical Society.*

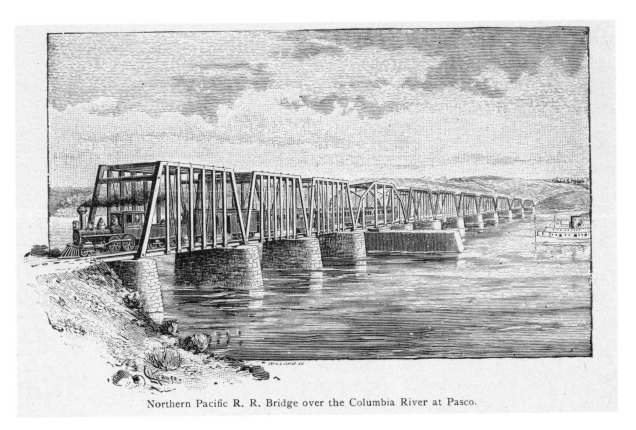

Northern Pacific R. R. Bridge over the Columbia River at Pasco.

newly bored tunnel nearly two miles long beneath Stampede Pass and the crest of the Cascade Mountains to create a major shortcut to Puget Sound. Tacoma residents took time to publicly celebrate the Northern Pacific's long-awaited but notable accomplishment. A good claim can be made that the name Pasco is railroad derived and signifies the place where Northern Pacific tracks "pass over the Columbia." As was predictable, the first bridge across the Columbia River within the United States had the same impact on cities of the far Northwest as the first rail bridge across the Mississippi River had on the cities of the Midwest.

Residents of Puget Sound communities, notably Tacoma and its rival, Seattle, had long dreamed of forging direct rail connections between the agricultural empire emerging from the farm and the ranch lands of eastern Washington and the ocean shipping companies that connected ports of the Pacific Northwest with California as well as the distant cities in Asia and Europe. The developing ports of Puget Sound had for years envied Portland, a city seemingly favored by nature and an extensive system of good river highways that brought prosperity with every boat that arrived or left its wharves. Now, with railroad technology and the new bridge across the Columbia River, cargoes could speed between the wharves of Tacoma and Seattle (bypassing Portland) on their way to Saint Paul, the end of Northern Pacific tracks, as well as continue to Chicago and cities of the East Coast over a variety of competing lines.

A familiar story was repeated in the late 1880s and 1890s: Just as in 1856 Rock Island tracks reached across the Mississippi to benefit rail-oriented Chicago at the expense of river-oriented Saint Louis, so too the rail bridge over the Columbia River at Pasco favored upstarts Tacoma and Seattle over river-oriented Portland. Like Saint Louis, Portland had grown smug and prosperous as a result of river commerce and the steamboat fleet that since the early 1860s had funneled gold, grain, and other valuable commerce through the city. But rail lines that extended east over the Cascade Mountains from Seattle and Tacoma in the 1880s threatened Portland's hegemony.

This is not to say that Saint Louis and Portland lacked rail lines of their own. During the expansive decade of the 1880s, Southern Pacific tracks linked Portland with San Francisco and Los Angeles, and Union Pacific tracks linked it to Denver, Kansas City, Omaha, Chicago, and Saint Louis. From Saint Louis, a number of railroads headed west: The Missouri Pacific (successor to the Pacific Railroad of Missouri) ultimately reached Pueblo, Colorado, but not the Pacific Ocean, and the Saint Louis-San Francisco Line reached western Oklahoma before it ran out of financial steam. Its tracks never reached San Francisco—or even the base of the Rocky Mountains. In extending the commercial reach of Portland and Saint Louis, in short, their respective railroads tended to offer too little, too late. To be sure, each city prospered, but neither dominated their respective regions the way Chicago and Seattle did after 1900.

C HICAGO FIRST SURPASSED SAINT LOUIS IN POPULATION IN the 1880 census, and after that year the Lake Michigan city never looked back over its shoulder to see if Saint Louis was gaining on it. Ten years later, Chicago boasted of a population of 1,099,850 to Saint Louis's 451,770. The same reversal occurred in the Pacific Northwest, where in 1910 Seattle for the first time surpassed Portland in population, and the metropolis of Puget Sound, like Chicago in the Heartland, never lost its front-runner status.[16]

Many forces, both natural and human, shaped the expanding network of tracks between the Great Lakes and Mississippi Valley and the Far Northwest, yet the essence of the story is urban rivalry—Chicago versus Saint Louis, and the Puget Sound cities of Seattle and Tacoma versus Portland—and rail bridges over the Mississippi River at Rock Island and Saint Louis and over the Columbia at Pasco fueled their spatial contests.

Back in the 1830s, during the earliest days of railroads in the United States, most visionaries, particularly those living on the East Coast, thought of railroads mainly as a way to expand the usefulness of the nation's superb network of waterways. The names they gave their early railroads were geographically evocative and addressed their role as supplements to the system of waterways: Delaware and Hudson, Hudson River and Lake Erie, Mohawk and Hudson, Baltimore and Ohio. The names refer not to states or Indian tribes but to the Delaware, Mohawk, and Ohio rivers.

The names of the transcontinental railroads that reached the far Northwest, with the exception of the Great Northern, spoke of a desire to reach the Pacific Ocean: Northern Pacific; Union Pacific; Southern Pacific; Chicago, Milwaukee, Saint Paul, and Pacific; and the Canadian Pacific north of the border. Their ambitions were as grand as their names, but, regardless of their stated geographic goals and well before they actually reached the ports of the Pacific, their tracks, wherever they extended across the West—and this was true even for the region's shortest carriers—profoundly transformed whatever they touched. What happened to the fortunes of Chicago, Saint Louis, Portland, Tacoma, and Seattle is merely an illustration of what happened to many other communities, both great and small, along the lengthening corridors of iron and steel.

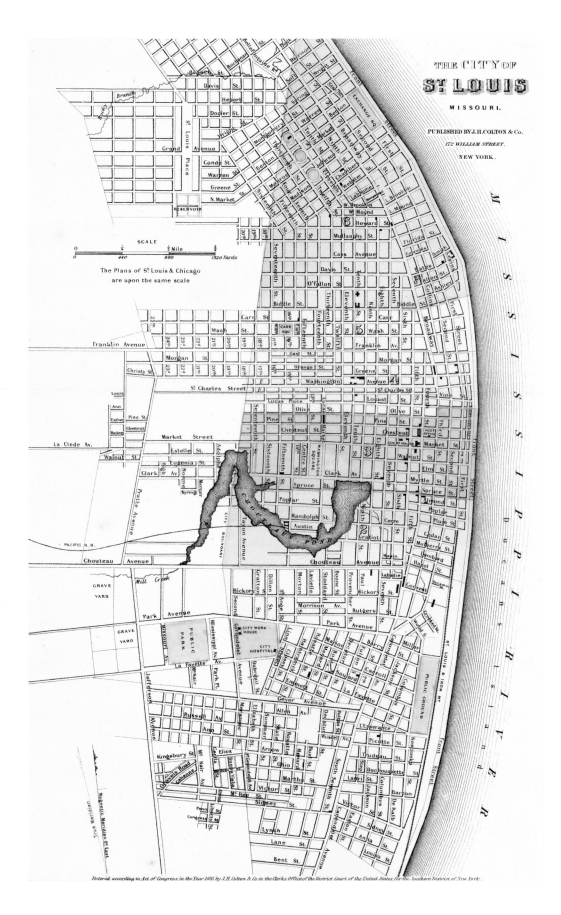

An 1855 map of Saint Louis highlights its location along the Mississippi River. *Courtesy of Special Collections, Washington State Historical Society.*

A companion map, drawn
to the same scale as the
Saint Louis map, high-
lights Chicago's location
on Lake Michigan. Note
the railroad lines on both
maps. *Courtesy of Special
Collections, Washington
State Historical Society.*

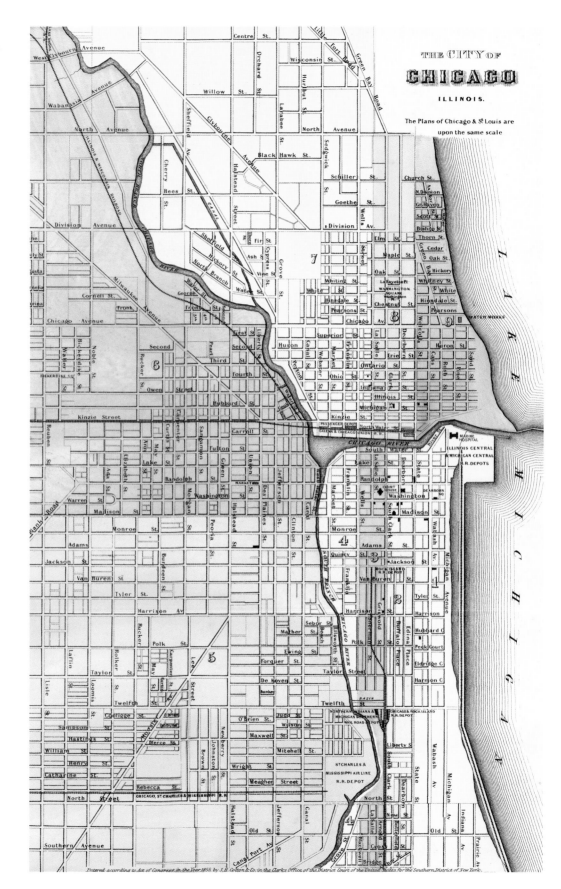

"How Science Aids the Traveler." This brochure cover shows the Milwaukee Road's transcontinental main line through mountainous central Montana in the early 1920s, when electricity powered the locomotives. *Courtesy of Special Collections, Washington State Historical Society.*

CONSIDER, FOR INSTANCE, THE FATE OF FORT BENTON, Montana. The surname of the expansion-minded senator from Missouri, Thomas Hart Benton, is today recalled by Benton County (both in Oregon and Washington), and the Montana village situated as far upriver as a steamboat could travel from Saint Louis or New Orleans. Fort Benton has been labeled the farthest inland port in the world. Its waterfront was once a hive of activity, especially during the feverish gold rushes to Montana and Idaho in the 1860s. From its levee "flowed the commerce of a great inland empire. From Wyoming deep into British North America, the plains country paid tribute to the little inland port," observed Paul Sharp in his classic history, *Whoop-Up Country.*[17]

During Fort Benton's heyday as the vital link between river commerce and the prairie and mountain outposts of the United States and Canada, the focal point of everyday life was its Grand Union Hotel, which boosters claimed featured

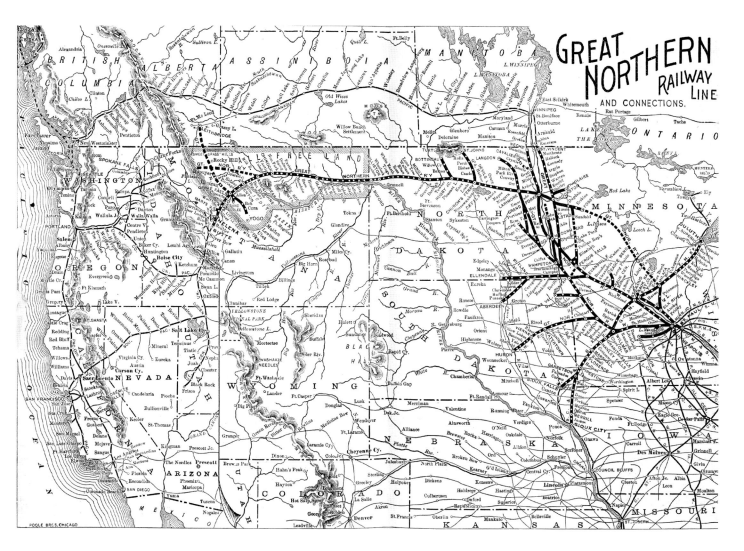

GREAT NORTHERN RAILWAY LINE AND CONNECTIONS.

A map of the Great Northern Railway in 1889 illustrates the great importance of the copper mines of Butte and the free land elsewhere in Montana. An extension of the tracks heading west to Seattle to tap the commerce of the Pacific Rim is shown almost as an afterthought. *Courtesy of Barriger Railroad Library of the St. Louis Mercantile Library.*

the finest accommodations between Minneapolis and Seattle. Their claim may have been true. This much is certainly true: after the tracks of the Great Northern Railway passed through Fort Benton to connect Saint Paul with the "world's greatest copper camp," booming Butte, Montana, in the late 1880s, river commerce effectively dried up. Though Fort Benton is no ghost town today, its quiet, tree-shaded streets and empty levee suggest that it is but a shadow of its former busy self. By the 1880s there was no doubt that the future of the West was what the railroads willed it to be. Their "magic" left no part of the region untouched. In ways both obvious and subtle, the railroads transformed established places, patterns, and relationships, even as they also created entirely new ones.

The new Garden of Eden, as depicted on the front cover of the Southern Pacific brochure *California for the Settler*. Courtesy of Barriger Railroad Library of the St. Louis Mercantile Library.

The truth is, that the completion of the railroad and the consequent great increase of business and population, will not be a benefit to all of us, but only to a portion.

—HENRY GEORGE, "WHAT THE RAILROAD WILL BRING US"

3

Tracking a Transformation

IN OCTOBER 1868, AS AMERICA'S FIRST TRANSCONTINENTAL railroad neared completion, Henry George's insightfully titled essay "What the Railroad Will Bring Us" appeared in the *Overland Monthly*, a popular California magazine. George predicted that tracks and trains would forever alter California. "All over it is felt that the old era of stagecoaches and ox and mule transportation is rapidly passing away, and that the locomotive, soon to penetrate the State in all directions, will in future carry the wheat to the wharf, the ore to the mill, the timber to the mine; supply the deficiency of navigable streams, open up millions of acres of the best fruit and grain lands in the world, and make accessible and workable thousands of rich mines." The coming transcontinental railroad, George confidently predicted, would "not merely open a new route across the continent; it will be the means of converting a wilderness into a populous empire in less time than many of the cathedrals and palaces of Europe were built, and in unlocking treasure vaults, which will flood the world with precious metals."[1]

George also pondered the power of a transcontinental railroad to transform radically both time and space: "We are so used to the California of the stagecoach, widely separated from the rest of the world, that we can hardly realize what the California of the railroad will be—the California netted with iron tracks, and almost as near in point of time to Chicago and St. Louis" as Virginia

City, Nevada, was to San Francisco when the great Comstock silver mining excitement commenced in 1859, "or as Red Bluff [California] is now."

The California of Henry George was only one example of the transformations wrought by tracks and trains. In Washington's Yakima Valley, as in most parts of the West once devoted almost exclusively to grazing, the railroad totally transformed the agricultural landscape. The fertile valley noted for its nutritious bunchgrass and mild winter climate had long been a paradise for raisers of cattle and horses. "Of course the railroad disturbed this cattle paradise. The land was too good to be thus given over to cattle and horses for the benefit of the lucky few, and so man has come in to increase and multiply and fill up the garden spots," observed one publicist in 1887.[2]

Transformation from "wilderness to empire" by the power of railroads was a popular topic during the last third of the nineteenth century. "A new age has happily dawned for Oregon and Washington Territory, as well as for other States of the grand Northwest. The era of railroads has opened for them, and the serious impediment to their progress will soon be removed."[3]

Residents need only ponder the many changes they witnessed around them to understand fully the West the railroads made in practical and personal

This helpful guide tells how to establish a home in the West that the Northern Pacific was fashioning along its tracks in the late 1890s. *Courtesy of Special Collections, Washington State Historical Society.*

terms—for good or for ill. Because of railroads, "the old channels of commerce are broken up, and the points which depended upon them are left to philosophize upon the mutability of human affairs in forgotten obscurity," observed Charles and Henry Adams in 1871.[4]

The railroad transformation of the West took many forms. Perhaps most dramatic was the emergence of substantial communities fashioned from brick and stone instead of from logs or rough-hewn lumber, as was the rustic hallmark of frontier outposts across the West. "Tacoma emerged by her own efforts from the condition of a straggling village to that of a large, self-reliant commercial town, with well-built banks, daily newspapers, steamboat lines, manufactories, and the finest hotel on the Pacific coast north of San Francisco," bragged the Northern Pacific in 1887.[5] The instant cities of the West invariably formed regional centers of commerce and trade. In addition to Tacoma and the original great metropolis of the West, San Francisco, other new cities transformed spatial relationships across the region: Portland, Seattle, Salt Lake City, Denver, and the gangliest and fastest-growing adolescent of them all, Los Angeles.

Along numerous rail lines that by 1880 bisected the Great Plains, new settlements sprang up like Kansas wildflowers—and some died just as quickly. Perhaps, however, what most impressed and sobered transcontinental train travelers was what was missing among the Great Plains wildflowers: By the late 1880s observers of the transformation of the American West fretted aloud over the rapid disappearance of wild animals. Where were the immense herds of bison that had only recently roamed freely across the prairies? Only a generation or two earlier, travelers by overland stagecoach had marveled as they paused to watch seemingly limitless herds of shaggy bison intersect their rutted trail and often block their way for minutes and even hours.

It had been easy for early travelers to imagine that western wildlife was abundant beyond belief, and that the trigger-happy man who relieved the boredom of an overland stage journey by using bison, antelope, prairie dogs, grouse, and other wild creatures for target practice could never diminish their numbers. Hunting for sport—if that is what one called randomly targeting wildlife from a slow-moving stagecoach or the deck of a Missouri River steamboat—was common on the long journeys that required weeks of hard traveling. Observers noted that many wild animals simply learned to stay out of range. Rather, it was the systematic slaughter of western wildlife, primarily bison, on an industrial scale that devastated the herds and transformed the natural landscape and ecology of the Great Plains.

Railroads in recent years, grumbled the journal *Forest and Stream*, had "sought eagerly for the transportation of meat and hides from the regions where

they were killed by hunters, forgetting that by thus encouraging the slaughter of this game, they were cutting off one of the greatest attractions to passenger traffic over their lines." For that reason the Northern Pacific Railway ceased quoting rates for wild meat in the late 1880s. The northern transcontinental realized almost too late that "to a very considerable portion of the traveling public, the game and fish of the region traversed by the Northern Pacific Railroads constitutes its chief attraction. This large and ever increasing class of travelers are well-to-do people, who have money to spend, and are thus desirable patrons of the road. Any course which will decrease the supply of the game which they see will tend to reduce the travel over the road by this class, who will go where they believe game to be most abundant."[6]

A Scandinavian engraving illustrates the railroads' impact on the wildlife of the West. *Courtesy of Barriger Railroad Library of the St. Louis Mercantile Library.*

EVEN AS RAILROADS "CIVILIZED" THE WEST BY LESSENING the region's perceived wildness, they imposed industrial uniformity in place of nature's unpredictability; and they took justifiable pride in engineering achievements that ensured the efficient, habitual, and safe operations of trains year-round. Sweaty construction crews sliced through and transformed thousands of miles of uneven terrain with precisely aligned cuts and fills to keep track grades and curves manageable by puffing locomotives. Trestles bridged deep ravines and tunnels bored through mountains to forge new transportation corridors that surpassed nature's own inadequate designs, and railroads added countless stations, roundhouses, switching yards, and other support structures to the landscape. In all they did, railroads dared leave nothing to chance. Everything from the roadbed to the locomotives was carefully and precisely engineered. Curves and grades conformed to exact mathematical calculations to ensure the repeatable and predictable results that safe and successful railroad operation demanded. Approximation was no longer good enough.

Railroads excelled at creating industrial order where no pattern of organization existed apart from nature, of being agents of change that, in the words of

The results of a successful hunt in the West in 1872 are perhaps typical of Gilded Age excess. Courtesy of Minnesota Historical Society.

historian John Higham, transformed the West from "boundlessness to consolidation." The thirteen massive volumes of the Pacific Railroad Surveys of the 1850s exemplify the initial stage of this process of reordering the West, because they classified and categorized as never before the innumerable natural features of the hitherto boundless region. The illustrations by skilled survey artists aided the transformation of popular perceptions of the landscape. The surveyors continued the process by using precisely calibrated instruments to quantify the West in terms of degrees and distance as they staked out prospective railroad lines. Never before had the West's landscape been defined so precisely.

The process of transforming the West continued, and even accelerated, once railroad operations began. Something seemingly so simple as the space between the two rails could not vary by more than a fraction of an inch, or the locomotives and cars would derail. Mile after mile, the transcontinental lines maintained a standard gauge of four feet eight and one half inches (though some mountain lines of the West saved money by using a narrow gauge of three feet between the rails).

Uniform gauge was only one example of an industry's passion for precision and standardization in all it did. When a railroad hired contractors to construct its right-of-way it provided them detailed specifications—even for the proper

Even the Great Plains of Kansas were not level enough for successful railroad operations. *Courtesy of Barriger Railroad Library of the St. Louis Mercantile Library*

Track Gauge and Urban Empires

Track gauge may at first seem like the dullest of subjects, but history reveals how the distance between the rails is rich in symbolism and suggests how even experts once emphasized the local, not the national, reach of American railroads. James P. Kirkwood, chief engineer for the Pacific Railroad of Missouri, addressed the company's board of directors in Saint Louis in June 1851 on the proper gauge for their as-yet unbuilt line. After noting that the prevailing track gauge in England and parts of the East Coast of the United States was four feet, eight and one-half inches, he nonetheless urged them to adopt what he considered the more practical gauge of five feet, six inches, noting that Saint Louis need not worry about its connections to other rail lines because of the Mississippi River. At the time the major cities of North America—including Montreal, Boston, New York, Philadelphia, Baltimore, Richmond, and Charleston on the Atlantic seaboard—still thought in terms of defending, dominating, and extending commercial empires connected to them by rail or water, not interchanging freight or passenger cars to forge a continent-wide network of railroad lines.

"In fixing upon a gauge for your road," observed Kirkwood, "you are not trammeled by considerations of convenience affecting your connection with other roads. You are so situated as to be able to choose the gauge best adapted, without much increase of expense, to the requirements of a railroad so far as we understand these now." History soon proved Kirkwood wrong, though in 1853 the Missouri legislature approved a law that fixed the gauge, "or width between the rails," of "all railroads in this State" at five feet six inches, just as he had recommended.

—James P. Kirkwood, *Report on Gauge of Track to Board of Directors of Pacific Railroad, Missouri* (Saint Louis: Intelligencer, 1854), 11.

The Union Pacific's impressive right-of-way across the Missouri River at Omaha, Nebraska. The railroad removed the massive buffalo head during World War II and donated the metal to make armaments. *Courtesy of Barriger Railroad Library of the St. Louis Mercantile Library.*

size and spacing of the cross ties. W. Milnor Roberts, chief engineer of the
Northern Pacific, specified in a construction contract let in 1878 for two hundred
miles across the High Plains between the Missouri and Yellowstone rivers that
"cross-ties shall be eight (8) feet long, six (6) inches thick, and six (6) inches face:
must he hewn, of White Oak, Rock Elm, White Pine or Tamarac, and must be
perfectly sound. Ties will be so spaced as to require twenty-six hundred and
forty (2,640) to each and every mile of main and side track."[7] Eventually, and
with occasional prodding from federal regulators, everything from paper thick-
ness to envelope sizes in company offices was standardized within the railroad
industry.

The railroad passion for precision extended even to uniforms worn by their
passenger-train personnel. The Northern Pacific, for instance, published a sar-
torial guide titled "Rules Governing Uniforming of Employes and Specifications
of Uniforms." The company advised its employees that they were "at liberty to
purchase materials for uniforms wherever they choose, but no deviation from
quality specification or color or cloth or other uniform materials hereinafter
specified, will be permitted." It required that all employees working aboard passenger trains "must wear clean white linen (shirts, collars, cuffs); and shoes
must be kept polished. Those who wear beards or mustaches must keep them

A web of standard-gauge tracks defined the urban landscape of Saint Joseph, Missouri, in 1887. In the distance is the Missouri River, the former highway to the West, which seems almost to fade away in this illustration from *Frank Leslie's Illustrated Newspaper. Courtesy of the St. Louis Mercantile Library.*

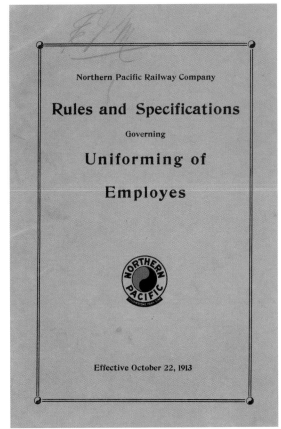

Northern Pacific Railway Company

Rules and Specifications

Governing

Uniforming of

Employes

Effective October 22, 1913

Standardizing Northern Pacific passenger train personnel. *Courtesy of Special Collections, Washington State Historical Society.*

neatly trimmed, otherwise must be cleanly shaven. The use of celluloid or rubber collars or cuffs will not be permitted." A Northern Pacific superintendent periodically inspected the appearance of all employees who dealt with the public aboard its passenger trains.[8]

While one lengthy set of rules governed employee grooming, another governed train operations—and even employees' leisure hours. No railroad company tolerated a drunken employee endangering the safety of passengers or fellow employees. One West Coast railroad rulebook in the 1880s warned that "the use of intoxicating liquors and frequenting of saloons is prohibited." Any employee "appearing in a state of intoxication" was to be dismissed immediately. Conversely, loyal employees who avoided intoxicating beverages received preferential treatment in promotion.[9]

*T*HE RAILROADS' MOST NOTABLE FEAT OF TRANSFORMATION was their adoption of the system of standardized time familiar across North America today. That action clearly epitomized their power to transform society through practical application of science and engineering. This was the most successful and far-reaching triumph of modernity (as epitomized by railroad-imposed order) over local and premodern ways governed by the rhythms of nature as represented by extremes of weather, seasonal changes, and even the contrast between hours of daylight and darkness. Railroad regularity invariably trumped nature's seasonal variations and weather eccentricities.

One particularly dramatic photograph dating from the early 1880s shows steam locomotives lined up like circus elephants atop the Northern Pacific's newly constructed bridge over the Missouri River at Bismarck, Dakota Territory. The image illustrates a common method railroads used at the time to field-test the strength and safety of bridges before the first passenger and freight trains chugged across them. Less obvious was that the bridge at Bismarck towered above the water corridor that Lewis and Clark had followed eight decades earlier and that steamboats based in Saint Louis had used in more recent years for fur-trade commerce and gold-camp traffic. Once again, as with the Mississippi River Bridge at Rock Island in 1856, feats of railroad engineering triumphed literally as well as symbolically over familiar steamboat technology and redefined spatial relationships—and yearly seasonal variations, too.

One reason that the Lewis and Clark Expedition had wintered at Fort Mandan, a historic site about fifty miles north of the new bridge, was that the Missouri River freezes solid and impedes water travel until the spring thaw six months later. In later years, the Missouri River commerce based in Saint Louis shut down each winter. On the Columbia River's water highway system west of the Rockies, winter ice likewise halted steamboat traffic between Portland and the inland port of Lewiston, Idaho, trailhead for the northern mines in the 1860s.

During the 1850s and 1860s, when steamboats and stagecoaches dominated long-distance travel across the West, their schedules varied according to the season. Not only did ice halt river travel for several months at a time, but ice and drifting snow in the high mountain passes greatly slowed the pace of overland stagecoaches and their vital cargoes of mail, or stopped them literally in their tracks. Stage operators commonly substituted horse-drawn sleighs for wheeled vehicles, but the fickle weather common in the Rocky Mountains might suddenly turn warm and trap a heavily laden sleigh in slimy mud and melting snow and ice. Then it was the long-suffering passengers' unstated obligation to climb

Using the weight of locomotives to test the Northern Pacific's new bridge across the Missouri River at Bismarck. The camera of F. Jay Haynes recorded this odd scene on October 21, 1882. *Courtesy of Haynes Foundation Collection, Montana Historical Society, Helena, Montana, H-815.*

down and help the driver push the sleigh through the cold muck, or simply to walk ahead to the nearest stage station and wait. Let rivers freeze solid and let sleighs carrying Uncle Sam's mail wallow through knee-deep muck or buck drifting snow. In the new railroad era, steam locomotives and their passenger and freight trains would roll with impunity across frozen waterways and through icy mountains passes to reach their destinations regardless of the weather, and generally on schedule.

American railroads had a long history of triumphing over nature. Starting in the early 1830s, they turned night into day by mounting massive headlights on locomotives, and thus operated trains around the clock. Likewise, they did not scale back operations or abandon their regular schedules with the first heavy snowfall of winter. Instead, the railroads used a combination of technology and muscle to triumph over nature. They dispatched snowplows of various types and armies of shovel-wielding workers to clear the tracks and keep trains moving. Only rarely did their best efforts fail. Whenever the railroads lost a battle with Old Man Winter, their temporary plight gladdened the hearts of local journalists eager to write maudlin human-interest stories about snowbound trains and marooned passengers.

With proper equipment on the job, there was no reason why winter operations should be any different from those of summer. Each season posed special challenges that the railroaders successfully met. Further, with a steady and consistent service that no previous mode of transportation could provide, railroads transformed or eliminated the seasonal variations once ingrained in Americans since birth. Only consider the nation's dietary habits. Fresh oranges and grapefruit, for instance, were once unimaginable luxuries on the breakfast table, especially in the Midwest during the long winter season. Yet, beginning with the widespread use of refrigerated cars in the 1880s, all kinds of fruit—from apples

Union Pacific used technology such as steam-powered rotary snowplows to remove snow drifts blocking its tracks and maintain regular train operations through the winter months. *Courtesy of California State Railroad Museum Library.*

and cherries to lemons and peaches—sped east from newly planted orchards in southern California or the Pacific Northwest to help provide wholesome and nutritious meals for families in places as distant as New York and Massachusetts. Perishable cargoes traveled inside insulated cars that protected them from the ill effects of the winter chill and the summer heat. In time, seasonal variations meant no more to the railroads of the West than differences between night and day.

I N THE FALL OF 1883 A GROUP OF WELL-DRESSED LADIES AND gentlemen gathered with much fanfare in the wilds of Montana Territory. In their stylishness and cool elegance they looked conspicuously out of place. Some had traveled from as far as England, the Netherlands, and Germany to this isolated patch of sagebrush and sand on the banks of the Clark Fork River, and they had done so willingly. Nearby stood a large sign that read "Lake Superior 1,198 miles / Puget Sound 847 miles." It reminded visitors that they had assembled almost literally in the middle of nowhere.

Among the various grandees present for the day's events were former president Ulysses S. Grant, former secretary of state William Evarts (the featured speaker), and the governors of the states and territories linked to this desolate site by the tracks that were the sole reason for the unusual gathering. The guests of the Northern Pacific Railroad had traveled to Gold Creek, Montana, aboard five luxury trains to witness the driving of the last spike that marked the formal opening of the first transcontinental rails linking the Midwest and the Pacific Northwest—the railroad-made West.

Despite historic ties of kinship and commerce, never before had the Midwest

The site of the Northern Pacific's last-spike ceremony in Montana Territory on September 8, 1883, was precisely 1,198 miles west of Lake Superior and 847 miles east of Puget Sound. *Harper's Weekly* published the large engraving on September 22, 1883. *Courtesy of Barriger Railroad Library of the St. Louis Mercantile Library.*

and Pacific Northwest been able to embrace more intimately than they did on September 8, 1883, when the Northern Pacific Railroad radically redefined the time and space that separated the two regions. More than ever before, boundless space became precisely definable time: the two regions now lay less than a week apart by passenger train.

After the loud band music, the flowery oratory, and the last sledgehammer blows drove a golden spike into place, the Glittering Ones reboarded their special trains and left Gold Creek, most of them never to return. The day had been rich in symbolism. For one moment, the old West of Indians, trappers, and pioneers had stood face to face with the new West of high finance, nationwide markets, and rapid advances in communication and transportation.

A little more than two months later, on another day rich in symbolism, North Americans collectively reset their clocks and watches to standard time—though traditionalists in the United States and Canada protested railroad imposition of uniform time standards by refusing to march in step with the majority. The completion of a northern transcontinental rail line in Montana in September 1883 and the reordering of timekeeping across North America the following November were not closely connected events—or were they? In fact, the system of timekeeping used in North America today, comprising Pacific, Mountain, Central, Eastern, and Atlantic (in maritime Canada) time zones is an entirely artificial creation. For certain, the system of timekeeping imposed by railroads and which we still utilize today was neither natural nor inevitable. Like the symbolism of business moguls driving a golden spike in the wilds of Montana, it is an unadorned statement of railroad power.

Our present time system was invented to resolve the confusion caused for the railroads of North America by hundreds of local time standards. Local time, based on the position of the sun, had worked well for countless generations who never traveled faster than a spirited team of horses or a swift sailing ship (if they traveled at all beyond the confines of their home villages), but it created confusion for travelers in a world that railroads caused to grow physically smaller by the day.

Back in the days of trail travel to Oregon and California, time needed only be measured casually by noting the position of the sun or by marking off each passing day. Every spring in the 1840s and 1850s, individuals and families traveled west by wagon train, leaving the familiar Missouri Valley and rolling slowly across the lush grasses of the Great Plains. Their collective goal was to reach golden California or fertile Oregon by September or October, before snowfalls blocked mountain passes. History remembers the Donner Party because it lost

Inset: A portrait of Charles Dowd (1825–1904), one of several fathers of standard time, appeared in *Harper's Weekly*, December 29, 1883, shortly after railroad managers reset their company clocks and watches across North America. Soon most people adapted to "railroad time." *Courtesy of Barriger Railroad Library of the St. Louis Mercantile Library.*

SYSTEM

OF

NATIONAL TIME

AND ITS APPLICATION, BY MEANS OF

HOUR AND MINUTE INDEXES,

TO THE

National Railway Time-Table;

ALSO A

RAILWAY TIME GAZETTEER,

CONTAINING ALL THE RAILWAYS IN THE UNITED STATES AND CANADA, ALPHABETICALLY ARRANGED,

WITH THEIR

STATIONS INDEXED

IN FORM FOR THE

NATIONAL RAILWAY TIME-TABLE.

BY CHARLES F. DOWD, A. M.,

PRINCIPAL OF TEMPLE GROVE SEMINARY, SARATOGA SPRINGS, N. Y.

ALBANY:

WEED, PARSONS AND COMPANY, PRINTERS.
1870.

the seasonal race to the West Coast and became trapped by deep snow in the Sierras during the winter of 1846–47.

As for keeping track of passing minutes, who really cared—except for fanatics of industrial order or religious zealots such as the Orthodox Jews, who sought to precisely mark the passage from secular to sacred time each Friday sundown, as they had done regularly for millennia? However, there were also the railroad managers, neither fanatics nor zealots, who wanted only to schedule their trains safely over single-track lines—the kind that predominated across America. That was impossible except by imposing a system of time discipline and educating employees to follow timetables and supervisory instructions known as "train orders" to the exact minute. Failure to observe accurate time might well result in a bloody head-on collision between two speeding trains occupying the same section of track at the same time. This was the kind of headline accident every railroad engineer feared most. A growing number of long-distance travelers cared about accurate timekeeping, too, because the numerous local time standards caused confusion that resulted in impossibly tight connections and missed trains.

These were some of the reasons railroad managers, acting without support from governments at any level, resolved the problem by introducing railroad time zones on November 18, 1883—the "day of two noons"—noon as defined by local time and by railroad time. Taking his cue from the railroad managers, Governor Thomas Crittenden encouraged Missourians to set their clocks and watches to the new Central Time.[10]

Across the nation there were pockets of resistance. To the critics, the action by railroad managers was high-handed and thus typical of the growing power of

The front cover of one of Professor Charles F. Dowd's treatises advocating standard time in 1870. Dowd taught in a women's seminary in Saratoga Springs, New York. *Courtesy of Barriger Railroad Library of the St. Louis Mercantile Library.*

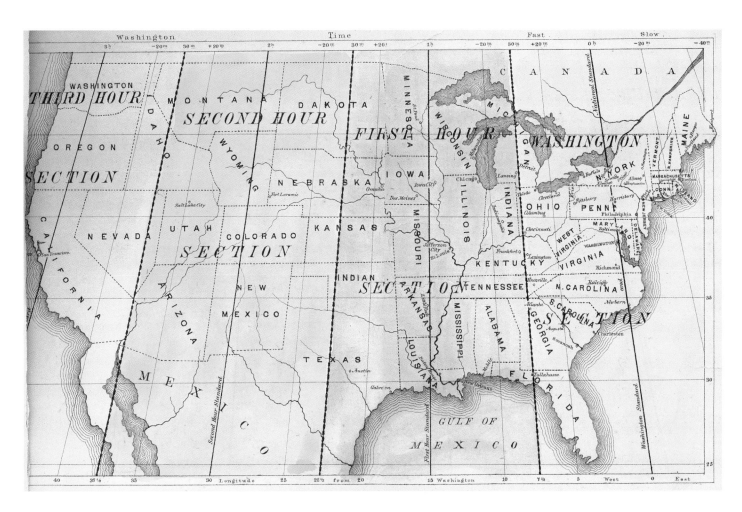

Dowd's proposed division of the United States into standard zones of time. When actually adopted, the time-zone boundaries turned out to be much more irregular; they tended to zigzag among rail division points located near the meridian divide. *Courtesy of Barriger Railroad Library of the St. Louis Mercantile Library.*

The front cover of the *Travellers' Official Guide of the Railways* for March 1875 illustrates the problem of local time differences that Dowd sought to address with his proposal for standardization. The two lengthy lists of city names that form the left and right columns of the ornate border note that when it is 11:17 a.m. in Chicago, it is 11:07 in St. Louis, and 11:24 in Indianapolis. No wonder railroad travelers became confused. *Courtesy of Carlos A. Schwantes, personal collection.*

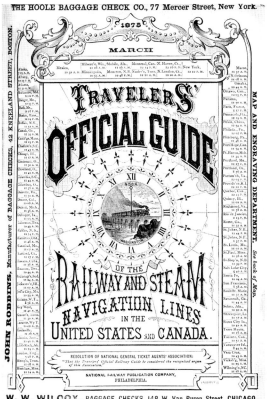

The Chicago-Portland Special on Lane Cut-off, near Omaha, Neb. Signals Indicate "Proceed!"

EN ROUTE TO SPOKANE

VIA UNION PACIFIC

"THE SAFE ROAD TO TRAVEL"

SEE THE WONDERS WROUGHT BY IRRIGATION

Union Pacific trains run through the richest and most beautiful part of the West.

Stopovers readily arranged at all points of interest including Omaha, or Kansas City, Denver, Salt Lake City and Yellowstone, Montana.

For full information relative to fares, routes, etc., call on or address any of the agencies shown on page 46.

Promoting automatic block signals as the "most perfect invention known to science" to protect railroad passengers from accidents. *Courtesy of Special Collections, Washington State Historical Society.*

Opposite: Time consciousness is implied rather than made implicit in this dramatic image of Seattle's railroad landscape wreathed in steam and smoke in the 1920s. The photographer was Yukio Morinaga, a member of the local camera club, which at the time encouraged soft focus ("pictorialist") images. *Courtesy of Special Collections, Washington State Historical Society.*

railroads to shape all phases of human existence. "Railroad time is to be the time of the future," grumbled the *Indianapolis Daily Sentinel*. "The sun is no longer to boss the job. People—55,000,000 people—must eat, sleep and work as well as travel by railroad time." The diehards kept their clocks and watches set on local time, but they were fighting a losing battle and they knew it. The *Indianapolis Daily Sentinel* protested: "It is a revolution, a revolt, a rebellion, anarchy, chaos. The sun will be requested to rise and set by railroad time. . . . People will have to marry by railroad time, and die by railroad time. . . . Banks will open and close by railroad time. . . . And it is useless to ask, What are you going to do about it?"[11] Symbolically, the railroads of the United States and Canada had collectively taken upon themselves a form of power that for millennia had belonged solely to God. What was the brave new world defined by railroads coming to?

RAILROAD TIMETABLES WERE ANOTHER MEASURE OF THE creative process involved in transforming boundless distances into precisely measurable space—the space necessary to operate two trains on the same track safely. Trains were required to wait on side tracks or speed along main lines according to the dictates of timetables and specific orders from supervisory personnel. Otherwise they ran the risk of collision. The related rise of safety consciousness offers an additional example of the thoroughgoing transformation wrought by railroads across the West. Freewheeling individuals temperamentally unable to follow rules and orders found no place among the employees of a modern railroad.

A song from 1897 called "Asleep at the Switch" addressed the issue of railroad safety in particularly maudlin terms: "The Midnight Express will be late here tonight, so sidetrack the westbound freight." Those were the orders that Tom the switchman, "with a heart true as steel," received. But Tom apparently fell asleep at the switch. Only his quick-acting daughter, Nell, prevented a head-on collision and consequent loss of life. Her father, it turned out, had not fallen asleep (an unforgivable breach of industrial discipline), but had been a faithful employee who died on the job from a heart attack.[12]

Safe operations by railroads did not just happen. They resulted from conscious campaigns by supervisors to impose order in place of indifferent or careless work habits. Railroads created detailed books of rules that they expected operating employees to know by heart. In time, safe operations became something to be valued as railroads advertised for passengers, as the Union Pacific understood when it publicly promoted itself as "The Safe Road to Travel."[13]

WHEREVER RAILROADS CHOSE TO RUN THEIR TRACKS, they transformed the West by naming (or renaming) what they perceived to be boundless and undefined space. "Some official put an inky finger on the map. 'There,' he said, 'is a good place for a city. Call it Smith's Coulee, after our master-mechanic.'" In his magazine account of the naming of fictional Smith's Coulee, the popular journalist Ray Stannard Baker sought to dramatize for Eastern readers the all-pervasive impact of railroads on the West, even to the naming of numerous features of that landscape. Although the town of Smith's Coulee existed only in Baker's imagination, he accurately described a process repeated countless times across the region.[14]

Names on the western landscape often attested to the transforming influence of various modes of transportation as they fostered the growth of new settle-

The railroad-made Milk River Valley in Montana. *Courtesy of Barriger Railroad Library of the St. Louis Mercantile Library*

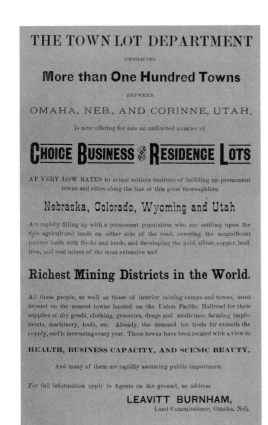

To promote the creation or expansion of more than one hundred towns along its right-of-way, the Union Pacific's town lot department issued this helpful brochure in 1878. *Courtesy of Barriger Railroad Library of the St. Louis Mercantile Library.*

ments or forged improved corridors of commerce. The name Fort Benton, as noted earlier, derived from Missouri River commerce at a time when the political influence of Senator Thomas Hart Benton extended from Saint Louis to the far boundaries of its vast hinterland (which, as imagined by Benton, extended to the Northwest Coast). Another set of names recall the supremacy of a generation of western railroad builders, promoters, financiers, and executives, all working tirelessly to transform the landscape. Billings, Montana, for instance, recalls Frederick Billings of Vermont, one of many Northern Pacific founding fathers; while Garrison, Montana, forever burnishes the name of railroad tycoon Henry Villard's father-in-law, the noted Boston abolitionist William Lloyd Garrison. Belmont, Washington, today hardly more than a wide spot in a rural road, was named by Northern Pacific officials to honor the influential Wall Street financier August Belmont. The town of Avery, Idaho, recalls that Avery Rockefeller once invested millions of his oil dollars in the stocks and bonds of the Milwaukee Road line, which located a roundhouse complex there at the western end of its electrified track over the Rocky Mountains.

Railroads claiming the right to inscribe names across the land made sense only because many parts of the West appeared far younger historically to the Euro-Americans doing the naming (or, from an Indian perspective, renaming) than comparable lands in the Great Lakes or Mississippi River country, and thus the West seemed wholly undeveloped when railroads first arrived. For that reason, vast portions of the modern American West were, in effect, children of the railroad parents who did so much to shape and transform them, and in many cases that included naming the land and its distinctive features.

WHEN RAILROADS FIRST APPEARED IN STATES SUCH as Pennsylvania, Maryland, New York, and Massachusetts during the 1830s, settlement on the East Coast had achieved considerable maturity during the passage of more than two hundred years since the first permanent European settlements in Virginia and Massachusetts Bay. Railroad builders wedged their tracks and support structures into an existing landscape composed of farms and towns, some of them already generations old. Montana, by contrast, was the last of the lower forty-eight states and territories to hear the whistle of a steam locomotive, that ubiquitous sound of modernity. That auditory milestone did not occur until 1880, the year the first tracks entered the still sparsely settled territory. By then half a century had passed since the first steam locomotives thrilled residents of the East Coast.

Montana Territory, like much of the West, had not experienced the shaping influence of two hundred years of settlement, at least not by Euro-Americans newcomers determined to change all they touched, nor could it claim large, established, and attractive communities fashioned from brick and stone and all-weather roads required for the steady flow of freight wagons and mail coaches among bustling population centers. Montana in the early 1880s had few real centers of population and no long-established financial and social networks. Montana settlements, like those in other frontier territories, were still fashioned mainly from locally sawed wood, and their streets and roads amounted to little

One of the crude new villages that developed during the early 1870s along the railroad tracks of the Great Plains. *Courtesy of Library of Congress.*

SKETCHES IN THE FAR WEST—AN UNDER-GROUND VILLAGE.

more than dirt and mud paths. Montana society, such as it was, remained for the most part transient and ill defined. Railroads reaching north from Salt Lake City and Denver and west from Chicago, Saint Paul, and Omaha transformed and modernized Montana during the relatively short span of the 1880s and 1890s.

*T*HE TRANSFORMATIVE PROCESS IN MONTANA AND THE rest of the railroad West, as already noted, invariably began as someone's dream. Over time, one person's dream might evolve and attract enough popular support to elevate it to the status of seemingly inevitable public policy. When early support for a transcontinental railroad grew powerful enough, Congress legislated the transfer of land resources and loans needed to transform the dream into reality. In other cases, however, seemingly good dreams died from lack of popular support and financial sustenance. And, in some cases, one person's dream turned into another's nightmare.

Native Americans, for example, rarely benefited from the dramatic transformations that the railroads wrought across the West. For example, in the mid-1880s the Northern Pacific Railroad issued special Indian tickets "good for one passage on car platforms," the drafty and dangerous open spaces between enclosed passenger cars. Furthermore, the railroad segregated its Indian riders to the platforms of head-end cars that carried mail, baggage, and express, but no other passengers.[15]

"Are the Indians troublesome to settlers?" rhetorically asked a Northern Pacific guide issued in 1873 to promote settlement of Washington and Oregon. "No. There are but few Indians in Washington Territory, and these have been for many years on reservations, living by fishing and agriculture. There are a few, scattered near the settlements, in some parts of the country, but their presence is viewed as an advantage, as they are, in some sections, the main reliance for hired help. They long since abandoned all thought of hostility to the whites, and have mostly adopted civilized customs and habits of industry."[16]

Transcontinental railroads increased Uncle Sam's ability to control Native American populations in the West and prevent conflict, or so claimed another of the Northern Pacific's 1873 brochures: "The Indian question in the Northwest cannot in any other way be so promptly, so thoroughly, so economically and so humanely settled as by the construction of the Northern Pacific Railroad." The company further claimed that the amount of money "thus to be saved to the Government by the completion of the Road—in the early reduction of the military force on the frontiers, the avoidance of costly Indian wars, the cheapening of government transportation throughout the Northwest, and the permanent

This lurid image of a violent encounter on the High Plains appeared in *Frank Leslie's Illustrated Newspaper* for March 26, 1870. *Courtesy of Barriger Railroad Library of the St. Louis Mercantile Library.*

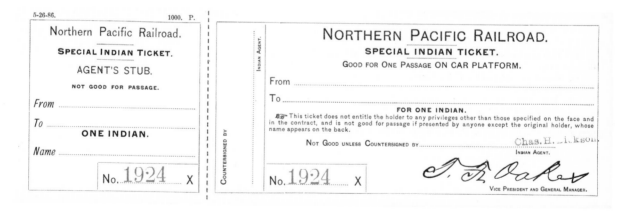

An Indian ticket. The Northern Pacific provided this free pass to Indians traveling between Toppenish, Washington, and the nearby Fort Simcoe Indian Agency. *Courtesy of Special Collections, Washington State Historical Society.*

Theodore Kaufmann's *Westward the Star of Empire*. His painting of Indians derailing the onrushing Iron Horse is a not-so-subtle representation of native resistance to the railroad-made West in the late 1860s and early 1870s. *Courtesy of the St. Louis Mercantile Library.*

One of many railroad brochures advertising the opening of Indian reservation land to settlement by non-Indians in the early twentieth century. *Courtesy of Special Collections, Washington State Historical Society.*

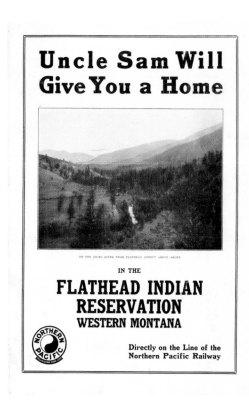

pacification of the Indians—may reasonably be estimated, as it is by officers of the Government, at several million dollars each year."[17]

Perhaps of even greater significance to Indians of the West was the impact of railroads on reservation lands. "Uncle Sam will give you a home in the Flathead Indian Reservation" in fertile western Montana, proclaimed one Northern Pacific broadside. If anything, the swelling stream of newcomers who traveled by train from the East Coast in the 1880s and 1890s only increased popular pressure to break up reservation lands held by Indians. Numerous large and colorful rail posters promoted settlement of former Indian lands by homesteaders. "Opening of Three Indian Reservations," proclaimed the bold red type of the railroad broadside that advertised land on the Flathead, Coeur d'Alene, and Spokane reservations to non-Indian settlers in 1909. "It costs nothing to register and you may get a farm cheap," proclaimed the Great Northern Railway. "These reservations contain some very choice agricultural, fruit and timber land."[18]

When in 1913 the Northern Pacific issued a brochure to promote summer vacations on the Pacific Coast, enough time had elapsed for Indians to be transformed from wild natives inspiring fear and loathing into stalwart agrarian capitalists—if not also into tourist attractions. The brochure writer jauntily observed that the railroad's main line "runs through the heart of the old Indian and buffalo country made historic by the many

encounters between the various Indian tribes and the old fur traders and early miners, and later by the campaigns against the Indians by Generals Hancock, Terry, Howard, Custer, Miles and Gibbon. Now the buffalo and other game are replaced by cattle, sheep and horses; the Indians and their tepees by white settlers and their comfortable homes. In a word, the country has been transformed by Immigration and Irrigation. Even the Indians now have their farms and irrigation works."[19]

EARLY FARMERS AND RANCHERS OF THE WEST, AT LEAST those of Euro-American ancestry, were usually overjoyed when the first tracks reached their hitherto isolated tracts of land. Likewise, would-be farmers and ranchers who arrived by emigrant

Portrait of W. Milnor Roberts in 1879. At the time, he did reconnaissance work for the as yet unfinished Northern Pacific in the Pacific Northwest. *Courtesy of Special Collections, Washington State Historical Society.*

train initially praised the railroad companies for making it easy for them to relocate "out west" and begin life anew. As the governor of Washington, Marshall F. Moore, phrased it in 1867, well before his remote territory contained many miles of track: "Railroads are not a mere convenience to local populations, but a vast machinery for the building up of empires. They are the true alchemy of the age, which transmutes the otherwise worthless resources of a country into gold."[20]

That is, railroads made it possible for settlers to grow grain, fruit, and vegetables and to raise sheep and cattle in areas once located beyond the limits of human perception, and to ship the most perishable commodities by train to once impossibly distant markets. W. Milnor Roberts observed in 1878 that farmers living near Colfax, Washington, could haul grain by wagon to steamboat landings on the Snake River, but that "the transportation charges by the time it reaches Portland or Astoria will nearly equal its value, leaving a very small margin for the farmer." Asking a farmer in that quandary if he wanted a railroad was like asking any candidate for political office if he wanted to be elected. "Everybody—men, women, and children— want a railroad." A "bright intelligent lady" assured Roberts that if the Northern Pacific would construct a line connecting eastern Washington farms with Puget Sound ports, "it would pay more than two hundred percent profit every year."[21]

Roberts, a civil engineer experienced in building canals and railroads, was residing in Saint Louis and assisting the often-ailing James Buchanan Eads on his Mississippi River bridge project when Jay Cooke recruited him to be chief engineer of the Northern Pacific Rail Road in 1869. That same year, Jay Cooke & Company accepted the job of selling Northern Pacific bonds backed by its landed empire to raise the money needed to build the railroad. Roberts immediately set out from Saint Louis to survey the western portion of the line and report to Cooke what he found. During the next ten years, the Northern Pacific's chief engineer observed firsthand how the railroad and its well-orchestrated advertising campaign dramatically transformed the landscape of the northern West.

IN RETURN FOR ALL THE PROFIT AGRARIANS EXPECTED TO EARN following the long-awaited arrival of Northern Pacific tracks, farm and ranch families anticipated that they would be able to peruse illustrated pages of catalogs issued by merchandisers like Sears, Roebuck and Company in Chicago and to order the latest fashions in dresses and suits, bigger and more efficient farm implements, or whatever else tickled their fancy, and have their prized purchases delivered in a timely manner to the nearest railroad station. Though Sears entered the mail-order business in 1886, even older was Montgomery Ward and Company, also located in Chicago, which originally benefited from agrarian discontent with local prices in states of the Midwest. Montgomery Ward rapidly expanded its mail-order business until small-town merchants across the United States began to fear its competitive prowess.[22]

Railroads contributed to the rise of nationally recognized brands, too. The Saint Louis brewery of Anheuser-Busch exemplifies how the transcontinental railroads enabled large-scale manufacturers to sell their consumer products in distant markets, and in return buy raw materials that brought prosperity to the western hinterlands. The entrepreneurial genius of Adolphus Busch was to combine the latest advances in brewing and railroad technology in order to ship quality beer from Saint Louis to distant markets. Busch pioneered the use of refrigerated railroad cars, which, when combined with pasteurization in the mid-1870s, made it possible to ship his beer to hot climates and keep it chilled and fresh. Busch introduced a beer called Budweiser in 1876, the same year Sioux warriors massacred General George Custer and his troops in Montana

Insulated carloads of beer traveled by rail from Saint Louis to distant markets. *Courtesy of Anheuser-Busch.*

Territory. The company soon distributed large and colorful prints of the instantly famous battle to drinking establishments across the United States. Each one carried the name Anheuser-Busch Brewing Association.

Business boomed, and starting in the mid-1870s the small Saint Louis brewer expanded into manufacturing facilities that within two decades covered a hundred acres. Budweiser became a popular beer in the Pacific Northwest, where Anheuser-Busch increasingly purchased the hops used in the brewing process, especially after World War I cut off its supply from Europe. Hop growing in the Yakima Valley dated from 1872, but did not amount to much until after the coming of a transcontinental rail line in 1886. In a relatively short time, the valley evolved from raising cattle and horses to growing hops, apples, and numerous other kinds of fruit and grain to be hauled by train to eastern markets, like the Saint Louis breweries.[23]

HOWEVER, WITH THE RISE OF NATIONAL BRANDS, AND the many advantages a national market conferred on sellers and buyers alike, came almost total dependence on railroad power. For agrarians, that power was best illustrated by the seasonal availability (or frequent lack) of freight cars needed to ship their commodities from farm to market, and the costs that transportation imposed on shippers (costs that were invariably part of the farm or ranch profit equation). The higher the freight rates, the less profit agrarians made from their potatoes, beans, or wheat. Rail freight rates were probably never low enough to satisfy cost-conscious farmers and ranchers of the West, particularly during the late nineteenth century, when commodity prices generally declined around the world. Until the early twentieth century, the railroads themselves set the rates, and their governing principle was often to "charge what the traffic will bear."

Shippers in the new territories and states of the West wanted the best of all possible worlds—the benefits that railroad connections conferred, but also the personal autonomy and freedom they formerly enjoyed in their geographical isolation. It was impossible to reconcile the two. In the eyes of commodity producers wholly dependent on rails to gain easy access to national and world markets, their former benefactor had been all too easily transformed into a grasping and heartless monopolist.

Thanks to the novelist Frank Norris, the octopus became a popular and highly potent symbol of the sinister and far-reaching power of rail barons to squeeze every last dime from hardworking and honest agrarians, or to use their multitude of arms to probe each pocket of a farmer's sweat-stained overalls in search of still more financial tribute. The result was a series of antirailroad political insurgencies. One was the farmer protest in the upper Midwest in the 1870s called the Granger movement. Another was the Populist revolt that raced like wildfire from the High Plains and Rocky Mountains to the far Pacific Coast during the 1890s. Such reform-minded political insurgencies ultimately led lawmakers to regulate the carriers, and in time this wholly transformed the way railroads did business. Rail regulation at the federal level began with the creation of the Interstate Commerce Commission in 1887. State and federal lawmakers greatly increased the power of railroad regulators during the early twentieth-century years known as the Progressive Era.

NATIVE AMERICANS AND WESTERN AGRARIANS WERE NOT the only groups who saw themselves at the mercy of railroad power. The railroad industry was at one time the nation's single largest employer. Even the smallest rural station—and once there were thousands of them—had to be staffed by one or more employees, usually a ticket agent and a telegrapher, often one and the same person. Agents and their families frequently resided on the upper floors of country stations. At any major classification yard, an army of rail workers toiled around the clock, shunting freight cars to make up trains for various destinations, maintaining and repairing locomotives and cars, restocking passenger dining cars with food fresh from the company's commissary and swank sleeping cars with clean linens from the company's laundry, or adding blocks of ice to chill refrigerated cars that hauled perishable commodities from fields and orchards to processing plants and breakfast tables.

In remote and recently settled parts of the West, train crews frequently lived in specially created railroad division towns. At the end of a day's run, they handed off their responsibilities to the next crew and went home to relax—if they were lucky. In the days before strict work rules and heightened safety consciousness, weary crew members might immediately be called back to work if the railroads were shorthanded.

In ways large and small, all railroad employees were reminded that their lives, both on the job and off, were enmeshed like cogs in a complex bureaucratic machine that functioned much like a military organization. It was no accident, perhaps, that the large railroads were organized into numerous divisions, or that power flowed from corporate headquarters down through the ranks to the lowliest employee—the railroad equivalent of an army private. The president of a large railroad traveled in regal style aboard his own private car to visit his troops in the field.

Locomotive engineers, in particular, were proud of their skills and bravery,

76

and, in turn, were admired by the general public, even by people who seldom rode the trains. In the age of steam, an engineer often developed a distinctive way of sounding his locomotive whistle so that even distant listeners could identify him by name. Self-assured engineers, train conductors, and other railroad workers formed some of America's oldest and most enduring labor unions, such as the Brotherhood of Locomotive Engineers, the Brotherhood of Railroad Trainmen, and the Order of Railway Conductors of America. The largest unions published monthly journals that included extensive sections for brotherhood wives, a feature that underscored the fact that railroading was a family occupation. The daily and seasonal tempo of a father's work on the railroad invariably governed family time and activity. Railroad work also linked the generations of the same family, because grandfathers, fathers, and sons might all work for the same railroad. Until recent years, railroad operations (except during the two world wars) remained a man's domain.[24]

One particularly vivid example of the power of the railroad to dominate a community of workers derives from Rock Springs, Wyoming, where the Union Pacific Railway mined coal to power its numerous locomotives. To keep wages low, it hired Chinese labor, but resulting tensions with workers of other nationalities led to a bloody riot and anti-Chinese agitation by labor protestors across the West in the mid-1880s.

Railroads were destined to wield inordinately great power for good or ill simply because they were invariably the largest business enterprise in any city, county, or state in the West. The primary exceptions would be seaports accessible by ship—cities such as Seattle, Tacoma, and San Francisco. Such was not the case for countless Northern Tier communities that typically were geographically scattered, landlocked, and lightly populated. Further, state and local government across the nineteenth-century West was invariably no match for railroad power. It has been claimed, for instance, that when Washington lawmakers gathered in Olympia in 1889 to write a constitution for the new state, railroad lobbyists practically surrounded the gathering to influence delegates by plying them with free food and liquor aboard private rail cars.

Even in isolated mining and timber towns, where companies producing the local commodity seemed all-powerful to their employees, railroads were more powerful still, because they had power to set rates for everything from the lead and zinc ore that flowed from Idaho's Silver Valley to a smelter located in distant Tacoma, to the hair pins and frilly aprons that traveled from a warehouse in Chicago to a merchant's clothing counter in Spokane. The number of such examples is practically infinite. With power this great came the chance for rail-

A postcard portrait of a railroad family living in an "outfit" car of the Oregon Railroad and Navigation Company. In 1906 the company maintained more than three hundred of these mobile homes for employees, scattered along isolated portions of its network of tracks serving Oregon, Washington, and Idaho. *Courtesy of Barriger Railroad Library of the St. Louis Mercantile Library.*

roads to transform huge parts of the West as had no other institution before or since. This was done either intentionally, as when subsidiary companies made the desert bloom by irrigating arid land, or by default, as exemplified by management's choice of where to run tracks across the West. And it was not transformation alone that was important. Railroads could also forge fundamentally new patterns of everyday life. Rail power to shape the modern West was thus creative as well as transformative.

*The Northern Pacific Railroad is now an accomplished fact. The region
it traverses, once decried as a cold, barren, useless zone, now possesses the
largest farms in the world, the greatest mines in the world, the noblest forests in the world, and the bravest people in the world.*

—OLIN D. WHEELER, *INDIANLAND AND WONDERLAND*

4

Lords of Creation

"THE IRON ARMS" OF THE RAILROAD, OBSERVED CHARLES and Henry Adams in 1871, "have been stretched out in every direction; nothing has escaped their reach, and the most firmly established institutions of man have proved under their influence as plastic as clay."[1] Construction of the Northern Pacific Railroad, its executives impressed upon skeptical members of Congress in 1868 (when the line remained unbuilt), "will change the whole order of things at the West. It will, in an inconceivably short space of time, convert these vast plains, now laying waste and unproductive, into fruitful fields; it will supplant the herds of buffalo, elk, and deer, with countless flocks and herds of domestic animals, it will occupy the streams of water now running waste with manufactories and mechanics shops, giving comfort and remunerative employment to thousands on thousands of intelligent citizens."[2]

Perhaps in no other part of the United States was the power of railroads to transform as well as create afresh more visible than in the nation's far northwest corner, its last frontier. "Railroads have been built, and the means of water communication have been extended, the result of which already has been the redemption and occupation of rich areas from the primitive wilderness," boasted an 1883 publication devoted to settlement of the Pacific Northwest. "Within the brief time since these enterprises began, the advancement of the country has been everywhere apparent, and what has been already accomplished is simply wonderful."[3]

Railroads Leave Nothing Untouched

"The Northern Pacific Railroad will change the whaling business of the United States. Puget Sound is only 18 days from the best ground left to the American harpooners. It is the cheapest and best place in the Pacific in which to fit out, refit, repair and discharge. If it shall be deemed economy to ship the proceeds of voyages home to New Bedford by vessel, Puget Sound is certainly a better place to do it from than the Sandwich Islands [Hawaii]. The business has already been planted on the Sound, and its growth to large proportions is certain."

—from *The Northern Pacific Railroad's Land Grant and the Future Business of the Road* (Philadelphia: Jay Cooke & Co, [1870]), 15.

From 1880, when remote Montana Territory became the last of the contiguous states and territories to awaken to the piercing shriek of a steam locomotive whistle, and the 1920s, Montana, together with its neighbors in the Northwest—Idaho, Washington, Oregon, Wyoming, the two Dakotas, and the western provinces of Canada—were all dramatically changed by what railroad leaders chose to do—or not to do. Something so basic as where a railroad located its tracks determined which communities prospered and which languished or were stillborn. Should an already established community try to force a railroad to do its bidding, the railroad lords of creation might retaliate. They could punish town leaders and bypass the place entirely, locating the nearest station some distance away on railroad-owned land.

That is what happened to the original community of Yakima, Washington. Residents learned about railroad power the hard way when they stood up to the Northern Pacific in the 1880s by refusing to donate land the railroad needed for a right-of-way and station. As a result, passenger and freight trains soon steamed through Yakima—and kept on going, because the Northern Pacific refused to build a station in old Yakima or stop its trains there. Its trains paused instead at a new station built on Northern Pacific land, where many chastened townspeople humbly chose to physically relocate their homes and commercial buildings and establish a new settlement properly deferential to the railroad and its all-powerful management. "Three years ago the place where the city [of North Yakima] now stands was a barren sage-brush plain without one of the thirty thousand shade trees which now lend their growing attractions to the streets and yards."[4]

Many Westerners in the late nineteenth century tended to measure progress

A Union Pacific map of Puget Sound in 1898, the year Seattle became a principal jumping-off point for the rush of gold seekers headed north by ship to Alaska. From the ports of Dyea and Skagway, they continued overland to reach Canada's remote Yukon Territory. *Courtesy of Barriger Railroad Library of the St. Louis Mercantile Library.*

Map of PUGET SOUND and Vicinity

SHOWING
ALL POINTS REACHED
BY THE
UNION PACIFIC SYSTEM.

in terms of statistics—and especially those statistics that tracked notable physical changes after a railroad came to town. The new town of North Yakima was no exception. "There are two brickyards, both of which have been kept busy since they were established, early in the summer of 1887, in making brick for the

WHAT UNCLE SAM AND AUNT COLUMBIA THINK OF THEIR N° 42
STATE OF WASHINGTON
N° XLII
Excel ! "Aye , Aye".
(for ever)

SEATTLE its chief city

FLOWERS ALL THE YEAR   FLOWERS IN ABUNDANCE

TIMBER FIR   BLACKBERRIES
CEDAR MAPLE   STRAWBERRIES PRUNES GRAPES
SOAPSTONE FIRE CLAY   PEACHES. PEARS. PLUMS APPLES
TREASURE
LIME KAOLIN   POTATOES HOPS
GOLD   COPPER
SILVER   LEAD
MARBLE SLATE   BARLEY HAY
from SEATTLE
to UNCLE SAM
IRON COAL   WHEAT OATS
Via N.P., C.M.&St.P. and VANDERBILT LINES
SALMON OYSTERS CLAMS HALIBUT COD MACKEREL ETC.

PUBLISHED BY THE
ESHELMAN–LLEWELLYN INVESTMENT Cº
SEATTLE. WASHN.
(COPYRIGHTED.)

THE SPIKE & ARNOLD MAP PUBLISHING Cº
DESIGNERS & ENGRAVERS.

The "commodification" of Washington, which became one of the nation's new states in 1889. *Courtesy of Special Collections, Washington State Historical Society.*

various substantial structures completed, and others began." A brochure promoting the wonders of the new community also noted that a local druggist had been first in town to construct an "iron-front" two-story brick building, a symbol of modernity.[5]

WESTERNERS ALSO TENDED TO LIVE IN THE FUTURE, no doubt a result of the impressive creative power of the railroads. Today was less important than what tomorrow would bring. "But, whatever shall be the future volume of the Asiatic trade by rail across this continent—and it will unquestionably be large—the Northern Pacific Road is sure of its full share," Jay Cooke & Company reminded investors in an 1873 promotional brochure.[6] Others observed how transportation created new cities of the West: "Meanwhile San Francisco and Chicago spring up like a very palace of Aladdin, and the center of population is transferred, as if by magic, to some point which existed in the school-books of the present generation of men only as a howling wilderness."[7]

Future thinking as a promotional tool also inspired individuals temped to

A DESCRIPTION OF THE STATE OF

TEXAS

TRAVERSED BY

THE
MK and T

MISSOURI, KANSAS & TEXAS RAILWAY.

WHERE, IN A PERFECT CLIMATE, MAY BE FOUND
CHEAP HOMES FOR A

MILLION PEOPLE

D. MILLER,
Traffic Manager, ST. LOUIS, MO.

H. P. HUGHES,   JAMES BARKER,
G. P. & T. A., M. K. & T. Ry. Co.,   G. P. & T. A., Missouri, Kansas & Texas
of Texas,   Railway System,
DENISON, TEXAS.   ST. LOUIS, MO.

Form 4.   Rand, McNally & Co., Printers, Chicago.

The railroad dream of a bright future for the West included Texas in this turn-of-the-century settlement brochure issued by the Missouri, Kansas, and Texas Railway. *Courtesy of Barriger Railroad Library of the St. Louis Mercantile Library.*

move west. "Success can be promised to energetic farmers. However modest their beginning, they can be sure of finding themselves in possession of a competency after a few laborious years," wrote one publicist in 1883, though he also warned that in the Pacific Northwest "idlers will only go from bad to worse, and adventurers will not prosper."[8]

Communities, too, lived in the future. "An advantage possessed by North Yakima, and one of great importance, is the fact that it lies in the path of all future railroads from the interior to the coast. It is confidently expected," continued one booster brochure, "that within a year or two at the outside" additional railroads would provide North Yakima with valuable new connections. "Irrigating schemes will play an important part in the future of the city." Page after page, the brochure presented its dream of expected prosperity. "Another project, lately set on foot, contemplates the opening of a coal deposit within five miles from the city, and steps have been taken to form a company for that purpose. Geologists predict a find of natural gas, also." No significant finds of coal or natural gas were ever made in the area, but Yakima (as the community was later named) prospered nonetheless.[9]

"I was at one little town on the Columbia," wrote another publicist in 1911, "a beautiful district of fruit growing where the farmers are growing wealthy. Five years ago—only five years ago!—it was a place where no one cared to stop for an hour. It was like the desert—hot, dusty, barren and desolate. But the irrigation ditch brought down the blessed water, and land that was a drug at $10 an acre is now held at $1,000—to $2,000—according to the age of the trees."[10]

Out-of-the-way Washington—which a Northern Pacific booster booklet in 1897 predicted was to become "the Empire State of the Future"—was introduced to the world at large primarily through an onslaught of railroad publicity, which included countless pamphlets and a traveling exhibition car that displayed the primary products of its forest and fields. Operated by the land department of the Northern Pacific, the car was a mobile cabinet of curiosities that included among the many agricultural and mineral wonders the stuffed heads

The Northern Pacific's mobile exhibit car advertised the West the railroads made. *Courtesy of Montana Historical Society, H-3313.*

of buffalo, mountain goats, and other wild animals of the northern West, and Indian artifacts popular with Gilded Age audiences. All of these items somehow related to the Northern Pacific landed empire.

Museum-like rail cars had a limited geographic range, however, and so railroads of the West published advertising brochures in different languages to attract settlers from western and northern Europe. These publications, which collectively numbered in the millions, featured a compelling combination of words and illustrations—photographs in many cases by Asahel Curtis or paintings by John Fery—that showcased scenic wonders, products of farm and factory, and the overall prosperity of the northern West. Still other brochures invited people to visit the natural wonders of the region as tourists, or, better yet, to move to the West's new Gardens of Eden as home seekers and grow rich and prosperous along with the vigorous young commonwealths.

Always the message was a variation on this basic theme: "The poor man, desirous of making a home for himself and family, and willing to work, can find no country which offers greater inducements than Washington Territory. He must not expect to find it an earthly paradise, but he will find it superior to any of the States on the Atlantic Coast. He can earn a living here easier than in the

GREAT NORTHERN STEAMSHIP COMPANY

Between Seattle, Japan, China, Philippines

With Connections at Hong Kong for the Philippines, Straits Settlements, Australia and all European and Asiatic Ports

The "MINNESOTA" was constructed in the
United States to meet the special requirements
of the Trans-Pacific passenger traffic from Seattle
to Japan and China.

PASSENGER accommodations unequaled by any vessels in the Trans-
Pacific trade and unsurpassed on the Atlantic.
All first cabin staterooms are outside rooms, located amidships. Un-
usually large and comfortable berths are provided. There are electric reading
lights in each stateroom as well as telephone. Staterooms are cooled and heated
by natural means and by electric power.
Other features of the superb passenger accommodations are the music room,
library, social hall, smoking room, children's play room and electric laundry.
The enormous dimensions of the Minnesota, combined with the bilge keels
with which it is fitted, insure a steadiness and comfort at sea which is not
obtainable on vessels of smaller tonnage, whilst its great beam provides spacious
and comfortable decks for promenade and amusements at sea.
Honorable Horace N. Allen, formerly American Minister to Korea, speaks
of his trip on the "Minnesota" as follows:
"I have made twelve trips across the Pacific on various lines, but for speed
and comfort, the last on the great 'Minnesota' was by far the best and most
enjoyable. I did not know that this trip could be made without a trace of sea-
sickness until we made that passage with no more motion than we would experience at anchor in the harbor."

One way rates from Seattle are as follows

	1st Cabin	2d Cabin	3d Cabin	Asiatic Steerage
Yokohama	$200.00	$160.00	$70.00	$51.00
Kobe	207.50	104.00	74.00	51.00
Nagasaki	222.50	110.00	80.00	51.00
Shanghai	225.00	115.00	85.00	51.00
Hong Kong	225.00	115.00	85.00	51.00
Manila	225.00	115.00	85.00	51.00

Round trip rates from Seattle are as follows

	First Cabin 4 mo.	12 mo.	Second Cabin 4 mo.
Yokohama	$300.00	$350.00	$200.00
Kobe	312.50	365.00	208.00
Nagasaki	334.00	393.75	220.00
Shanghai	337.50	393.75	230.00
Hong Kong	337.50	393.75	230.00
Manila	337.50	393.75	230.00

For detailed information, berth reservations, etc., inquire of any steamship
representative or agent of the Great Northern Railway, or

A. L. CRAIG, Genl. Passenger Agent,   W. C. THORN, Trav. Passenger Agent,
Great Northern S. S. Co.   209 Adams Street,
St. Paul, Minn.   Chicago, Ill

W. A. ROSS, Asst. Genl. Passr. Agent,
Seattle, Wash.

3

Steamship "Minnesota"
(28,000 tons)

SAILINGS WESTBOUND, 1909.
(Subject to Change Without Notice.)

STEAMER	Leave Seattle about	Arrive Yoko-hama about	Arrive Kobe about	Arrive Nagas-aki about	Arrive Shang-hai about	Arrive Manila about	Arrive Hong-kong about
S. S. MINNESOTA	June 10	July 3	July 6	July 11	July 14	July 19	July 22
S. S. MINNESOTA	Sept. 18	Oct. 2	Oct. 6	Oct. 11	Oct. 14	Oct. 19	Oct. 23
S. S. MINNESOTA	Dec. 22	Jan. 5	Jan. 9	Jan. 13	Jan. 16	Jan. 21	Jan. 24

East, as labor is in demand, wages are good, and provisions are cheap. A man
can subsist bountifully by his rifle and fishing-rod alone, so that the procuring
of food need give him no trouble."[11] It could be argued that none of today's states
were more dramatically impacted by the creative genius of railroads than Washington, Idaho, Montana, Oregon, Wyoming, and the two Dakotas. The nation's
Northwest quadrant thus offers a particularly compelling example of the West
the railroads and their publicists made.

THERE WAS A COMPELLING REASON FOR RAILROADS TO
devote so much effort to advertising the lands and scenic attractions
of the West. To encourage the railroads' construction, Congress had
given the earliest transcontinental railroads enormous land grants,
and none was larger than the landed empire it gave to the Northern Pacific, con-

sisting originally of 470 million acres. In reality, the lawmakers gave railroads only alternate sections of land, and retained the rest for Uncle Sam, thus fashioning immense checkerboard swaths of railroad land across the West. The Northern Pacific grant extended from Minnesota all the way west to the Pacific Coast. Curiously, when the Northern Pacific first advertised its landed empire, it depicted its grant as a solid corridor of railroad land, a visual blunder that critics later used to advantage when they denounced the vastness of its landholdings and the baronial power Congress thus conferred on the company.

Initially, railroads used their land holdings to raise capital to build their lines. Once they had trains running on regular schedules, they needed to generate business by populating the land along the tracks with farmers, ranchers, and townspeople of various trades and skills. The tourist business became important, too. For all such reasons, railroads hired creative wordsmiths, artists, and photographers to sell the West to the world, especially during the years of extraordinary growth from the 1880s through the 1930s. Boosters used inventive combinations of text and illustrations to transform harsh and even sinister landscapes into mountain paradises and geyser-punctuated wonderlands. A skilled rail promoter could artfully transform any sagebrush wilderness into a new Garden of Eden—though in arid portions of eastern Montana and central Oregon, many of the gardens withered when the rains stopped, and gullible settlers cursed the railroads for having lured them out West in the first place.

When the Northern Pacific Railroad staged its grand celebration in the wilds of Montana in September 1883 to commemorate driving a final spike to open a continuous line of tracks between Saint Paul and Puget Sound, the person who probably did most to orchestrate the splendid "wedding of the rails" was Henry Villard. An immigrant from Germany, he had worked industriously over the years to transform himself from a penniless teenage runaway into one of North America's most esteemed captains of commerce and industry. Villard earned his entrepreneurial laurels by transforming railroads in Oregon's Willamette Valley from woebegone paper dreams and streaks of rust into smartly stepping carriers that earned fortunes for canny investors. He then shouldered the burden of completing the long-stalled Northern Pacific.

Villard apparently relished the challenge of impressing Wall Street investors, but this time he overreached his talents by attempting to do too much, too quickly. Only days after the final spike triumph in Montana, his financial empire collapsed like the proverbial house of cards. Villard suffered a nervous breakdown, the first of two. However, as frequently happened during the era of freewheeling capitalism, after a period of restorative relaxation an ambitious person might rise above periodic health troubles and financial adversity, which Villard

The cover of a Great Northern brochure issued in 1908 conveys an unmistakable message about the beauty and productiveness of Washington farmland. *Courtesy of Special Collections, Washington State Historical Society.*

did. He returned later to serve as chairman of the board of the Northern Pacific from 1888 to 1893 and as president of the newly formed Edison General Electric Company from 1889 until 1893, when the young enterprise was reorganized as the General Electric Company.

It might be noted that Captain James Buchanan Eads, the self-educated engineer in charge of construction of the Mississippi River Bridge at Saint Louis,

THROUGH THE

American Wonderland

THE PACIFIC NORTHWEST

also suffered a nervous breakdown. Nervous complaints and physical breakdowns of various types were not uncommon during this time of strenuous activity and rapid change. Likewise, the process of building the American West in the late nineteenth century dramatically impacted communities and landscapes along the railroad right-of-way no less than it did the lives of individual movers and shakers, and sometimes the results were equally stressful. The nation's economy, too, suffered a couple of major nervous breakdowns during this era of frenzied finance, notably in 1873 and 1893. Both periods of hard times resulted from the freewheeling nature of the nation's rapid growth and development encouraged by railroads. Creation was not without pain and suffering.

The modern West was in many ways the outcome of a massive sales campaign, though railroad publicists were not alone in boosting the region. It was in the economic interest of every westerner to brag about the seemingly unlimited resources of his or her newfound home. Regional boosterism became a public profession of faith, or so it often seemed. Historian Earl Pomeroy perceptively noted that by 1912 fully one-quarter of all chambers of commerce in the United States were located in the far-western states and territories, though collectively they contained scarcely one-seventh of the nation's total population. Like the railroads, the chambers of commerce were passionate and creative publicists.

Long before Villard's final spike celebration took place in 1883, the Northern Pacific had been required to triumph over negative perceptions of the American West, a process that meant overcoming several decades of ingrained popular prejudices. Zebulon Pike and Stephen Long, two explorers to leave Saint Louis for the West after Lewis and Clark, returned home with disparaging assessments of the Great Plains environment—the "Great American Desert," they often called it. "There was a time—not so very long ago, either—when the meager word 'Wyoming' conjured visions of a howling wilderness, bewildering solitude, unimagined deeps of mountain recesses—and the world-famed bad town—the one wickedest spot on earth—Cheyenne," recalled a Union Pacific publicist in 1910. "What do you want of that vast and worthless area," he recalled Daniel Webster addressing his Senate colleagues in 1843, "that region of savages and wild beasts, of deserts, of shifting sands and whirling winds, of dust, of cactus and prairie dogs? To what use could we even hope to put those great deserts and those endless mountain ranges, impenetrable and covered to their very base with eternal snow? What can we even do with the western coast, a coast of 3,000 miles, rock bound, cheerless and uninviting?"[12] Undaunted, the Union Pacific and other transcontinental railroads created a new "Empire of the West," the title of this booster pamphlet.

The high plains region destined to become the Dakotas and Montana (through which Northern Pacific tracks had to run) needed to overcome the popular perception that it was too cold or too dry to farm that far north. No railroad could be built across the northern West unless it overcame the negativism. It simply had no other choice if it expected any person of sound mind to buy the stocks and bonds it sold to raise money for construction or to populate its landed empire.

In order to get the Northern Pacific built, Congress took the dreams of visionaries like Samuel Parker and Asa Whitney and the surveys of army officers like

"Washington, the Land of Fruit," a folding novelty issued by the land department of the Northern Pacific Railway in the late 1890s. *Courtesy of Special Collections, Washington State Historical Society.*

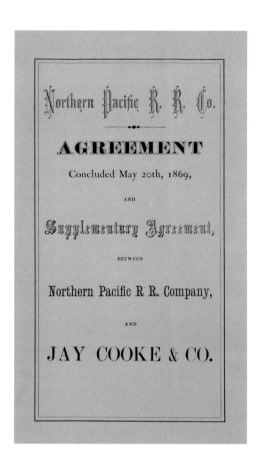

A copy of the Northern Pacific's agreement with America's preeminent financier in the late 1860s and early 1870s, Jay Cooke. *Courtesy of Special Collections, Washington State Historical Society.*

Isaac Stevens and transformed them into public policy. Hindsight suggests that that may have been the easy task. It became the job of Philadelphia financier Jay Cooke in 1869 to transform the immense grant of land into the capital essential to build and operate the railroad. To do that, Cooke needed to create a positive image of land scorned by most people as cold, barren, and generally worthless—except on the rare occasions when grizzled prospectors unearthed valuable minerals, such as the colossal copper deposit in central Montana that made Butte world famous. A member of the Stevens survey in 1853 wrote his father from a camp along the "Ya-Ka-Ma River" in September 1853 that he would "stake my reputation on the assertion that the railroad to the Pacific will not come this way. The Territory of Washington is worthless for agricultural settlements. Puget Sound offers magnificent commercial advantages, but there is no back country to support it with agricultural products. Except for a few narrow strips on the streams and lower down a few small prairies the country is barren, rocky and desolate and beyond all power of cultivation."[13]

The work of creating a positive public impression of Washington probably began in earnest with field observations of its eastern half by the railroad's chief engineer, W. Milnor Roberts. During the summer of 1869, in a letter to his wife in Saint Louis (relevant portions of which she was to forward to Jay Cooke to further his promotional activity), Roberts noted that "this is a strange country. Our old notions about it, that because it is so far north it must be proportionately cold and barren, must give way to the truth that it is very much milder and more fruitful than the region on the Atlantic Slope of the same Latitude."[14]

Cooke's exuberant promotion of the Northern Pacific's huge landed empire as the embodiment of Jefferson's Garden of Eden for ambitious farmers and ranchers became so legendary that cheerful skeptics labeled the region "Jay Cooke's Banana Belt." They could laugh if they wanted, but the indefatigable Cooke raised the initial capital needed to launch construction of the railroad. Unfortunately for Northern Pacific's boosters and builders, Cooke's banking firm fell victim to the nation's economic breakdown in 1873. In fact, the collapse of the prestigious House of Cooke so unnerved Wall Street investors that the nation's economy remained chronically ill for several more years. All over the United States, railroad construction clanked to a halt.

Seeds planted by early rail promotional activity germinated nonetheless. Rob-

Inside what is probably a downtown ticket agency during the golden age of rail travel. Note the display rack at the left, offering travelers a variety of free promotional literature. *Courtesy of California State Railroad Museum Library.*

erts observed in 1878 that when he had first crossed eastern Washington on horseback a decade earlier, he found only one ranch along the road between Waitsburg and Lake Pend Oreille, and not a single settlement. Only ten years later, he observed "continuous fences" for thirty miles from Walla Walla to Dayton, and fields of wheat extending as far as the eye could see. The road was "almost choked with two and four horse teams hauling through six inches of dust to Walla Walla to be shipped over Dr. Baker's narrow gauge railroad and thence by the O. S. N. Co.'s river and portage system to Portland and Astoria."[15]

Roberts recalled that during an earlier encampment on the Touchet River, "no sound of church bell or factory bell or stage coach horn with six prancing horses, as now, then reached our ears." Roberts wished for a telephone line to connect the new town of Dayton, Washington, with the Northern Pacific's headquarters on Fifth Avenue in New York "so that you might hear the difference in the *sound* of things at least."

Indeed, the railroad era produced many distinctive sounds, and not just the sounds of construction. Communities measured progress in terms of the sound of a locomotive whistle: "There are two transcontinental passenger trains passing daily, and freights so frequently that there are few hours of the day or night during which the whistle of a locomotive whistle is not heard," observed one North Yakima booster.[16] All across the West, steam locomotives huffed and puffed like powerful beasts of burden as they moved cars heavily loaded with the region's freight. One writer described the Iron Horse as "blowing its nostrils with awful noise, making the hills and dales resound with the echo of its strange and uncouth sounds."[17]

Another familiar sound of the railroad era was that of freight cars banging one after another along the length of a train as a locomotive pulled the couplers tight and began to move the cargo. Wheels squealed around tight curves. Bells rang aboard locomotives as they approached stations, and inside the ticket office the telegraph sounder clicked commands reduced to the staccato of dots and dashes. The coded language made sense to a telegrapher's trained ear, and so did railroaders speaking to one another in the words of a distinctive work lingo that was unintelligible to less favored mortals. In big city stations of the pre-electronic era, men used megaphones to drone out the destinations of each train. On station platforms, a blue-uniformed conductor shouted "All aboard!" to warn last-minute passengers before visually signaling the engineer to proceed. Out of the hearing of passengers, a workman might curse a recalcitrant piece of equipment.

*M*UCH MORE COMMONLY, PEOPLE DESCRIBED development activity in terms of the visual changes they witnessed on all sides. Roberts in 1878 noticed many families relocating to eastern Washington from Oregon's Willamette Valley "because they think it is better, and where land is at present cheap." He also observed many settlers arriving "in the old fashioned way" across the Great Plains by wagons, "occupying months, because they cannot raise money enough to pay their way out by the route of the Union and Central Pacific railroads."[18] Roberts attributed the many changes he witnessed in eastern Washington in the late 1870s to "the prospect of the Northern Pacific Railroad." He met one farmer who settled there in 1870 in anticipation of a railroad, but because the Northern Pacific had yet to be completed and his farm was too far from water transportation, he was "raising wheat for shipment as grain. He feeds it to cattle and hogs—in which shape it can carry itself to some market. If the railroad were built he would be within 14 miles of it, and then he could dispose of all the wheat he could raise, at a profit." Roberts observed that the "rapidity with which settlements are taking place in anticipation of a railroad is marvelous."[19]

Rail baron Henry Villard (1835–1900) and his business associates. *Courtesy of Special Collections, Washington State Historical Society.*

IN MOST INSTANCES, RAILROAD COMPANIES PERFORMED FEATS of creation through the subsidiary companies they organized to encourage agricultural development or irrigation of sizeable tracts of desert land. Working closely with company-paid agriculturalists, the railroads of the

West sought to create all kinds of new farm landscapes, as when a Union Pacific subsidiary published its *Corn Primer* in 1916 to promote increased production of corn in the Pacific Northwest, a proposal that invariably brought the negative response, "You can't grow corn in this country." When in the fall of 1912 the railroad suggested holding a "corn show" in the Pacific Northwest, "skeptics ridiculed the idea and asked the question, 'Where will you get the corn to show?'" Though railroad management grew "nervous" in the face of popular ridicule, its corn shows in Pendleton, Oregon, and Colfax, Washington, were successful.[20]

The list of railroads actively promoting the West is a lengthy one. It included not just the Northern Pacific and the Union Pacific lines opened between the Midwest and Pacific Northwest in 1883 and 1884 respectively, but also the Great Northern, completed between Saint Paul and Puget Sound in 1893, and the Chicago, Milwaukee, St. Paul, and Pacific, completed to Puget Sound in 1909. Southern Pacific tracks at long last linked Oregon with California and the Southwest in 1887. At its greatest size, in the 1920s, an extensive web of tracks joined together distant parts of the Pacific Northwest. Some tracks also belonged to several regional and local carriers that complemented the large networks fashioned by the great transcontinental railroads. All had land or services to sell.

Promotion of the Northwest grew especially intense in the early 1880s as the main line of the Northern Pacific neared completion. One man who picked up where Cooke involuntarily left off was Henry Villard, a self-taught journalist before he became a self-taught financier and prominent railroad executive. In his younger years, in 1858, he reported on the historic Lincoln-Douglas debates in Illinois for German-language newspapers across the United States, and later he wrote text for the promotional brochures the Northern Pacific sent to Germany by the tens of thousands.

Overcoming popular perceptions that much of West, apart from a few well-watered anomalies like Oregon's lush Willamette Valley, was a sprawling and barren desert inhospitable to Euro-American settlement remained Villard's and his successors' and competitors' single greatest challenge into the twentieth century. To address the public's dismissive attitude toward arid lands in the Pacific Northwest, the Oregon-Washington Railroad & Navigation Company issued an imaginative brochure in 1911 aptly titled "The Old Timer and the Homeseeker." It stands out among countless booster publications because it consists of a conversation between two strangers in the smoking compartment of a Pullman car crossing the desert West. "The Homeseeker drew back from the dust-dimmed window with an exclamation of disgust. Well, of all the God-forsaken countries I ever saw! If the West is all like this, none of it for me." Smoking contentedly, the old-timer, a newly wealthy fruit grower from the Yakima Valley of Washington, gently responds to the skeptic by explaining how a garden can easily be created from a desert. "All it needs is water." The Homeseeker facetiously begins to respond that that all hell needed was water. But "It's a fact," the old-timer interrupts. "When I came to the Yakima Valley in ninety-seven, mighty near all of it was just like that—just as dry and dirty looking. There wasn't much there but coyotes and Indians. And look at it now. I've traveled around quite a bit the last few years, and for right-down money-making productiveness, I ain't seen much that can touch it." The homeseeker immediately becomes interested, explaining to the old-timer that he was from Missouri, "the 'show me' State, you know. That's what I'm out here for—to be shown. Some of our neighbors went out to the Northwest and they've been writing all about the climate and the crops, and so on, so my wife wouldn't be satisfied until I came out to look it over."

The fifteen-page pamphlet ends with the old-timer bragging about North Yakima. "There's one little old city for you. The census people gave us a population of 14,082, and I've been in cities with 30,000 that didn't look as big. In 1900 we had 3,156. We've got everything that makes a city, too—miles of paved streets, fine churches, up-to-date hotels, public building, an $80,000 Y. M. C. A., and all the rest."[21]

RAILROADS LARGE AND SMALL WORKED TO FASHION THE type of West that was clearly in the best interest of a business enterprise intended to make a profit for stockholders. To that end, rail companies advertised extensively for the kind of people their newly planted communities desired (or at least the kind of people the railroads most desired to populate communities along their tracks). To create an entirely new community, railroads might advertise for a specific number of merchants, doctors, dentists, and so forth, willing to relocate to the settlement. On a larger scale they advertised for immigrants from Europe to populate empty railroad lands—but not from all parts of Europe equally, because of the ethnic prejudices of the era.

Journalist-entrepreneur Henry Villard himself wrote some of the early advertising copy that appeared in railroad brochures intended to entice Germans to migrate to lands held by the Northern Pacific. Other brochures sought to lure settlers from the various Scandinavian countries, England, and the Netherlands. Railroads deliberately sought to create settlements of hardworking and thrifty settlers along their tracks by playing upon national and ethnic stereotypes popular in late-nineteenth-century America. Few if any of their advertising booklets targeted would-be immigrants from southern and eastern

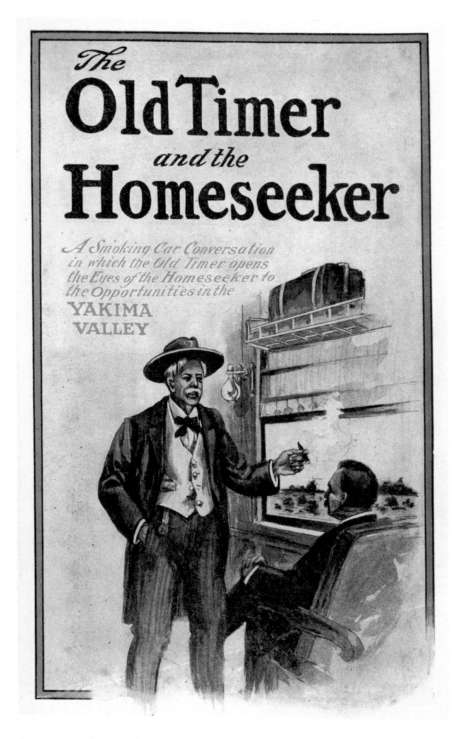

Europe—and certainly not residents of Asia, though railroads might hire Chinese and Japanese men to do track maintenance or mine coal in places like Rock Springs, Wyoming.

Using sex appeal, a Northern Pacific brochure advertises the beauty of eastern Washington and northern Idaho. *Courtesy of Special Collections, Washington State Historical Society.*

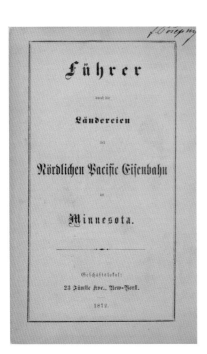

The Northern Pacific appealed specifically to Germans (as well as to Swedes and Norwegians) to settle Minnesota in the 1870s. *Courtesy of Special Collections, Washington State Historical Society.*

No one can say for certain how many millions of advertising brochures the railroads' various settlement campaigns generated. A single shipment of printed matter to the Northern Pacific's emigration agent in Tacoma, Washington, in 1901 included multiple copies of at least twenty-two different pamphlets. Among the titles listed on the invoice were "How and Where to Secure a Home" (German edition), "Progress made by Farmers in N. Dakota," and "Yakima Valley leaflets."[22] Most such pamphlets were free for the asking, though the Northern Pacific charged fifty cents for a booklet titled "Wild Flowers from Yellowstone." What made it so expensive was that its pages contained "pressed wild flowers from Yellowstone Park, showing the real flowers in their natural colors. This is a dainty and beautiful souvenir—has twelve specimens of flowers and six full page illustrations of Park scenery."[23]

Railroad brochures competed with one another for the attention of would-be settlers of the West. Just in case thickheaded agrarians missed its "come-on" message, the Milwaukee Road issued a brochure the front cover of which shows a farmer plowing gold coins from a Montana field. Another publicist determined to boost Washington, Oregon, and California (though he apparently was not directly connected to any railroad), wrote a pamphlet in 1911 called "The Golden West: 'Where Money Grows on Trees.'" Greed, no less than competition, fueled the seemingly nonstop publicity campaigns, which at times seemed to devolve into contests of one-upmanship waged between rival towns or railroads.

No one could anyone say with assurance how effective the advertising was in luring settlers west, but judging from the masses of new settlers, it was highly effective. Nonetheless, in some cases the hired wordsmiths appear to have been

Apple Talk

Using apple recipes, the Union Pacific and Northern Pacific competed with one another in the early twentieth century. Take the apple, for instance, "one of the masterpieces of nature." Those words come from a flowery tribute the Northern Pacific issued in 1915 called "Apple Talk: Recipes for 55 ways to serve the Apple." Ten years later, when the agricultural department of the Union Pacific system issued a brochure on the "king of fruits," it chose the title "150 Recipes for Apple Dishes." And so competition went all across the West.

King of Fruits

APPLE TALK

Recipes for

55 Ways to serve the Apple

READ AND PRESERVE

NORTHERN PACIFIC RAILWAY

The front cover from one of the many railroad brochures promoting apples from the Pacific Northwest. *Courtesy of Barriger Railroad Library of the St. Louis Mercantile Library.*

overly imaginative with their facts and figures. Some publications attracted settlers onto marginal land that could produce crops only intermittently during wet years. In some places, notably central Oregon and eastern Montana, rain did not fall frequently enough to sustain a farmer and his family over the long haul.

One particularly pernicious notion fostered by railroads of the northern West was that rain followed the plow. That is, if new settlers would only plow the virgin prairies of eastern Montana, for example, exposure of dark soil beneath the grassy sod would foster the increased rainfall that made it possible to grow lush crops of wheat and other grains. Thousands of settlers acted on this creative fic-

tion and moved to eastern Montana only to learn to their dismay, after a string of dry years beginning in 1917, that no amount of plowing could stave off drought and withering summer heat. Giving up the struggle, many hapless agrarians abandoned everything, including hopes for a better life in Montana. Ironically, some would-be farmers ended up working as laborers for the railroad companies whose creative words first lured them west.

RAILROADS ALSO DIRECTED THEIR PUBLISHING EFFORTS AT tourists. Unlike potential settlers, tourists came as visitors to the land served by the railroads. They nonetheless generated valuable passenger revenue for the railroads, which expended considerable creative energy promoting tourism. The wordsmiths worked diligently to create tourist wonderlands of the mountains, lakes, and river valleys that lay along the right-of-way. "Wonderland" was, in fact, the title of a series of brochures the Northern Pacific issued annually to promote the tourist attractions of Yellowstone National Park.

Gushing descriptions of the passing landscape seemed to almost exhaust the descriptive possibilities of the English language: "The slow approach to the summit [of the Cascade Mountains on the Northern Pacific] dragged by another team of iron monsters hitched in tandem; the view from the car window over the wide wastes of mountain billows, where a yawning gulf below or a towering cliff above intensifies the chaotic jumble about us; the plunge from daylight into night as the tunnel hides us from the world, and then the swift rush out, and down the mountain, racing time itself as we swiftly descended into the wild and weird gorge of Green River, forms an episode in the long journey to be remembered."[24]

Other railroad brochures specifically directed toward tourists emphasized
special opportunities to hunt and fish in areas near the tracks—such as a brochure issued in 1915 by the Northern Pacific called "Fishing and Hunting on the
Headwaters of the Columbia in Northern Idaho." Other pamphlets invited tourists to explore the countryside on foot, or camp out with their families. As in the

case of their settlement brochures, the various railroad companies exercised considerable creativity in luring tourists west. Once again, this genre of railroad publication numbered in the millions and covered topics ranging from the pleasures of dude ranching in Montana to fossil hunting in Wyoming. If there was money to be made from a western landscape—or from what lay beneath it, in the case of Wyoming fossils, railroads were interested and creative publicists.

MANY OF THE FIRST TOURISTS TO TRAVEL WEST BY train were wealthy Americans and Europeans, but by the early years of the twentieth century, budget-conscious travelers headed west, too. Railroads recognized the new economic reality by issuing brochures with titles like "Short Jaunts for Little Money in Glacier National Park," published shortly before World War I by the Great Northern Railway.[25] Tourists of all income strata filled passenger trains, and settlers contributed to the swelling tonnage of finished goods for railroads to haul west to consumers and commodities to haul east to producers.

Early on, railroads of the West became conscious of the fact that where they ran their tracks created lasting impressions of the passing landscape on passengers. The scenery was for many travelers, in fact, part of the special appeal of a journey across the American or Canadian West. Journalist Richard Harding Davis observed in 1892 that a passenger riding a train as it threaded its way through the mountains ranges of Colorado "commits a sin if he does not sit day and night by the car window."[26] The Northern Pacific Railway once advertised itself as the "Scenic Highway" and noted that the traveler aboard its trains "passes through a region replete with fine and varied scenery, rich in historic incident, and interesting from an agricultural and industrial viewpoint, as well. For many miles the route coincides with that followed by the first great explorers of the Northwestern territory, Lewis and Clark."[27]

A traveler aboard a Northern Pacific passenger train crossing the Great Plains in early 1883 noted, "Our time on the cars, although there was considerable monotony, did not seem to drag at all heavy." He observed that the "prairie would frequently be lighted up by distant fires, and then again all would be darkness except from the faint light that was still left from the sun's departed rays. Finally the darkness would be complete, the porter would light the lamps and the brilliancy of the scene within would be in startling contrast to the camp fires of some of the settlers, who had not as yet had time to build a house to cover their heads, and who sat quietly around their wagons probably wishing for the morrow's sun when they might resume their labors in establishing their homes."[28]

When trackside settlements fostered by railroads were still new, every passing

Notes by the Way was one of many brochures the railroads of Canada and the United States issued to tell passengers what they were seeing along the right-of-way. *Courtesy of Special Collections, Washington State Historical Society.*

Koch and Oakley's was one of many regional guides once published monthly in the United States. *Courtesy of Special Collections, Washington State Historical Society.*

passenger was a potential resident, or a settler on the surrounding farm and ranch land. Rail brochures recognized that fact. In the words of what was perhaps the first pamphlet issued to promote a rail line in the trans-Mississippi West (in 1852): "Nature, beautiful in itself, still remains indebted to human skill for the many advantages, with which it can show itself off."[29] In some cases, the railroads formally noted that the lands traversed by their tracks were not particularly appealing to settlers—as in the case of the dry coulees of eastern Washington through which tracks of the Northern Pacific ran, but would-be settlers were invited to find their agrarian paradise just over the horizon in the fertile Palouse country served by a Northern Pacific branch line.

B Y THE EARLY TWENTIETH CENTURY, THE RAILROADS OF the West no longer wielded power with impunity. Slowly but surely, federal and state laws during the Progressive Era had eroded once-absolute corporate power to the point that after 1914 railroads earned only a meager return on investment that left them unable to compete successfully with new modes of transportation that appeared at much the same time. During the height of its power, from the 1920s through the 1960s, the Interstate Commerce Commission probably compiled a trillion regulations—or so it seemed to harried railroaders—to govern every facet of their industry.

Ironically, though many people in the early twentieth century sought to limit railroad power by supporting punitive legislation, in the end the most effective restraint proved to be unfettered competition and the power of the marketplace. Automobiles, which first bounced along the primitive roads of the American West in the early twentieth century, were initially seen as playthings of the idle rich, but of no practical value for the working masses. That once-popular idea disappeared as automobiles became cheaper and more reliable due to mass production and technical improvements that increased reliability. Roadways grew better, too, and that further encouraged automobile ownership, which in turn encouraged road building. The cycle of improvement seemed to be self-perpetuating. By the 1920s, automobiles had become a serious competitive threat to passenger trains. National parks were forced to open their gates to tourists arriving by automobile. By the end of the 1920s, far more vacationers traveled by car than by train, and that never changed.

In many newly established cities of the West, railroads had built imposing stations that now stood half empty. Most such structures had originally been built to make an impressive architectural statement, mutually edifying to the community and the railroad. Such was the case for Seattle's King Street Station, an elegant building opened in 1906 and featuring a 245–foot clock tower modeled after the campanile in historic Piazza de San Marco in Venice, Italy. Ostentatious stations might also testify to a railroad's confidence in a community's future prospects, as the Milwaukee Road's impressively overbuilt station obviously does for Great Falls, Montana. The largest and busiest union station in the world opened in Saint Louis in 1894. All such stations, large or small, bustled with activity. Many contained the best restaurant in town, or the best-stocked newsstand. Everybody who was anybody arrived and departed by train.

A railroad's best trains, like its largest stations, were intended, at least in part, to impress travelers with their grandeur. Aboard the Northern Pacific's luxurious North Coast Limited, the 1910 traveler could expect to find that a "clothes-

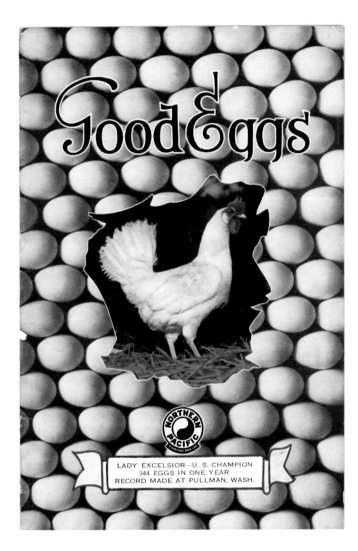

LADY EXCELSIOR—U. S. CHAMPION
344 EGGS IN ONE YEAR
RECORD MADE AT PULLMAN, WASH.

Nothing, not even eggs, escaped the notice of a good railroad publicist. *Courtesy of Special Collections, Washington State Historical Society.*

pressing service, a barber, a bathroom (with shower), a buffet, where are served fine cigars and beverages—leave nothing to be desired." The railroad further noted that it owned a fifty-two-acre farm seventeen miles east of Seattle that "affords the supply of fresh eggs. Each egg is stamped N. P. R. P. & D. F., meaning Northern Pacific Railroad Poultry and Dairy Farm. The dairy farm, with 300 thoroughbred milch cows, provides the milk and cream supply, which is constantly inspected and tested."[30] The railroad added that it was installing an extensive garden in Paradise, Montana, to supply fresh vegetables for its dining cars. Further, "afternoon tea with fruit cake is served gratuitously upon request to standard sleeping car patrons on all five transcontinental trains. Haviland chinaware decorated with a dainty Scotch thistle design is used on all Northern Pacific dining cars." No detail was too small or mundane to escape the eye of an avid rail publicist: "The toilet rooms are kept thoroughly clean and disinfectant is liberally used to preserve the proper degree of sanitation during each trip," noted a 1915 Northern Pacific brochure extolling the virtues of travel aboard an economy or "tourist sleeping car."[31]

Every transcontinental railroad serving the West had its flagship train. For the Great Northern that was the Oriental Limited and later the Empire Builder. The Northern Pacific competed with its posh North Coast Limited. The Milwaukee Road was proud of its Olympian and later Olympian Hiawatha. The Union Pacific's finest train serving the Northwest was at one time the City of Portland. In addition, the major railroads of the West operated numerous local trains, but these plodding and unglamorous beasts of burden were omitted from the tourist brochures, and frequently they became the objects of popular humor if not scorn for their unfashionably homespun ways.

The best transcontinental trains were rolling palaces on wheels. "The physical comforts and the aesthetic beauty of the Men's Smoking Room are of the highest order and every want is carefully provided for," bragged a Milwaukee Road brochure that introduced the railroad's latest "Olympian" in 1927. "In architectural line, decoration and lighting the Spanish influence is dominant." Bringing up the rear, the Olympian's observation parlor car featured a "powerful moveable flood light with which to view the passing scenery at night."[32]

As one might expect, local trains were first to fall to the rising popularity of automobiles. In community after community, the filling station and not the railroad station became a popular focal point for travelers. In many cases the local filling station served as the bus depot too. Railroads frequently utilized buses in the 1920s to replace local trains. A growing number of bus operations with no railroad connections presented additional challenges to local passenger trains. Increasingly, as state roads improved, buses competed effectively with the

Northern Pacific Railway
Dining Car Service

Relishes

Head Lettuce with "Our Own" Dressing, 40c; Half Portion, 25c
Queen Olives, 25c   Sweet Mixed Pickles, 15c   Chow Chow, 15c

Soups

(Our Soups Are All Freshly Made—Not Canned)
Hot Chicken Broth, in Cup, 20c   Chicken Broth with Rice, 30c
Consomme, Clear, in Cup, 20c   Tomato Bouillon, in Cup, 20c
Puree of Split Pea, 30c   Clam Chowder, 30c

Fish

Fresh Fish in Season, 70c; Half Portion, 50c   Imported Sardines, 50c

Meats

Mutton Chops (one) 40c; (two) 75c   Sirloin Steak, $1.00
Milk Fed Chicken (one-half), 90c   Broiled Pork Chops (2), 75c
Fried Calf's Liver and Bacon, 70c   Salisbury Steak, Creole Sauce, 65c
Rasher (Two) of Bacon (Served with Meat or Fish Orders Only), 25c

Vegetables

Early June Peas, 20c   Stewed Corn, 20c   String Beans, 25c
Boiled Potatoes, 15c; Mashed Potatoes, 15c
Hashed Brown Potatoes, 20c   Lyonnaise, 20c
French Fried Potatoes, 25c

Salads

Celery and Apple Salad, 35c   Cold Asparagus Vinaigrette, 45c
Potato Salad, 20c

Entremets

Orange Marmalade, 25c   Preserved Figs, 40c (with Cream) 50c
Guava Jelly, 30c

Breads and Pastries

"Our Own" Plum Pudding, Fruit Sauce, 20c
Bread and Butter, 10c   Apple Pie, 20c   Fruit Cake, 20c
Paul's Assorted Fruit Jams, 25c

Cheese

Anona Cheese with Crackers, 25c; Half Portion, 15c
Roquefort Cheese, 30c

Beverages

(Hot Water for Drinking Purposes Furnished Our Guests on Request)
Coffee, Per Pot, 15c   Tea, Per Pot, 15c   Chocolate, 15c
Cocoa, 15c   Instant Postum, 15c   Cream, Per Glass, 35c
Milk Served in Individual Bottle, 15c   Malted Milk, 15c

L. K. OWEN, *Superintendent Dining Cars,* **St. Paul, Minnesota**

*Mailing envelopes for this genuine photograph
may be had on application to the dining car conductor*

The Great Northern issued a colorful brochure to advertise its new Oriental Limited of the 1920s. The premier train linked Chicago and Seattle. *Courtesy of Special Collections, Washington State Historical Society.*

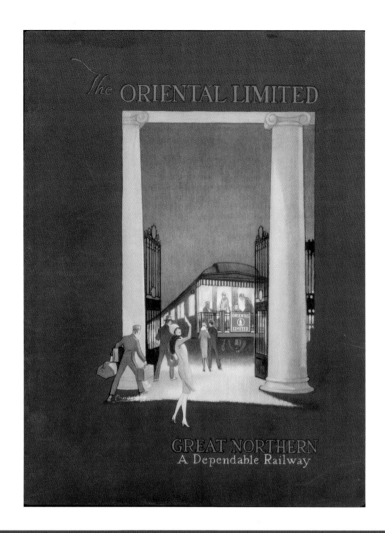

A Visual Delight

"Spick, span—shining in dark green dress, the New Oriental Limited awaits the Conductor's 'high ball' to galvanize into action. Brilliant with electric lights except for the softly shaded glow from the dining car tables, it radiates a spirit of traveling hospitality. The crew veterans all natty in their dark blue uniforms with silver lettered arm bands are all attention to welcome the Oriental's guests."

"A concession and a most important one, has been made to the feminine passenger; a daintily furnished traveling boudoir and lounge room with its decorations and furnishings in blended harmony of tones and colors. Inside a most comfortable sofa, upholstered seats for six, softly shaded light, a toilet table and large mirror; in a convenient annex a shower bath, while in constant attendance a maid who is also a hairdresser, a manicure and a masseuse."

—from *The New Oriental Limited* (St. Paul: Great Northern, [1927]).

long-distance trains too. In the late 1920s, the first commercial airlines took to the skies, though they presented no commercial threat to railroads until after World War II. Given the primitive highways and skyways of the early 1920s, it is not difficult to see how railroad executives imagined that their companies would remain the West's primary long-distance carriers, even if they lost local passenger and freight business to automobiles and delivery trucks.

In 1919, shortly after the end of World War I, the United States Army decided to run a convoy of military vehicles overland from Washington, DC, to San Francisco to see if it could be done. Military planners expressed some reserva-

The Great Northern advertised vacations in Glacier Park and adjacent Waterton Lakes National Park in Canada in the 1920s and 1930s. *Courtesy of Barriger Railroad Library of the St. Louis Mercantile Library.*

tions about the army's over- reliance on railroad transportation should war come to America again, and they wanted to test an alternative. The trip should have been an eye-opener. Even the main roads were terrible, and many bridges were unable to sustain the weight of military vehicles. It took weeks to travel from one coast to another. One soldier who went along was a young lieutenant named Dwight David Eisenhower. Later, in the mid-1940s General Eisenhower observed just how good the German autobahns were compared to the slow and over-crowded highways in the United States. Still later, as President Eisenhower he helped to launch the Interstate Highway System in 1956. The network of new interstates effectively marked the end of the railway era.

IN THE PACIFIC NORTHWEST, SIGNS THAT THE RAILROAD ERA WAS passing were probably evident as early as 1930 and the coming of the Great Depression. It would be massive government projects like the building of Grand Coulee Dam or the Hanford Project, both in eastern Washington, that would create the region's new communities. Railroads no longer did that. In fact, it would be hard to point to a single community born after 1920 that owed its origin to railroad activity.

Further, railroads no longer served as publicists for the West. For obvious reasons, the number of rail brochures devoted to settlement dwindled notice-ably during the 1920s, though a joint campaign launched in 1923 by Northern Pacific, Great Northern, and Burlington publicists represented a major effort to promote the Pacific Northwest. One example of their creativity is a well-illus-trated brochure called "There is a Happy Land: The Pacific Northwest." "Not an American but thrills to the story of the Empire Builders! Those brave men who, first by sheer man-power and later by the daring of modern engineering genius, conquered the great Pacific Northwest . . . , men who developed the riches of a land fat with the wealth of forests, mines, soil, shipping and trade—the memory of their achievements in eneffaceable—as deep-cut as the marks they left on the mounts of rock that barred their progress."[33]

Tourism brochures remained popular through the 1940s and 1950s, though they were not nearly so elaborate, colorful, or informative has they had been in the early twentieth century. The same was true of the on-board brochures rail-roads used to describe the passing scenery to their passengers. Neither passen-gers nor scenery were as important to railroads after the late 1960s.

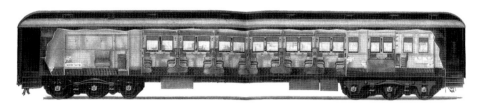

Cut out and plans of Twelve Section One Drawing Room Standard Pullman Sleeping Car showing roomy dressing rooms for both sexes and details of car's convenient arrangement.

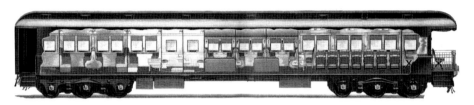

Cut out and plans of Compartment Observation Car showing roomy observation end and general lounge, women's shower bath and lounge, men's smoking and club room, buffet and other features of travel comfort.

RAILROADS DESERVE CREDIT FOR HAVING FASHIONED A firm foundation upon which the modern states of Washington, Oregon, Idaho, Montana, Wyoming, and North and South Dakota constructed their futures. That is also true to varying degrees for other states of the West. What gave the Lords of Creation this kind of power was the West's geographical isolation from the economic and political power centers of the United States as well as its long-time isolation from the nation's historical mainstream.

One telling example of how railroads effectively laid an enduring foundation derives from the history of the early airmail flights across the West—from Chicago to San Francisco. The victory that Chicago won over Saint Louis during the railroad era was reinforced when federal officials designated the first transcontinental route for airmail pilots in the early 1920s. Official guidebooks instructed Uncle Sam's airmen to follow the tracks of the Chicago & Northwestern, Union Pacific, and Southern Pacific railroads between Lake Michigan and the Pacific Coast. In other words, their flights duplicated the route of the nation's first transcontinental railroad. Pilots referred to the ribbon of rails below their wings as the "iron compass." The iron compass showed them the way west, just as it had done earlier for entrepreneurs, tourists, and settlers seeking a new fortune, a new adventure, or a new life beyond the Missouri River.

On the Saint Louis waterfront in 1910. The Eads Bridge is in the background. *Courtesy of the St. Louis Mercantile Library.*

In the late 1920s and the early 1930s, railroads and the nation's infant airlines worked together to define new spatial relationships in many different regions of the United States. Several companies cooperated to provide the fastest transcontinental passenger service to date by linking New York and Los Angeles by plane and train in little more than two days. *Courtesy of Barriger Railroad Library of the St. Louis Mercantile Library.*

When the Pacific Railroad is completed to San Francisco, a new era will be inaugurated. The road will then be the grand artery of the country."

—SAMUEL BOWLES, *ACROSS THE CONTINENT*

5

Manifest Destinies:
The Railroad West and the Modern World

HALF A CENTURY AFTER ENGINES TOUCHED PILOT TO pilot at Promontory, the imprint of the railroad was nearly everywhere in the American West. Some enthusiastic real-estate promoters and railway officials even claimed that the railroads invented the West—or at least the national image of the West. With the exception of the federal government, no one institution more fully shaped the appearance and character of the West than the railroad. Evidence was everywhere. The presence and power of the railroad could be seen on every farm and ranch, in every booming western city and sleepy tank town, and in the lives of the natives and countless newcomers. Ralph Waldo Emerson's prediction about the railroad as a "magician's rod" seemed to have come true in the West. Writing about Seward County, Nebraska, at the end of the 1880s, local historian W. W. Cox portrayed a West transformed by the railroad when he informed his readers that "a new railway has been commenced and completed, . . . opening up a great new artery of traffic, and bringing in its train joy and gladness for thousands of our people." Joy and gladness were invisible emotions, but Cox assured his Seward County friends that a new railroad was "building up three new villages along the way, and infusing new life and activity into a fourth, and adding new life to the city."[1] Cox was sure that the earth itself would be touched by Emerson's magic rod.

But the railroad did more than simply give the West a new look. Trains and

208.—*Westward, the Monarch Capital Makes its way*

209.—*Laying the rails of U. P. R. R.—two miles a-day.*

tracks out beyond Chicago and Saint Louis symbolized progress, prosperity, and the promise of the future. For many Americans, railroads and the West seemed the embodiment of the American Dream. Even if some westerners questioned the dream and feared its consequences, no one doubted that railroads in

the West represented a power for change that was undeniable and perhaps even irresistible.

The West the railroads made showed itself in many ways. At its most visible, the railroad West could be found along the right-of-way, the Iron Road. Two photographs taken in 1866 at the beginning of the railroad West catch the spirit of the tracks on the Great Plains. Standing on the line of the 100th meridian at what is now Cozad, Nebraska, Union Pacific vice-president and general manager Thomas C. Durant surveyed a trail of ties without rails heading west to the horizon. In the next photograph, Jack Casement's track gang sets rails to ties, tracking the West and laying the foundation for the railroad landscape. Railroad prophets in the age of Parker, Whitney, and Loughborough might have promptly given the photographs a grand caption: "Here is the IRON ROAD, the Pathway for Progress, Profit, and Civilization."

The initial right-of-way landscape soon expanded to include telegraph poles and wires. Tracks, poles, and wires were just the beginning of that railroad landscape. Many westerners simply thought of the railroad and the telegraph as a single line of communication. That "line of communication" was a phrase and an idea that Thomas Jefferson used in his instructions for Lewis and Clark. Western terrain demanded much from Jefferson's travelers; it asked even more of railroad planners and builders. Most of the West did not offer as level a country as the Union Pacific had followed through the Platte River Valley. Mountains, rivers, gullies, and ravines all stood as obstacles to be overcome by engineering skill and backbreaking labor. Soon enough the railroad landscape was filled with bridges, tunnels, cuts, and embankments. Here was an engineered West, a place as complex as any cluster of cities and factories. It seemed as if all of this had been done just for the benefit of an American empire. More than one Fourth of July orator could not resist the temptation to declare the railroad West the most manifest expression of America's continental destiny.

No matter how central the Iron Road was to the railroad West, every alert westerner knew that the railroad had created more than something built with wooden ties and steel rails. As historian Maury Klein put it, each railroad imagined itself as "a sovereign state."[2] The visible manifestation of that sovereignty came in what we might call the railroad establishment. In shops, sheds, roundhouses and freight houses, the railroad placed itself firmly at the center of western life. Little wonder that so many towns laid out Main Street to run directly to the company buildings on Railroad Avenue. Main Street recognized the power and promise of Railroad Avenue. For every expectant immigrant or restless young person, the railroad was the way into the West or the way out of town to a wider world. The railroad was foreground; everything else was background.

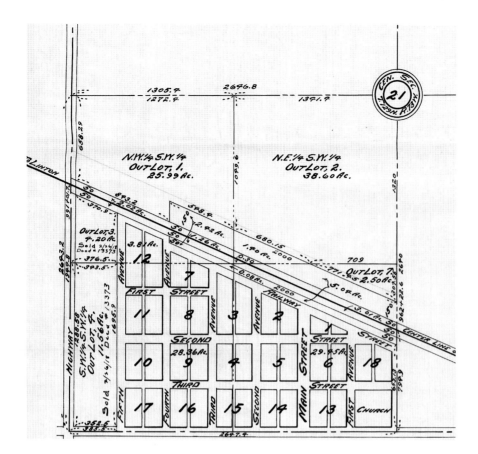

A map of Zeeland, one of numerous railroad-created towns that dotted the Great Plains. Note the location of Railway Street. *Courtesy of Barriger Railroad Library of the St. Louis Mercantile Library.*

No single building was more important in that railroad establishment than the depot. At the simplest level, the depot was where the company conducted its daily affairs. Here emigrants from a dozen places stepped off the cars and into a new life. Here townsfolk waited anxiously for the night express or knew it was time for bed when the Fast Mail whistled its way out to Denver or Seattle. Here a company man checked in freight, handed up orders to an engine crew, and presided over the telegraph key and sounder. At first glance the depots at Deadwood, South Dakota, or Casper, Wyoming, were all about business, the business of profit in an orderly railroad universe.

But for all its air of commerce on "railroad time," the depot meant more than stamping tickets, writing train orders, and marking up waybills. Writing about one small town at the end of the nineteenth century, Frances Weston Carruth put in words what everyone from Lexington, Nebraska, to Pullman, Washington, already knew: "The railroad station was [the small town's] one connecting link with the outside world."[3] That link made the station both center and gateway. Like the town square in more eastern places, the western depot was a public space—a place to get the latest news and hear the freshest gossip. This was the place to

ON THE PLAINS.—A STATION SCENE ON THE UNION PACIFIC RAILWAY.

A sea of humanity surged through a station on the Union Pacific to catch a waiting train. The date is probably 1869, the year that trains first crossed the United States to serve California and the Pacific Coast. *Courtesy of Library of Congress.*

check the time, inquire about the arrival of the new Sears catalogue, and argue about politics or the weather. Here were message blanks for Western Union and carts ready for stacks of boxes from Railway Express. Heading up Main Street to Railroad Avenue meant connecting to a wider world. No place seemed more alive, more up-to-date than the depot. For many westerners, the sound of the modern world was the locomotive whistle and the click of the telegraph sounder.

If the depot and its freight house were the town's real center, then they were also the gateway to both town and countryside. Nearly everything that came into Bennett, Nebraska, or Granger, Wyoming, passed through the station house gateway. Ready-made clothing, farm implements, seeds for new crops, pianos, books, and the entire stock for hardware stores, mercantiles, and millineries came by rail, entering western life on the platform and through the door. The social distances seemed less as farm families and merchant households enjoyed the benefits of the same stoves, washing machines, and bed frames—all brought by rail and passing through the depot gateway. Waiting "down at the depot," all could see the wonders of Chicago and New York reach places like Havre, Montana, and North Yakima, Washington.

T HOSE MAIL-ORDER TREASURES—BOXES OF THE NEW Gem Safety Razor or jars of Pompeian Massage Cream—were perhaps luxuries. Life in town or on the farm might get along without the latest razor or face cream. But on the Great Plains and into eastern Montana and Wyoming, there was one essential commodity that came by rail and changed the face of the western landscape. It might have been the Age of the Iron Horse and the Iron Road, but the Great Plains West was also a world in search of wood. As historian William Cronon writes, "For the first time in the history of North American frontier settlement, would-be farmers and town-builders had moved out of the forest and into a grassland" where ample supplies of lumber were beyond easy reach.[4] No variety of wood was more desirable for lumber to build houses than the white pine of northern Michigan, Wisconsin, and Minnesota. Chicago was the place where trees became wood and wood became lumber. And it was Chicago railroads that took the forest to the plains. In 1880 a journalist for the *Northwestern Lumberman* neatly summarized the relationship between northern forests, Chicago, railroads, and the changing appearance of the West: Every new settler on the plains "means one more added to the vast army of lumber consumers, one more house to build. But it means more, it means the extension of railroad lines" to carry lumber to an ever-expanding market.

In a rhetorical flourish so typical of the time, the writer conjured up the image of "churches, school houses and stores, sidewalks, paved streets, and manfactures" all built on the foundation of lumber carried west by rail.[5] In many ways this grand prophecy came true. The sod house frontier— so much a part of Great Plains mythology—quickly came and went. Settlers on the Great Plains—especially women— longed for the comfort and status of a frame house. Few things changed the architectural look of the interior West more than a frame house, a sound barn, and a windmill—all made possible by lumber from Chicago. The settlers' West was built with wood from logged-over forests of the Great Lakes.

Advertising Washington's impressive timber resources. *Courtesy of Special Collections, Washington State Historical Society.*

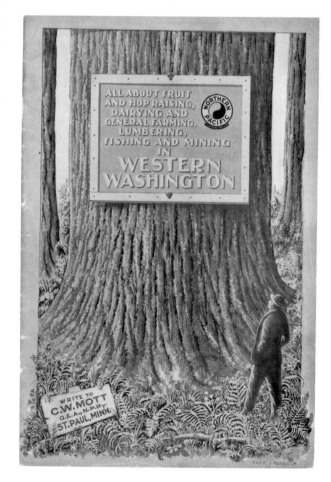

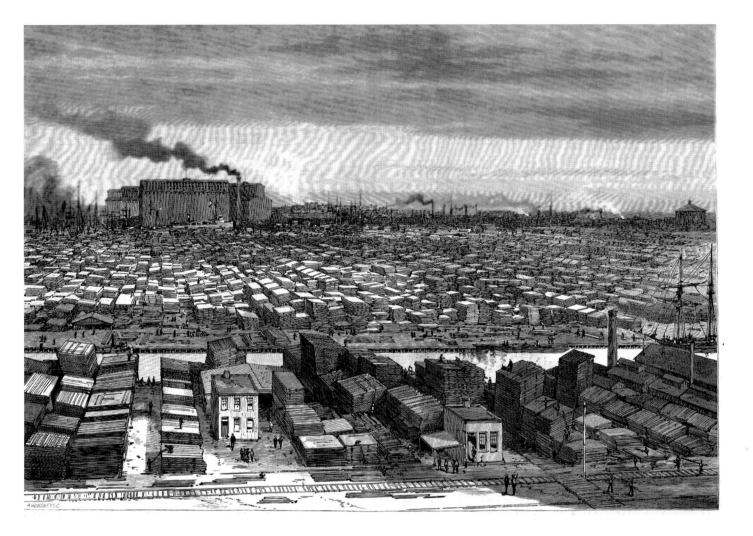

Some twenty years after he watched the golden spike ceremony at Promontory, Union Pacific contractor Sidney Dillon confessed that "none of us
dreamed that the future of the Pacific roads depended on the business that
would grow out of the peopling the deserts it traversed."[6] Visions of Pacific
trade did not vanish, but they were increasingly supplemented by strategies to
extract what the interior West grew, grazed, or mined, and turn them to profit.
The West could provide the things that things were made of. That business—
the wheat, cattle, and minerals that flowed out of the West—also passed
through the station gateway. If the actual objects were loaded somewhere down
the rail line, it was at the depot that the market information began the process
of turning Nature into commodities. Markets need information and the depot
was "Information Central." Just as the natural world of northern forests
became lumber for sale, western nature was transformed to become bread
and meat for eastern markets. The railroad was at the heart of all those
transformations.

Some called wheat "the golden stream." Others cursed it for promises unfulfilled and dreams betrayed. In O. E. Rolvaag's epic novel *Giants in the Earth*, Norwegian emigrant farmer Per Hansa and his sons reverently sorted the kernels of wheat on a white cloth as if in some sacred ritual. With each kernel, dreams of "bright dollars" and "a great store of riches" danced in Hansa's mind. No agricultural crop more fully dominated the lives of Great Plains farmers and railroaders than wheat. There would be other crops—rye, corn, cotton, and sugar beets—but none held the fascination and promise of wheat. Immigrants, including German Mennonites, brought the hardy Turkey Red wheat to Kansas. Turkey Red was well suited to the harsh plains environment. It came as no surprise that the empire of Turkey Red soon expanded to Nebraska and what is now Oklahoma. Not much later the empire of wheat reached the Palouse Hills of southeastern Washington State. Where once there had been an ocean of grass now wheat waved in the prairie wind.

Railroad "commodification" of the "Great Wheat Region" of the trans-Missouri country. *Courtesy of Barriger Railroad Library of the St. Louis Mercantile Library*

Railroads and wheat traveled together. Both promised a bright future. But the golden stream brought unequal measures of profit and loss to farmers, elevator operators, milling companies, and the railroads. Sacks of wheat on their way to becoming bread sparked years of intense controversy as western farmers, Chicago businessmen, railroad officials, and politicians argued about wheat and profit. Populist orators raged against those they called "thieves in the night" while corporate interests defended the right to make a profit in what they claimed was an open market. Railroad companies fought endless and sometimes destructive rate wars over Wheat Country. Those same companies encouraged the expansion of Wheat Country, never counting the cost of a falling market or the inevitable drought years. Like trees, wheat became not a living thing but commodity futures to be traded on the floor of the Exchange in Chicago, which traders and speculators called "the Pit." In his compelling novel *The Pit: A Story of Chicago*, Frank Norris put in words all the excitement and scheming that boiled in the Pit. "All through the Northwest, all through the central world of the Wheat, the set and whirl of that innermost Pit made itself felt, and it spread and spread and spread till grain in the elevators of Western Iowa moved and stirred and answered."[7] For Norris, the Pit had a roar and a rumble that shook the earth from the fields of California to the hungry streets of London. None of that—whether protest or profit—would have come to life without the railroad. Here, as elsewhere, the railroad blurred the distinction between city and country, changing each and making each dependent on the other.

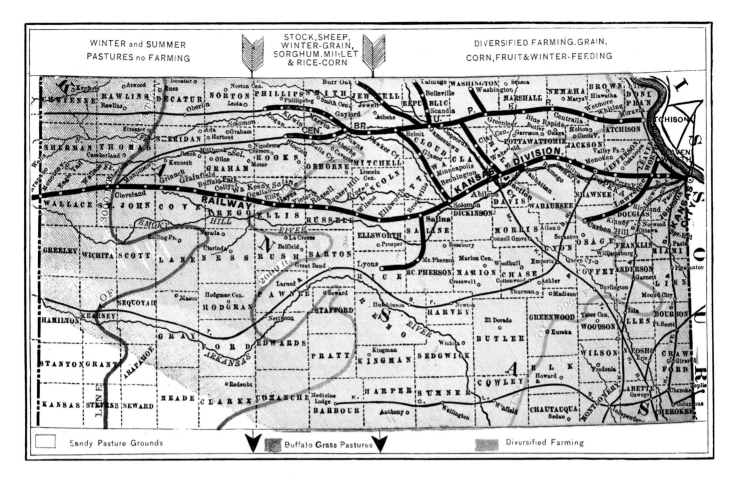

The Union Pacific's "Golden
Belt Lands" of the 1880s produced numerous agricultural
commodities. *Courtesy of Barriger Railroad Library of the
St. Louis Mercantile Library.*

THANKS TO THE HOLLYWOOD B MOVIES ENDLESSLY RERUN
on cable television and now-banned cigarette ads, no image more
fully represents the West in popular culture than the cowboy.
Adventure and romance seem just ahead as cowboys drive longhorns
up to Newton or Ellsworth, Kansas. More than a century after the last of the
long drives, nothing still says "West" more than cowboys, cattle, and the Long
Branch Saloon at the end of the trail. But behind every cowboy was a cattle
company with ranch house managers, bankers in Chicago or New York, and
investors on the other side of the Atlantic. And in front of every longhorn stood
the Chicago stockyards, slaughter houses, and packing plants all presided over
by the real cattle barons—Gustavus Swift and Phillip Armour. By the 1880s
turning sun and grass into living animals and sides of beef was a vast process
that involved Texas trail hands, Kansas pleasure-palace women, Chicago-bound
locomotive engineers, and Polish meat cutters.

Railroads were fundamental in that process. Without railroad stock cars,
Texas cattle could not reach Chicago abattoirs; without railroad refrigerator
cars, dressed meat could not arrive fresh at Boston butcher shops; without this
system, beef could not reach dinner plates in London or Glasgow. While other

entrepreneurs in the years after the Civil War undoubtedly saw the potential in connecting east-west railroads to northbound trail drives, it was Illinois meat dealer Joseph McCoy who first made that transportation idea a commercial reality. McCoy already knew about the shift in the American diet from pork to beef and the role of Chicago in supplying that growing market. In 1867 he persuaded the Kansas Pacific Railroad to build stock pens and loading chutes at a remote spot on the Kansas prairie called Abilene. Abilene became just the first in a series of cattle and rail towns that served as junctions between stock cars and locomotives. McCoy's transportation scheme was not an instant success, but over the next twenty years some two million cattle made the trip up the trail, by rail to Chicago, and on to the plates of beef-hungry Americans.

The cattle-railroad connection had profound consequences for the shape of the western landscape. Some of those transformations were soon visible. Where once there had been vast herds of buffalo, now cattle grazed, each competing for the grass. Range lands—increasingly divided up into pastures and fenced with barbed wire—made the plains part of an industrial landscape. And that feeling of an industrial landscape was emphasized by a growing number of cattle pens, loading chutes, and stock tanks. It was as if railroads had extended the Chicago stockyards to Kansas and Wyoming. But nothing more fully exemplified the way railroads and the cattle trade transformed the West than those

This illustration of grain dealers and speculators at the Chicago Board of Trade appeared in *Harper's New Monthly Magazine*, June 1886. *Courtesy of the St. Louis Mercantile Library.*

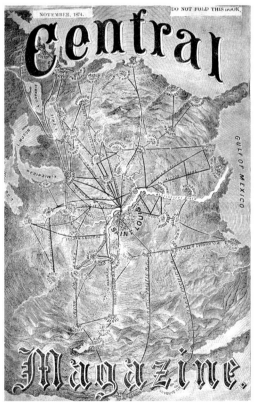

Shipping cattle to market from Abilene, Kansas. *Courtesy of Barriger Railroad Library of the St. Louis Mercantile Library.*

The oddly positioned map of the United States on the front cover of *Central Magazine* for November 1874 testifies to Saint Louis's enduring ambition to dominate commerce in the nation's vast middle section. Note, too, that the Saint Louis-based publication wishfully seeks to relegate Chicago to a tributary role. *Courtesy of St. Louis Mercantile Library.*

Kansas cow towns. Places like Ellsworth, Hays, and Newton all grew, prospered, and declined with the fortunes of the cattle trade. As rail lines gradually moved south from Saint Louis to tap Texas cattle country, and northern ranges were fully stocked, the days of the long drive and wild times in Dodge City were numbered. But in their heyday, the pens, loading chutes, dance halls, and saloons made the cow towns a testimony to the power of the railroad to create a new western landscape.

Sidney Dillon was right. In the half century after Promontory railroads fashioned a new West—a West increasingly industrialized with bonanza farms, corporate ranching, large-scale mining enterprises, and the beginnings of the first western oil boom. Hard rock miners, pipe fitters, and shop girls soon outnumbered rowdy cowboys and gun-toting sheriffs. Just a year after Union Pacific surveyors laid out Cheyenne's first town lots, J. H. Voorheis's auction and commission house offered "the largest supply of out-fitting goods to be found West of Chicago, and is prepared to Sell at New York prices." Rogers and Company bank promised customers ready access to "all the principal cities of the United States and Europe." Citizens of "the Magic City" could buy "a magnificent assortment of the latest and most popular Poetical Works, and Standard Novels" as well as "the latest eastern Daily Newspapers by every Mail" at R. M. Beers and Company at the Cheyenne post office.[8] Like so many other places, Cheyenne became an extension of distant markets. Standing trackside and waiting inside a small town depot, all these changes were visible to even the most casual observer. Stock cars filled with cattle and sheep, boxcars with grain sacks and cartons of books, train loads of lumber and farm machinery, and passenger cars with wide-eyed emigrants—all revealed the railroad West.

Bringing the world to the West: Whether in Cheyenne, Laramie, or another part of the interior United States, the variety of manufactured goods displayed on store shelves offered irrefutable evidence of the value of good rail connections. *Courtesy of Barriger Railroad Library of the St. Louis Mercantile Library.*

The Trabing Commercial Co.

Wholesale and Retail Groceries, Wines, Liquors, Tobacco, Pipes, Wood and Willow Ware.

Trabing Block, Corner South C and Second Streets, and "Blue Front" Warehouse, 312, 314, 316 & 318 Front St.,

Laramie, Wyoming.

B UT THE INVISIBLE CHANGES WERE PERHAPS MORE important. They were the pervasive ones, the ones that became part of daily life. That they came so swiftly made them even more powerful. By the time railroads came west, arguments about how to calculate and display time were commonplace. So were complaints about differences in local times, with missed connections and sometime terrible accidents. "What time is it?" became something of a national joke. Benjamin Franklin's adage "time is money" rapidly took on new meaning as labor on the farm and in the factory moved to the discipline of the clock. And as the railroad network expanded south and west, the complexities of differing local times posed not only an inconvenience but a threat to safety.

The story of the railroads and the creation of standard time zones in 1883 is a familiar one, effectively told here in chapter three. What the railroads brought west was new meaning to the phrase "on time." Standard Time was Railroad Time. But standardized time meant more than reliable clocks displaying predictable, uniform time. The standard time zones represented a growing standardization in all of American life. What began with Eli Whitney's idea about interchangeable parts for firearms soon spread to everything from tin cans and window frames to shoe sizes and rolls of barbed wire. The railroad, with its standard track gauge, required goods of common sizes. At the simplest level, that meant wrenches that fit bolt heads, steam gauges that were all marked in the same scale, and rails of predictable length and weight. In all of this, the message was clear. The individual quirks and eccentric ways so beloved in Henry George's "Old California" had to make way for a machine-made West that required uniformity, predictability, and respectability.

Few places along the railroad corridor made the power of standardization more visible than the depot. Many western railroads, including the Soo Line and the Chicago & North Western, used standardized depot designs. A town got a station based on population size and economic potential. The Chicago & North Western had two depot sizes. Smaller towns were given size number two, with a common waiting room for both men and women. Larger towns were blessed with size number one, offering a larger building and a separate "ladies waiting room." Building across North Dakota, the Soo Line had three depot grades. In the first years of the twentieth century, the Soo Line built more than two hundred standard-size stations throughout the state. Since many companies also used common color schemes, this was yet another example of the railroad as an agent for uniformity andstandardization.[9]

But the most pervasive force for standardization brought by the railroad was the mail-order catalogue. As former railroad depot agent Richard W. Sears

TABLE OF GRADUATIONS

FOR THE

BALTIMORE AND OHIO RAIL ROAD,

tween Baltimore and Cumberland. Computed for equal resistance in both directions.

		OUTWARD TRANSPORTATION. Weight of Carriages, 3 28125 tons / Do of Freight, 1.96875 tons / Amount of Friction, 0.08499 tons				Amount of resistance or power required for transportation in either direction		RETURN TRANSPORTATION. Weight of Carriages, 3.28125 tons / Do of Freight, 9.84375 tons / Amount of Friction, 0.08799 tons					
Statements	Horses	Inclination of plane in feet per mile	Inclination of plane in degrees and minutes of a circle		Gravity of the load, or its tendency to descend, expressed in parts of a ton	resistance in parts of a ton	resistance in pounds	Gravity of the load, or its tendency to descend, expressed in parts of a ton	Inclination of plane in degrees and minutes of a circle		Inclination of plane in feet per mile	Horses	Statements
No	No	Feet	dg	min	prtsof a ton	Ton	Po'nds	prts of a ton	dg	min	Feet	No	No
1	0	35.2	0	22.9	0.035			0.088	0	22.9	35.2	0	1
2	1	15.08	0	09.8	0.015	0.05	112	0.038	0	09.9	15.08	1	2
3	2	65.37	0	42.5	0.065	0.10	224	0.012	0	03.2	5.02	2	3
4	3	115.65	1	15.3	0.115	0.15	336	0.062	0	16.3	25.14	3	4
5	4	165.94	1	48.0	0.165	0.20	448	0.112	0	29.4	45.25	4	5
6	5	216.22	2	20.8	0.215	0.25	560	0.162	0	42.5	65.37	5	6
7	6	266.51	2	53.5	0.265	0.30	671	0.212	0	55.6	85.48	6	7
8	7	316.79	3	26.3	0.315	0.35	748	0.262	1	08.7	105.59	7	8
9	8	366.08	3	59.0	0.365	0.40	896	0.312	1	21.8	125.71	8	9
10	9	416.37	4	31.7	0.415	0.45	1008	0.362	1	34.9	145.82	9	10
11	10	466.65	5	04.5	0.465	0.50	1120	0.412	1	48.0	165.94	10	11
12	11	516.94	5	37.2	0.515	0.55	1232	0.462	2	01.1	186.05	11	12
13	12	567.22	6	10.0	0.565	0.60	1344	0.512	2	14.2	206.17	12	13
14	13	617.51	6	42.7	0.615	0.65	1456	0.562	2	27.3	226.28	13	14
15	14	667.79	7	15.5	0.665	0.70	1568	0.612	2	40.4	246.40	14	15
16	15	718.08	7	48.2	0.715	0.75	1680	0.662	2	53.5	266.51	15	16
17	16	768.37	8	21.0	0.765	0.80	1792	0.712	3	06.6	286.62	16	17

quickly recognized, the mail-order business depended on railroads for efficient, low-cost distribution. What Sears, Roebuck and Montgomery Ward catalogues offered was not merely an entire department store between book covers for rural America but a compelling social message. Selling ready-to-wear clothing with common colors, standard sizes, and the latest styles told western farmers and small-town business folk that they could be like their eastern relatives. In sometimes invisible ways, the mail-order catalogues spelled out the rules for respectability in everything from dress to home furnishings. A sample order form

The front cover of a 1912 catalogue boasting that Saint Paul was the "home market of the Great Northwest" left no doubt as to the importance of railroads in creating business for Minnesota merchants. Saint Paul itself was tributary to Chicago. *Courtesy of Special Collections, Washington State Historical Society.*

printed in the 1902 Sears, Roebuck catalogue says it all. One William Johnson, living in Cherry County, Nebraska, ordered the following items: a book on blacksmithing, a gold-filled bracelet, a twelve-gauge shotgun, ten pounds of coffee, and 100 bars of laundry soap. Johnson could be confident that when the railroad delivered his box at the station in Valentine, his bars of soap would be just like those sold in any city and that the shells for his shotgun would fit any twelve-gauge in western Kansas or northern Idaho. And if the gold-filled bracelet was for his wife, she could be sure that it might also grace the wrist of any woman in Portland, Maine, or Portland, Oregon. American identity might be expressed by everyone dressing in respectable, middle class ways, drinking the same coffee, and washing dirty clothes with the same soap. The railroad and the catalogue created a vast rural "common market" that shaped a common culture. What took the catalogue to thousands of western customers and then delivered their orders was the Iron Road. The arrival of each season's catalogue became a

fig 191

SEARS, ROEBUCK & CO., Cheapest Supply House on Earth, Chicago. CATALOGUE No. III. 13

The National City Bank
of New York.

CAPITAL FULLY PAID, $10,000,000.
SHAREHOLDERS' LIABILITY, $10,000,000.
SURPLUS & UNDIVIDED PROFITS $5,700,000
CABLE ADDRESS "CITIBANK"

New York

We also refer by special permission to the largest bank in the United States, The National City Bank of New York, with a capital and surplus of Fifteen Million, Seven Hundred Thousand Dollars.

THIS IS AN EXACT COPY OF AN ORDER WRITTEN ON OUR REGULAR ORDER BLANK.
A CAREFUL STUDY OF EACH POINT WILL AID YOU IN MAKING YOUR OWN ORDER.

ORDER BLANK OF SEARS ROEBUCK AND CO
73-87 N. Desplaines St.
74-96 N. Jefferson St.
68-96 Fulton St.
1-31 Wayman St.
CHICAGO, ILL.

OUR ONLY TERMS ARE CASH WITH THE ORDER. WE GUARANTEE ENTIRE SATISFACTION OR IMMEDIATELY RETURN YOUR MONEY. WE DO NOT ACCEPT ORDERS FOR LESS THAN 50 CENTS. OUR REASONS ARE EXPLAINED IN THE INTRODUCTORY PAGES OF OUR LARGE CATALOGUE.

HOW TO ORDER.

NOTICE TO CUSTOMERS. Don't fail to read the instructions on this blank before ordering, as a careful observance of our rules will greatly aid us in filling your orders in a satisfactory manner, AND BE SURE TO MENTION, IN SPACE PROVIDED BELOW, THE NUMBER OF CATALOGUE, CIRCULAR, OR NAME OF PAPER FROM WHICH YOU SELECT YOUR GOODS.

PLEASE SEND TO *June 3* 1902 (Date of this order.)

NAME *William Johnson*
POSTOFFICE *Fort Niobrara*
STREET AND NUMBER
COUNTY *Cherry* STATE *Nebr.*

BELOW GIVE SHIPPING POINT IF DIFFERENT FROM POSTOFFICE.

NAME
SHIPPING POINT *Valentine*
COUNTY *Cherry* STATE *Nebr*
RAILROAD CO. *F. E. & M. V.* EXPRESS CO.

Is there a Freight Agent at Your Shipping Point? *Yes* (State Yes or No)

	DOLLARS	CENTS
Draft or Check		
Postoffice Order	10	11
Express Money Order		
S. R. & Co's Check		
S. R. & Co's Credit Draft	1	60
Currency		
Postage Stamps		
TOTAL	11	71

THESE GOODS ARE SELECTED FROM CATALOGUE NUMBER OR NAME *111* CIRCULAR PAPER

Number of article in Catalogue.	Quantity desired.	NAME OF ARTICLES WANTED	Sizes, Colors, etc.	Price of each, or per dozen		Extend totals here and then add this column.	
				Dollars	Cents	Dollars	Cents
3R1394	1	Book "Modern Blacksmithing"			68		68
4R2114	1	Gold filled Bracelet		2	00	2	00
6R401	1	Long Range Winner gun 12 gauge 30 in.		3	98	3	98
7R117	10	Spcl. Griddle Roasted Coffee			21	2	10
7R1751	100	Bars SRT Co's Family Laundry Soap				2	95
						11	71

This is only a fac-simile order.

NOTE. IF ANY OF ABOVE GOODS ARE OUT OF STOCK MAY WE SUBSTITUTE? *Yes*
IF SO KINDLY MENTION SECOND AND THIRD CHOICE. *Use your best judgment*

If You Do Not Use This Order Blank at Once, Preserve it for Future Use, AS WE CAN FILL ORDERS better and quicker if written on our regular order blanks, and they are MORE CONVENIENT FOR YOU. We will be only too glad to send you a new supply when these are gone, if you will drop us a postal card, or will include them in your next order.

NOTE THAT CATALOGUE NUMBER IS WRITTEN OUT IN FULL. DO NOT FAIL TO WRITE EVERY LETTER AND FIGURE IN THE CATALOGUE NUMBER.

Railroads made the products of the Industrial Revolution part of daily life in the West. Sears, Roebuck catalogue order form, 1902.

much-anticipated event, one that is chronicled in George Milburn's now forgotten novel *Catalogue*. The first transcontinental visionaries thought the railroad itself would be a nationalizing force. But even more powerful than the rails themselves was what came in boxcars and baggage cars.

Writing in 1869, journalist Samuel Bowles predicted that the completion of the new Pacific Railroad would be the "revelation of a new Empire."[10] Manifest Destiny had found its true highway. The fabled Northwest Passage was once thought to be a waterway; now it was surely a "steel Nile."[11] By 1900 Bowles' prophecy seemed reality. With the exception of three territories that were not yet states—Arizona, New Mexico, and Oklahoma—the domestic Amer-

Opportunity beckons: advertising a million acres of land in the Redwater Valley of Montana in the early twentieth century. *Courtesy of Special Collections, Washington State Historical Society.*

ican empire appeared complete. Census figures for that year counted a total population of over 76 million. The nation's economy seemed on the mend after the devastating Panic of 1893. American railroads, hard hit by the Panic and the Pullman strike the following year, pursued a recovery strategy based on mergers and consolidations. The last great western railroad building boom was over, leading some to think that the West had finally been completely tracked. William McKinley, the very image of prosperity and respectability, had defeated William Jennings Bryan, a man many thought was a dangerous western radical. And all of this came at a time when the nation was still celebrating the Spanish-American War and the promise of American power in the Pacific and the Caribbean.

The packed and noisy interior of an immigrant car headed West. *Courtesy of Barriger Railroad Library of the St. Louis Mercantile Library*

If the nation seemed ready for the new century, so did the railroads. There were more than a thousand railroad companies of all classes and sizes. The American rail network seemed virtually complete, with some 193,000 miles of track. West of the Mississippi, only Oklahoma Territory and Nevada had less than a thousand miles of track. Railroad lines filled the map in 1900, thinning a bit in the middle, but thickening along both coasts. In its tangle of lines and routes, the map offered a reassuring message: The national project begun in 1803 to conquer the West and tame it now appeared complete. For most Americans, the map's rail lines represented conquest accomplished. If the census of 1890 announced that the frontier was "closed," the railroad map showed that the West was now fully part of the nation. If nothing else, the map reaffirmed the primacy of Chicago in the railroad West. As consumers of steel and coal as well as employers of a vast labor force, railroads dominated the economy. More than a million workers drew railroad paychecks, and a few short years later, one out of every twenty-three American workers found employment in the railroad world. Growing up along the Union Pacific in Ellis, Kansas, young Walter

Chrysler knew the power and promise of the railroad. Writing later in life, he recalled being drawn to the railroad and loving "to see the engines with their mysteries exposed."[12]

As the new century began, railroads west of Chicago and Saint Louis were part of two interconnected operating systems. These systems were not abstractions; they shaped the lives and fortunes of thousands who called the West home. The first of those systems spread across the Great Plains from Chicago to the Front Range of the Rockies. This was the world of the Granger railroads, domain and battleground for the Chicago & North Western; the Milwaukee Road; the Rock Island; the Chicago, Burlington, and Quincy; and the Missouri Pacific. Through a spreading web of branch lines, the Granger railroads carried wheat, cattle, and corn to Chicago. In the last years of the nineteenth century, Granger companies aggressively expanded to defeat rival lines, all the while encouraging town building and arranging for immigrants to find new homes on the prairie.

The second western operating system was the one envisioned by Asa Whitney and his generation of dreamers and promoters. This was the transcontinental territory, the main lines from a midcontinent terminal like Omaha or Saint Paul to California and the Pacific Northwest. In this busy corridor, the Union Pacific, the Santa Fe, the Northern Pacific, and the Southern Pacific all fought for long-haul dominance. But nowhere was the competition more intense than in the Pacific Northwest. Once the Canadian Pacific was built to Vancouver, the Union Pacific reached Portland, the Great Northern came to Seattle, and, in 1909, the Milwaukee Road arrived in Seattle, Tacoma, and Everett, the competition for through traffic was ferocious and eventually destructive. At heart, the competition was all about integrating the Pacific Northwest into a national and eventually a global economy. Rival transcontinentals fought to bring everything from prospective settlers to farm machinery into the region while carrying agricultural products out from it. The constant rate wars hurt railroad profits but enhanced the influence of Seattle and Tacoma. The good fortune of those cities came at the expense of Portland and its Columbia River transportation system. Seattle and Tacoma gathered in the bounty of Wheat County brought by the railroads and shipped it to distant markets in England, Australia, and elsewhere. In all of this, Chicago remained the unquestioned gateway to the interior West—the one place where the Granger railroads and the transcontinentals met the East Coast trunk lines.[13]

I N 1900 THE NORTH AMERICAN RAILROAD WORLD LOOKED prosperous and secure. Railroads had made the West part of a larger world. Ranchers and farmers, shopkeepers and schoolteachers—all lived in a West where railroad time shaped the work day. New stoves, the latest fashionable hats, and children's toys for Christmas were brought by rail to become part of everyday life. Letters from distant friends and relatives arrived by way of the Railroad Post Office car. The West's cattle, wheat, and fruit were staples of not only the American diet but that of England and much of western Europe. If all this came at the price of political corruption and ruinous competition, many Americans seemed ready to pay the bill. Directors who looted company treasuries and speculators who defrauded investors were part of the Gilded Age preached against on Sunday and tolerated for the rest of the week. Despite the ill-concealed anger of some Populists and reform-minded journalists, the railroad West seemed something nearly eternal, something that was ever-present and beyond the hand of change.

A half century of dramatic railroad expansion seemed to justify Samuel

Bowles' confident declaration that the Iron Horse would provide the energy for "the creation of a new civilization."[14] Federal census official Robert P. Porter explained how railroads would bring Bowles' "new civilization" to the West. "The modern system of railroads are of broader scope than mere State lines. They are planned with a national purpose, to bring together the products of labor in the forest, the mine, the shop, and the farm, far removed from each other, and bind them together in ever strengthening ties of commerce and ready social and political intercourse."[15] What railroad journalist Henry Varnum Poor had written half a century before now seemed a settled fact of western life: "The age of locomotion is the era of progress. Wherever the railway extends, knowledge and civilization advance in geometrical ratio."[16] But in the years after 1900, a thoughtful observer might have seen that the railroad West was heading for trouble around the next curve.

Intense, unregulated competition had created a tangle of lines and routes, many of them soon unprofitable. The expansion eagerly planned by railroad executives and warmly welcomed by small town farmers and merchants came at a high price. While no railroad official would dare admit it, there were too many main-line transcontinentals in the United States. Once there had been one; by 1909 there were six. Three of them—the Northern Pacific, the Great Northern, and the Milwaukee Road—served the northern Great Plains and the Pacific Northwest. As market realities soon made clear, this was at least one too many. Nowhere was the overbuilding more evident than in the world of the Great Plains branch lines. The wheat boom prompted an unprecedented decade-long burst of building that began in 1879. The annual report for the Northern Pacific Railway in 1883 pronounced all of this "a marvel of the times."[17] The Granger lines—especially those serving the northern Great Plains—rushed to capture the golden stream of wheat from Nebraska and the Dakotas. The Burlington pursued an expansionist scheme west of Lincoln. Even the transcontinentals hurried to profit from Wheat Country. The Santa Fe's main line from Chicago to Hutchinson, Kansas, quickly grew branches in the country west of Wichita. The Great Northern's line through North Dakota sprouted eleven northbound branches before reaching the state border at Williston. The bumper wheat harvest of 1890 in the Pacific Northwest seemed one more reason for rivals like the Northern Pacific and the Oregon Railway and Navigation Company to push hard into the Palouse country. The *Railroad Gazette* reported in 1884 that "never before in the history of the world was so vast a territory made accessible in so short a time."[18] No matter how grand the promises and how promising the future, this was a western strategy bound to produce red ink and, eventually, wholesale abandonments. The same issue of the *Railroad Gazette* that reported

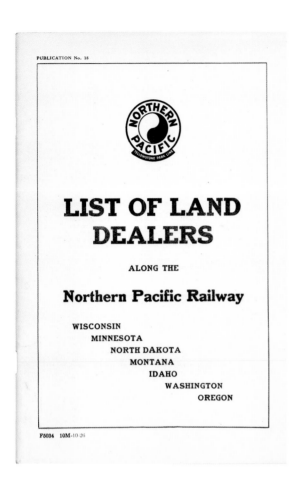

A list of land dealers along the Northern Pacific Railway in 1921. *Courtesy of Barriger Railroad Library of the St. Louis Mercantile Library.*

Although many railroads aspired to reach the Pacific Ocean, the Denver and Rio Grande remained a regional carrier that sought to develop the central Rocky Mountains, an area rich in gold and silver. *Courtesy of Barriger Railroad Library of the St. Louis Mercantile Library.*

on railroad expansion on the northern plains predicted a coming crash: "We may safely say that the construction now is at a rate which cannot be possibly kept up for many years without grave disaster."[19]

ANYONE LOOKING AT A RAILROAD MAP IN 1900 MIGHT be led to believe that the country finally had a national railway system. That "system" appeared to link the West to both coasts and beyond to Atlantic and Pacific markets. If the railroads had brought the world to the West, it now seemed as if the West was part of the world. But that cartographic expression of "system" was an illusion. At the end of the 1880s, Interstate Commerce Commission statistician Henry C. Adams offered this blunt assessment. "One frequently hears the expression 'railway system of the United States,' but the truth is that no such thing as a railway system exists in the United States."[20] Lines on the map that appeared connected were often not physically joined. Perhaps the classic example was the key city of Chicago. In the 1890s the city had seven main line passenger stations. While this

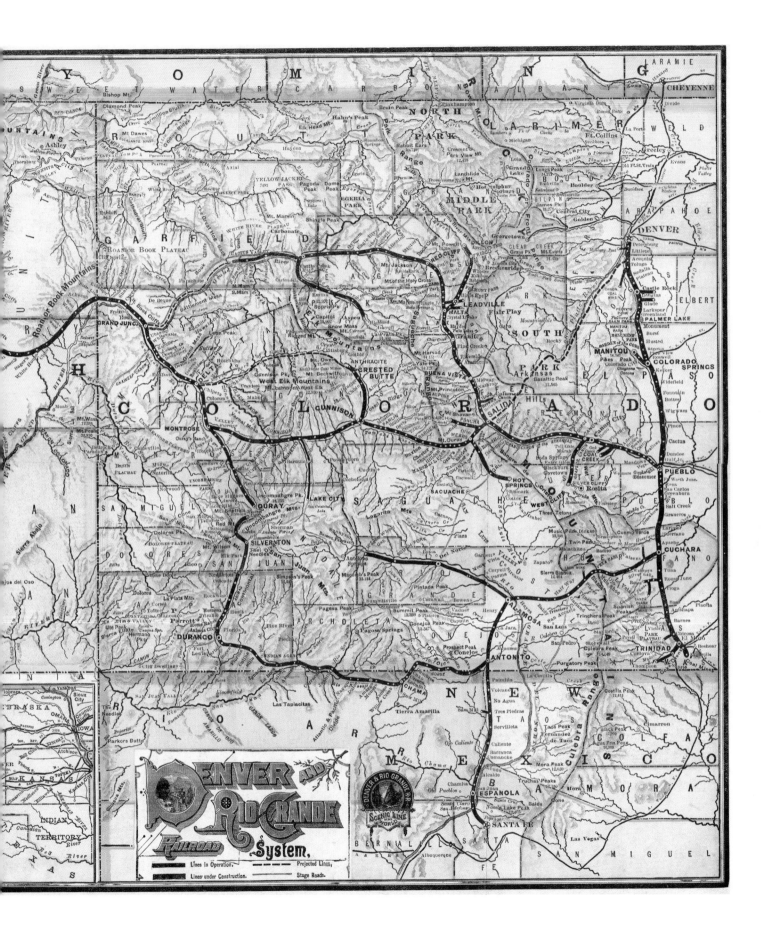

DENVER AND RIO GRANDE RAILROAD System.

Lines in Operation.
Lines under Construction.
Projected Lines.
Stage Roads.

DENVER & RIO GRANDE R.R.
SCENIC LINE OF THE WORLD.

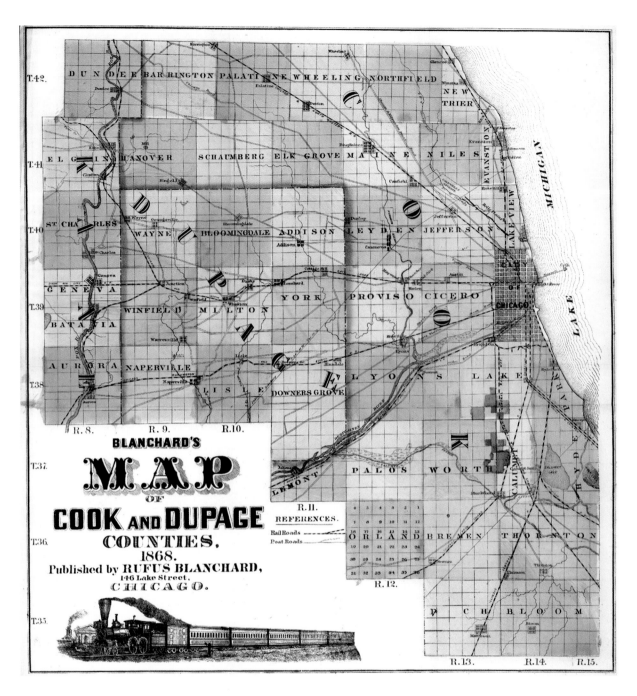

benefited the city's venerable Parmelee Transfer Company, passengers found making connections difficult and sometimes impossible. The story for freight traffic was often just as complicated. A traffic snarl in Chicago or a boxcar shortage in Omaha at harvest time spelled economic trouble throughout the West. The traffic flow problems experienced in Florida during the Spanish-American War were just a hint of things to come. If boxcars of important military supplies

By the time this map of Cook and Dupage counties was published in 1868, Chicago was clearly the railroad hub of a resource-rich hinterland. *Courtesy of Barriger Railroad Library of the St. Louis Mercantile Library.*

Chicago's smoky Wells Street Station in 1894, as depicted by its primary railroad tenant. Opened in 1881, the station served the needs of countless travelers until 1911, the year the Chicago and North Western terminal replaced it. *Courtesy of Barriger Railroad Library of the St. Louis Mercantile Library.*

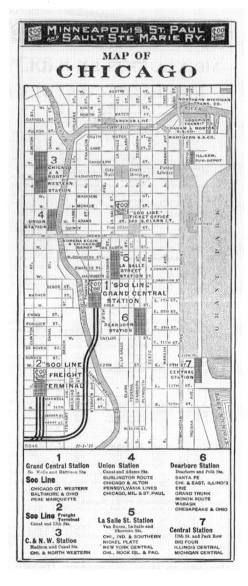

A complimentary pass for Frank Parmelee's Chicago Omnibus Line, which shuttled connecting passengers among the city's most important railway stations. *Courtesy of the National Museum of Transportation.*

This map of Chicago's main stations and their many railroad tenants comes from a public timetable the Soo Line issued on July 12, 1920. The Soo Line used Grand Central Station. *Courtesy of Barriger Railroad Library of the St. Louis Mercantile Library.*

went unloaded for want of adequate yard and dock facilities during the "splendid little war," what might happen if the nation waged a full-scale modern war?

But perhaps the most serious weakness in the world of the western railroads was a set of values and behaviors buried deep within the railroad business. These patterns of thinking and acting had consequences far beyond corporate boardrooms, engine houses, and small-town depots. In a national culture that put competition at the heart of the American Dream, railroad companies made it the centerpiece of corporate strategy and company life. Each line saw itself as a nation with a set of battle plans and an army of disciplined workers. In the railroad rhetoric of the time, each company waged war on its rivals for control of profitable territories. As one railroad warrior put it, "having been reluctantly compelled to fight, we did not feel safe to lay down our arms till a treaty of peace seemed probable." The same Burlington traffic official promised: "we will defend ourselves if attacked"[21] After an attempt to settle rate wars failed in early 1886, the *Railroad Gazette* reported that "for the first time in their history the transcontinentals engaged in open warfare."[22] Whether the territory promised wheat, corn, or cows, each railroad wanted the lion's share, if not the entire prize. These railroad wars guaranteed overexpansion in the West, shrinking profits thanks to rate competition, and making cooperation in times of crisis nearly impossible.

On the eve of America's entry into World War I, the grand railroad enterprise began to falter. In 1916 American railroads counted a record 254,037 miles of track. But that staggering number was hardly reason to celebrate. Fully one-sixth of all rail mileage was in receivership and every company, no matter how powerful, suffered from the consequences of overexpansion and profit-draining rate wars. Perhaps few noticed that the nation had registered more than 3 million automobiles that year. Western farmers and merchants enjoyed a moment of prosperity thanks to a war-hungry European market, but railroad profits did not keep pace. The ever-present issue of freight rates, especially in the West, became even more contentious as the Interstate Commerce Commission set rates that railroads considered far too low. Threats of strikes from the principal railroad brotherhoods seemed a distinct possibility in 1916—a possibility averted only when Congress passed and the Supreme Court upheld the Adamson Eight Hour Act. Swirling around all this was a steady shift in public opinion. Once cast as empire builders and national benefactors, railroads were increasingly portrayed as greedy corporate giants unconcerned with the public good. It was a blistering indictment: Railroad companies corrupted western political life, oppressed workers, and, despite efforts at regulation, still behaved like monopolists. From Frank Norris's powerful novels about wheat, California, and the railroad trust to muckraking articles in *McClure's Magazine*, the tide had steadily turned against the railroads. Few were more passionate in their denunciation of western railroads than Norris. Intent on exposing the political intrigues of the Southern Pacific in California, he lashed out at what he called "the great iron hand" that held the state and the nation in a crushing grip.[23] There was an irony in all of this probably not lost on railroad executives. Farmers and merchants wanted the railroad, campaigned for it, and bargained for it. But once it arrived, it was easy to hate, a ready-made target for growing western discontent with a market system far beyond the control of ordinary citizens in Kansas or Oregon.

THE YEAR 1869 WAS ONE DEFINING MOMENT FOR RAILROADS and the West. The year 1917 was another. As early as December 1915 President Woodrow Wilson publicly worried about the capacity of American railroads to handle massive wartime traffic demands. Some months before, a Special Committee on Cooperation with the Military Authorities was created, linking prominent railroad leaders to the War Department. At the time such a voluntary, industry-dominated approach seemed most workable. But when Wilson came before Congress at the end of 1916, he put railroad matters at the top of his State of the Union agenda. Heated debates about railroad regulation, the powers of the Interstate Commerce Commission, and labor-management tensions were in the public press and on the nation's mind. With the European war dragging on month after bloody month, the president asked Congress to grant him authority to take control of railroads "in case of military necessity."[24]

In April 1917 the United States entered what so many came to call the Great War. Just a month before, a national rail strike had been narrowly averted. Now, with the nation at war, rail traffic—especially bulk commodities shipped from the West to eastern ports—increased dramatically. Throughout the fall harvest season, railroads struggled to match available freight cars to shippers' demands. At the same time—thanks to an effective German submarine presence along the Atlantic coast—unloaded boxcars piled up in rail yards all along the eastern seaboard. This was a national economic and transportation crisis that struck western farmers, ranchers, and merchants especially hard. Despite the efforts of railroad leaders to deal voluntarily with the problem, the situation grew steadily worse. In the face of a severe winter and a nearly deadlocked rail system, it was estimated that on November 1, 1917, the freight-car shortage reached some 158,000 cars. Woodrow Wilson's worst fears had come true. Despite their best efforts, American railroads simply could not meet the challenges of modern war. On December 26, 1917, the president issued a proclamation placing

Overleaf: A 1926 map of the territory the Burlington route wanted to defend from competitors. *Courtesy of Barriger Railroad Library of the St. Louis Mercantile Library.*

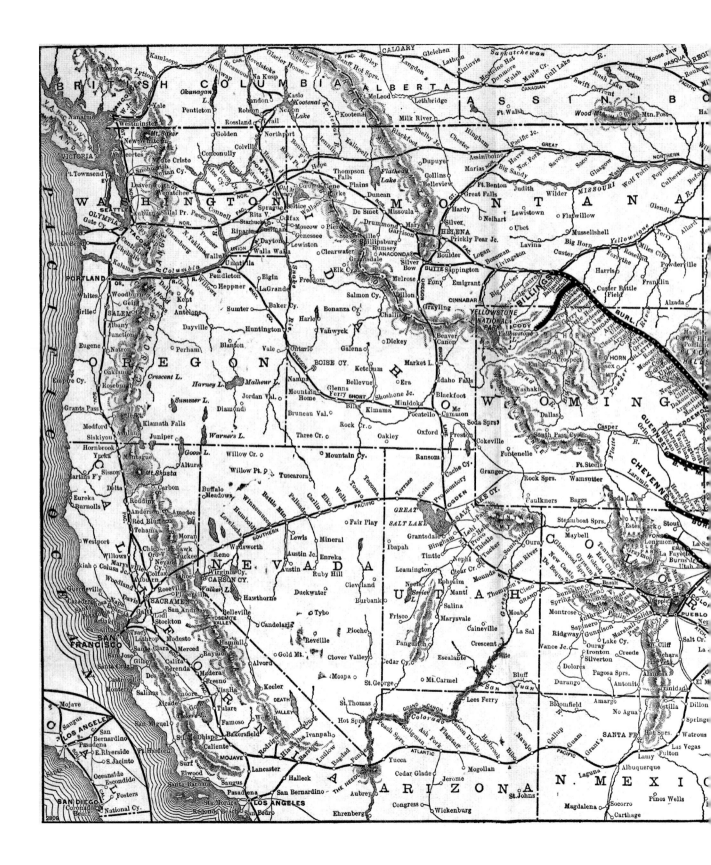

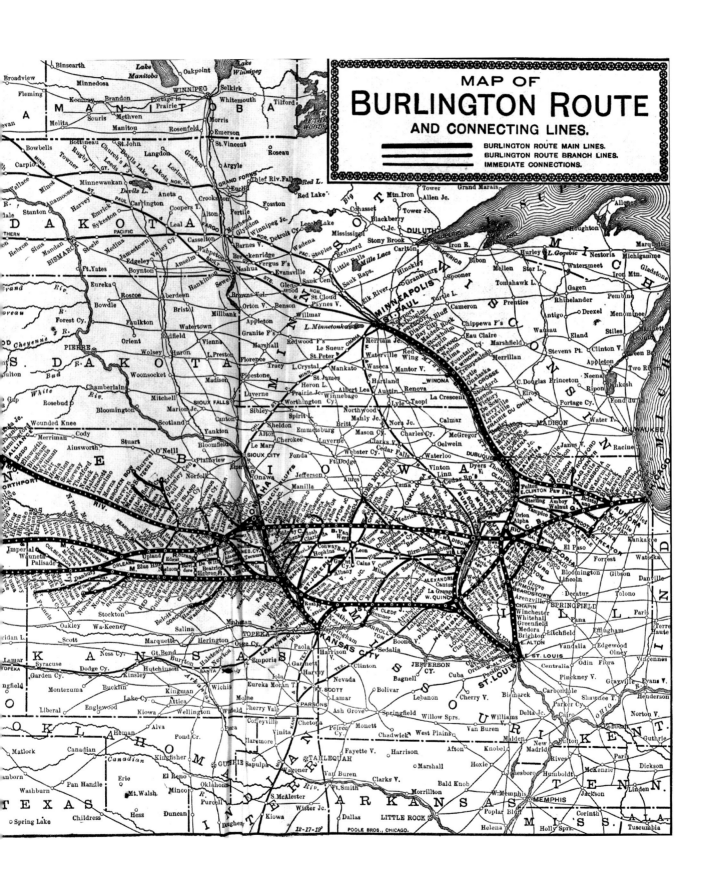

MAP OF
BURLINGTON ROUTE
AND CONNECTING LINES.

BURLINGTON ROUTE MAIN LINES.
BURLINGTON ROUTE BRANCH LINES.
IMMEDIATE CONNECTIONS.

American railroads under government control. That decision was based not only on the immediate situation but also Wilson's own ideas about efficient management and the value of centralized decision making. Turning to Secretary of the Treasury William G. McAdoo, Wilson made him director general of railroads and head of a new agency called the United States Railroad Administration. The USRA ran the nation's rail system until 1920.

Wilson's action in 1917 was both inevitable and appropriate. Under McAdoo's leadership, economies of scale in traffic routing were imposed, in many cases benefiting western agricultural interests. McAdoo instituted standardization in everything from paperwork to locomotive design. And, perhaps most significantly, he adjusted wages and freight rates to match current economic conditions. Historians have long argued about the decisions made by the USRA and the consequences of those actions for the future of American railroads. But one thing is clear. The confusions of the First World War and the presence of the USRA temporarily masked the emergence of a new transportation technology, a technology that would displace the world of steam and rails in the American imagination. Walter Chrysler knew that. Beginning with his first job as a sweeper

Smoke, the more the better, symbolized prosperity during an age when heavy industry added a dramatic new dimension to railroad landscapes of the West. Metal smelters provided some of the grandest displays of smoke, regardless of its impact on the environment. *Courtesy of Barriger Railroad Library of the St. Louis Mercantile Library.*

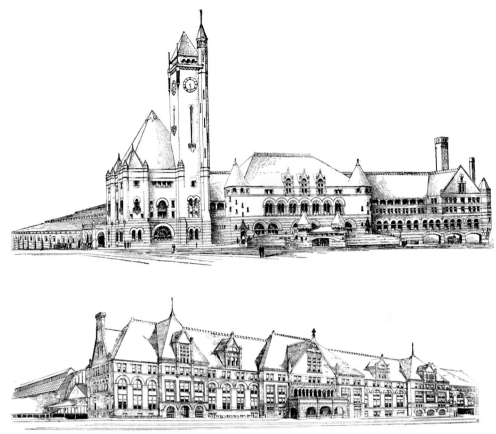

Fig. 654. – Perspective.

at the Union Pacific's Ellis shops, Chrysler became a major figure in several railroad companies. But in 1908 he went to a Chicago automobile show, saw a Locomobile touring car, and fell in love. He later said he was "hypnotized" by the car and "hopelessly infatuated" with it.[25] Chrysler always called himself a "transportation man." Once it had been the mysteries of a steam locomotive that had fascinated him; now the fascination moved to the Locomobile and all its cousins. Walter Chrysler would not be alone in his love affair with the automobile.

Warren G. Harding never had a reputation as an astute observer of the American scene. But in his 1921 State of the Union address, Harding pointed to a fundamental shift in American life—a shift that would leave its imprint on the West as surely as did the railroad. "The motor car," Harding declared, "has become an indispensable instrument in our political, social, and industrial life."[26] Congress evidently agreed, and promptly appropriated seventy-five million dollars a year for federal highway construction. Just a few years earlier, Woodrow Wilson might have said that the railroads were the "indispensable instrument" in the life of the nation.

Even during the belt-tightening of World War I, the United States Railroad Administration maintained an industry tradition of annually publishing brochures to lure trainloads of tourists west to vacation destinations. *Courtesy of Special Collections, Washington State Historical Society.*

Harding had the numbers on his side. As railroad mileage began a slow decline after 1916, American automobile production and sales steadily advanced. Nowhere was this automobile revolution more evident than in rural America, in general, and the Great Plains in particular. Kansas, Nebraska, and South Dakota—states shaped by the railroad—tell the story. In 1900 Kansas had 220 registered automobiles. That number increased to 1,750 in 1905, and five years later, to a remarkable 10,490. South Dakota experienced a similar growth pattern: 50 cars in 1900, 550 in 1905, and 3,240 by 1910. But no Great Plains state witnessed as dramatic a growth in automobile registrations as Nebraska. In 1900 the state had 60 registered cars. Five years later that number reached 570. By 1910 Nebraska had 11,340 automobiles, a number no other Great Plains state matched. While Lincoln and Omaha undoubtedly accounted for many of these cars, Nebraska farmers were plainly finding automobiles a useful part of rural life. In fact, during the first years of the automobile revolution, it was the rural market that kept the developing auto industry alive.[27]

No enterprise took greater advantage of that rural market than the Ford Motor Company. Although Henry Ford had left the farm early and always professed to hating farm work, he skillfully promoted himself as a country boy who loved to tinker with machinery that was sure to make farming a bit easier and certainly more profitable. With the introduction of the Model T in 1908, Fords became the farmer's friend of choice. Of the 34,000 automobiles sold in Kansas in 1915, most were Fords. And farmers put those Tin Lizzies to work powering saw mills, pulling plows, and hauling goats and chickens to market. One automobile historian called the Model T "a farmer's car for a nation of farmers."[28] Ford dealers and service stations were everywhere and soon the "Ford Garage" could be found from Madison, Nebraska, to Tacoma, Washington.

Just as tracks and trains shaped the West in the second half of the nineteenth century, what historian John C. Burnham called "automobility" transformed the western landscape in the twentieth century.[29] While the adoption of the automobile was neither automatic nor geographically uniform, rural folk felt the changes produced by the automobile more directly than did city dwellers. Automobility gradually lessened the isolation of farm life in a way that the railroads could not. Cars promised—and seemed to deliver—independence and personal choice. Chrysler expressed that American passion for going where you want to go when you want to go when he simply said "Just ask yourself what this country will be like when every individual has his private car and is able to travel anywhere."[30]

But it was more than choice, independence, and mobility that made farmers east and west embrace the car. Automobiles provided direct access to Saturday market days and increased their importance in regional economic development. A Saturday trip to town meant shopping for merchandise that could be seen and touched. Ordering by catalogue and waiting for shipment by rail amounted to delayed gratification. Goods bought in town still came by rail, but shopping now promised what is the foundation of the consumer culture—instant gratification. No catalogue or boxcar could compete with that. The expanding use of automobiles in the Rural Free Delivery system meant that farmers no longer had to go to the post office for mail. And there was one less reason to go down to the depot to pick up the occasional package from Sears, Roebuck when the RFD carrier could bring it right to the mailbox or the doorstep. All of this came at a time when there was a change in how many Americans imagined the shape of the Future and the machines that powered Progress. In the nineteenth century—especially in the West—railroads promised Progress. Every small town printer

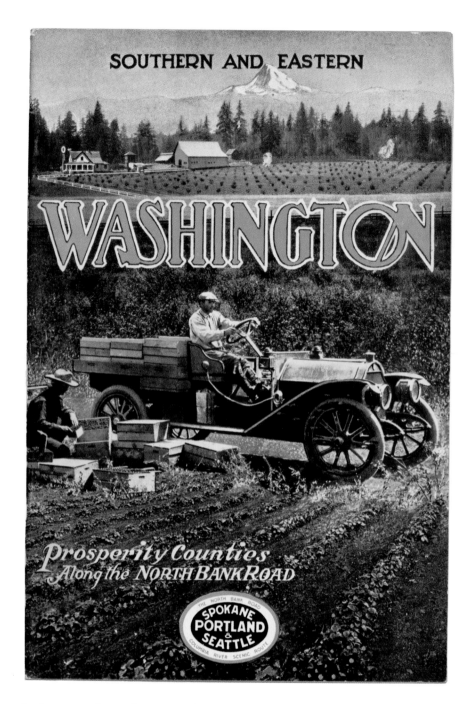

The automobile in the garden. *Courtesy of Special Collections, Washington State Historical Society.*

had a piece of type depicting a locomotive. Stock certificates, advertising posters, and even fillers between newspaper stories carried the locomotive image. Nothing said "modern machine" and Future more than that familiar shape. But by the time Harding called automobiles "an indispensable instrument" in American life, good roads began to signal Progress and cars were the symbol of a

bright future. As photographer David Plowden writes, the nation's "symbolic iconography" was shifting from trains and tracks to cars and roads.[31]

American railroad executives were not unaware of the challenges posed by automobility. But their capacity for quick change and creative response was sharply limited. The Interstate Commerce Commission made branch lines difficult to abandon. The very nature of the railroad meant that routes and times were largely out of the hands of travelers and shippers. Schedules were written for the convenience of the metropolis, not the small town. Railroad planners always expected that customers would come to them. Overconfident railroaders joined the Good Roads Movement in the first decades of the century, thinking that those roadways would simply lead farmers more quickly and directly to the depot door or the grain-elevator loading ramp.

But it was the urban market, with its emphasis on image and status, that the railroads most wanted to recapture. Locomotives once symbolized speed and the Future. But with their pipes, pistons, and side rods all visible, those same engines now seemed to represent the past. In the 1930s the Future was embodied in the sleek industrial design called "streamlining." With swept-back lines, rounded corners, and shiny metallic finishes, streamlined cars and airplanes advertised speed and the modern world. Not wanting to be left behind, railroad executives turned to industrial designers like Raymond Lowey, Otto Kuhler, and Henry Dreyfuss to give passenger trains a new face. What the designers produced were trains that appeared fast, even when stopped at a station. Beginning in 1934 with the Union Pacific's M-10000 and the Burlington's Zephyr, the railroad world was soon filled with locomotives that looked like rocket ships and passenger cars that seemed more like airplanes. The Union Pacific's advertising slogan for the M-10000 said it all: "Tomorrow's train Today." Perhaps no experiment in streamlining was more visually striking than the Southern Pacific's Daylight trains. Powered by high-speed GS-4 locomotives, the Daylights were a flash of orange, red, silver, and black. Even the railroad's advertising posters portrayed the Daylights as speed and modernity on rails. Despite these efforts, passenger-train travel increasingly seemed a relic from a distant age. In a culture that idealized speed, worshipped the idea of saving time, and was dazzled by new technology, railroads seemed locked in the embrace of the past.

If streamlining the railroads was an experiment doomed to failure, the massive capital improvement projects launched in the 1920s were more successful, upgrading locomotives, rolling stock, and improving road beds. Those investments paid off in World War II when the companies avoided federal control and successfully delivered the wartime goods. But for a public drawn to something new each year, all these projects meant little. More powerful locomotives and better roadbeds had a hard time competing with new styles from Detroit and highways without potholes.

In the long run, all the railroad's experiments, investments, and sales campaigns failed to change the public's mind. By the 1950s, postwar boom railroads—and certainly travel by rail—seemed a survivor from a distant past. Railroads in the West put a brave face on all of this. The Union Pacific assigned dome coaches and dome-lounge observation cars to the City of Los Angeles and other name trains in 1955. Some years earlier the Burlington polished its Zephyr tradition with the magnificent California Zephyr train sets. Not to be outdone, in 1956 the Santa Fe's final version of the El Capitan boasted innovative hi-level

The new face of the railroads: The Santa Fe used colorfully garbed Native Americans to introduce streamlined diesel locomotives from General Motors that in the 1930s replaced steam power on its best trains. Santa Fe diesels featured a visually appealing "war bonnet" design that still appears on locomotives of today's Burlington Northern Santa Fe. *Courtesy of Barriger Railroad Library of the St. Louis Mercantile Library.*

cars. But passenger revenues continued to fall. More troubling, so did profits from the freight business. Just as automobiles drained passengers from the railroads, trucks steadily encroached on both local and long-haul business. Pipelines seemed more efficient than tank cars; bulk commodities might be shipped to some markets more cheaply by barge; and trucks promised flexibility in pickup and delivery schedules. Perhaps nothing was more symbolic than the post office's decision to send increasing amounts of first-class mail by air. Mail by rail once promised speed and efficiency. The Railroad Post Office cars, carrying armed postal clerks busily sorting the mail, had been a mark of prestige for rail companies. Now that too was slipping away.

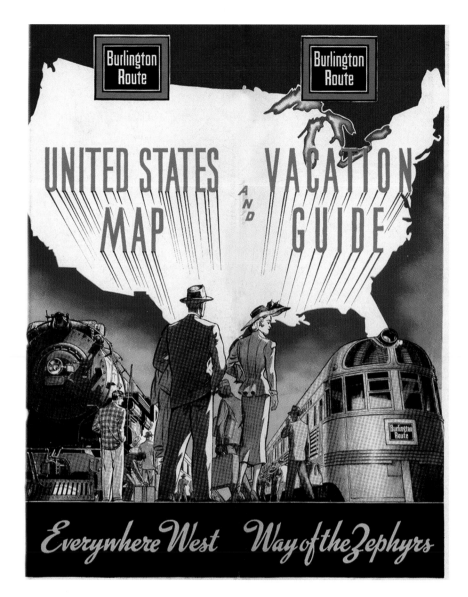

Although this illustration dates from 1951, the illustration of a steam locomotive typical of the pre-streamliner era adds a jarring visual element to a brochure cover clearly intended to showcase the modernity of Burlington's passenger service. *Courtesy of Barriger Railroad Library of the St. Louis Mercantile Library.*

The Pacific Railroad Act of 1862 had signaled the official beginning of a West made by railroads. The Federal-Aid Highway Act of 1956—sometimes known as the Interstate Highway Act—seemed to mark the end of one era and the beginning of another. The visionaries had once been Samuel Parker, Asa Whitney, and Theodore Judah. Now the prophets were countless lobbyists from the American Road Builders Association, the Automobile Manufacturers Association, and the American Association of State Highway Officials—all led by the indefatigable Thomas Harris MacDonald. Longtime head of the federal Bureau of Public Roads, MacDonald was an experienced highway engineer, skilled bureaucrat, and passionate promoter of a national highway system. As early as 1924 he

On a wintry day, the post-World War II modernity of a Great Northern streamliner contrasts with the timeless stubble of a corn field in the upper Midwest. *Courtesy of Barriger Railroad Library of the St. Louis Mercantile Library.*

called for an "interstate" system that would provide "a complete and economical highway transport service throughout the nation."[32] Virtually unknown today, MacDonald proved to be one of the architects of modern America. Almost without realizing it, MacDonald and his supporters picked up the language used to promote the first transcontinental railroad and applied it to the world of concrete and cars. Like railroads, the interstate highways promised safe and rapid travel, expanded markets, and the ability to move goods quickly in times of national emergency—all of this wrapped up in the glowing language of automobility. By the time President Dwight Eisenhower signed the bill creating the Interstate Highway System, MacDonald and his staff had already mapped out the network that many came to call the "I-roads."

In many ways the I-road network in the West followed the routes of the transcontinental railroads. Using Chicago as the gateway to the West, I-94 paralleled the Great Northern and Northern Pacific across the northern Great Plains and Rockies to Seattle, via I-90. Isaac I. Stevens, who championed that route during the Pacific Railroad Surveys of the 1850s, would have been pleased. I-90 also headed west out of Chicago, pushing over the plains and Rockies to Seattle following the route of the last transcontinental line, the Milwaukee Road. Like the Union Pacific, I-80 took the Platte River Road, skirted Denver, and headed to Salt Lake City and Sacramento. Saint Louis was the hub for I-70 across the central plains to Denver and into Los Angeles by way of I-15. Surveyors working for the Missouri Pacific and Union Pacific would have recognized that way west. In the 1850s Memphis put in its bid as the eastern terminal for the first transcontinental railroad. A century later that city found its western connection in I-40, reaching to just outside San Bernardino, and on to Los Angeles by way of I-15. That southern plains roadway followed a tangle of rail lines that included the Missouri Pacific and the Santa Fe.

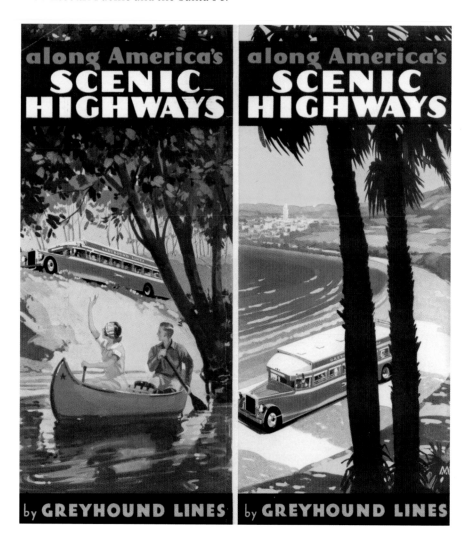

Travel brochures issued by Greyhound bus lines in the 1930s continued an advertising tradition begun by the railroads. *Courtesy of Special Collections, Washington State Historical Society.*

Writing about the interstate revolution, geographer Pierce Lewis put the matter in sharp focus: "Over the full span of American history, one is hard-put to find a single legislative act that so profoundly altered the face of the American landscape, did it so quickly, and yielded so many unexpected and unintended results."[33] Those alterations and transformations could nowhere be more clearly seen than in the small towns of the railroad West. North Platte, Nebraska, was a Union Pacific town in 1867, and in many ways remains one today. In 1956 North Platte was connected to the outside world by U.S. Highway 30 and the Union Pacific. Along with scores of freight trains, nearly a dozen passenger trains—including name trains like the City of Denver, the City of San Francisco, and the City of Los Angeles—made stops at the imposing brick station on Front Street near the north edge of the business district. The station, later the site of the famous World War II North Platte Canteen, was a key point in the city's life. But in 1956, when the route for I-80 was selected, North Platte's downtown was bypassed. For most travelers on I-80 today, North Platte is a familiar green sign and an exit outside of town at the junction of U.S. 83 and the Interstate. Like so many other Nebraska towns created by the Union Pacific—towns like Cozad, Lexington, and Grand Island—the Interstate left them just off the new main stem of the nation.[34]

What happened in North Platte was duplicated throughout the Great Plains. Hays, Kansas, is a typical plains town initially shaped by the railroad, cattle drives, and the presence of a nearby military outpost. The Union Pacific came to Hays in 1867. Cattle, cowboys, and a town marshal named Hickock soon followed. By 1956 those days were a memory, but the railroad depot at 10th and Walnut was still busy with trains like the Portland Rose, the City of Saint Louis, and local runs. Going to Denver by rail meant passing though downtown Hays. Travelers bound by car for Salina drove through downtown, perhaps stopping to buy gas and have a quick lunch. But when I-70 came to Hays in 1966–67, all that began to change. The Portland Rose and the City of Saint Louis still stopped at Hays, but most travelers increasingly took the Interstate. For them as for travelers today, Hays meant the intersection of I-70 and U.S. Highway 183, an interchange surrounded by an expanding number of motels, fast-food restaurants, and service stations. Hays became less a town or a downtown and more a place outside of town to buy gas, find a quick meal, or a bed overnight. The railroad has not left Hays; the Union Pacific is still there today, serving the elevators of the Midland Marketing Cooperative. But for most adventurers heading to the Rockies, Hays is the highway on the edge of town, not the railway downtown.[35]

ERHAPS NO ENTREPRENEUR BETTER UNDERSTOOD THE changes in transportation and distribution in rural America than Sam Walton. From his small-town origins in Oklahoma, Missouri, and Iowa, Walton saw those markets as great opportunities in the same way as Richard Sears had nearly a century before. Sears had grasped the meaning of the railroad; Walton did not miss the significance of the highway, the expansion of long-haul trucking, and the growing network of interstates. When major trucking companies were unwilling to serve Walton's small-town customers, he moved to create his own inter-modal system. Walton's first distribution center, built outside Bentonville, Arkansas, had a rail siding that allowed buying in bulk quantities. Especially in the years before completion of the Interstate Highway System, boxcars could bring more goods at lower prices than trucks. From there, Walton's own truck fleet could deliver shipments directly to the growing number of Wal-Mart stores. As the Wal-Mart empire expanded, trucks and interstates became an essential part of the distribution system. Some of the most recent distribution centers do not have direct rail access, but nearly every item sold at Wal-Mart—and certainly those goods from the Pacific Rim—comes into the Wal-Mart world by rail.[36]

When John Stover published his pioneering railroad history in 1970, the book was titled *The Life and Decline of the American Railroad*. In the railroad West of the 1960s, the word "decline" seemed especially apt. Beginning in the 1950s, many secondary lines dropped off railroad employee timetables and out of the *Official Guide of the Railways*. Eventually more than 8,000 miles of track would be ripped up. Great Plains states like Oklahoma, Kansas, Nebraska, and Texas all lost more than a thousand miles of track. The railroad landscape of the West visibly changed as highways replaced roadbeds, distribution centers took the place of freight houses, and gas stations edged out locomotive shops and servicing facilities. The Burlington Lines' proud slogan "Everywhere West" might have better read "Nowhere West" as far as passenger travel was concerned.

Few events were more symbolic of this change than what happened on August 22, 1986. That day, outside Salt Lake City, the last section of I-80 was complete. Thirty years and fifty-five days after Eisenhower had signed legislation creating the Interstate Highway System, the first transcontinental highway became something more than MacDonald's dream. No newspaper reporter missed a telling coincidence. Seventy-five miles north of I-80, and 117 years earlier, Promontory had been the site of the golden spike ceremony. The ritual had once been all about tracks and locomotives; now it was concrete and cars.

Opposite: Before Wal-Mart there was Montgomery Ward; its Chicago distribution center was described as a "busy bee hive" in this cutaway illustration. *Courtesy of Chicago Historical Museum.*

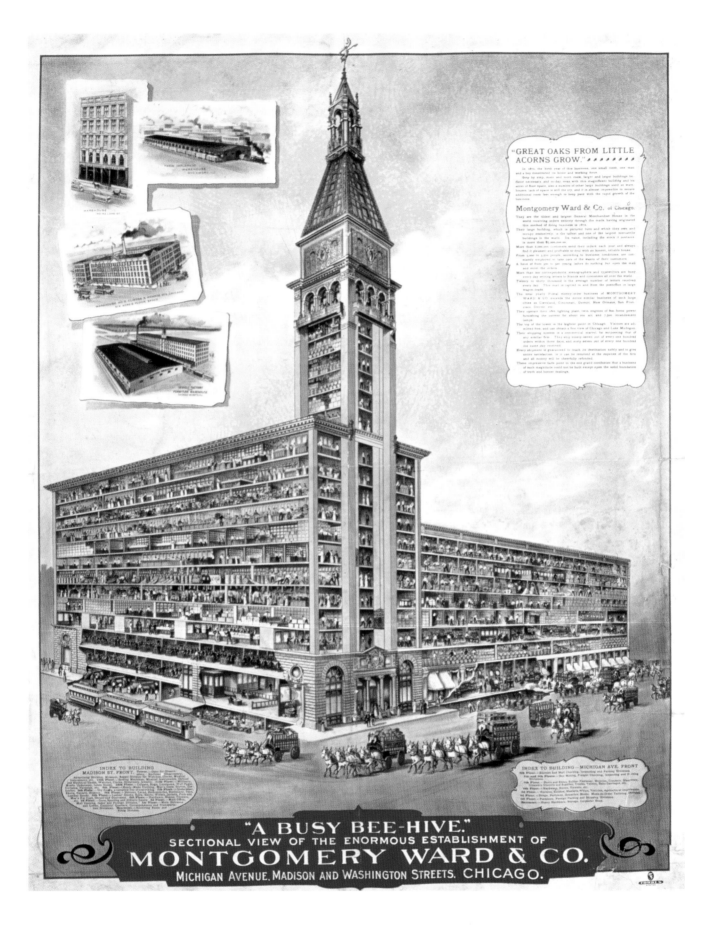

The Burlington route once
advertised, "We'll show you
the West." After most railroads
of the West transferred their
remaining passenger service
to Amtrak in 1971, this slogan
seemed sadly ironic. *Courtesy of
Barriger Railroad Library of the
St. Louis Mercantile Library.*

T HE RAILROAD WEST WAS BECOMING THE AUTOMOBILE
West, but railroads had not vanished from the world between
Chicago, Saint Louis, and the Pacific Coast. Perhaps the revived
fortunes of western railroads began in 1970 with the emergence of the

Burlington Northern—a merger of the Chicago, Burlington, and Quincy; the Northern Pacific; the Great Northern; and the Spokane, Portland and Seattle Railway. Ten years later, at the time the Staggers Act diminished the power of the Interstate Commerce Commission and opened the way for long-blocked mergers, the Burlington Northern purchased the Frisco. Fifteen years later the Burlington Northern acquired the Santa Fe to become one of the West's super-railroads. Watching from its headquarters in Omaha, the venerable Union Pacific was not about to be left behind. Following the same merger and consolidation strategy, the Union Pacific added the Missouri Pacific and the Western Pacific in 1982. The Union Pacific reached superrailroad status with the addition of the Denver and Rio Grande Western and the Southern Pacific in 1996. Freed of passenger obligations with the creation of Amtrak in 1971, the Union Pacific and the Burlington Northern Santa Fe developed a simple but effective business strategy. They would become what some called "dry canals," carrying bulk commodities like coal and grain from the interior West to mid-western and eastern markets.

Few places are more representative of the way railroads continue to shape the West than the Powder River Basin of eastern Wyoming. In August 1811 a fur trade expedition led by Wilson Price Hunt made its way through the vast grasslands of the basin. Searching for a route over the mountains and to the Columbia River, Hunt and his men could not have known they were walking over what is probably the world's largest reserve of low-sulfur coal. Hunt had fur on his mind. Later adventurers sought coal. If Hunt retraced his steps today, he would see one of the West's most industrialized landscapes.

Prompted by the requirements of the 1970 Clean Air Act and the threat of continued oil embargos, mining companies began building a series of deep shafts, strip mines, and towering coal loaders. These mining complexes dot the basin country from Douglas north to Gillette. The coal mines are the largest in the world. To bring that "PRB" coal to power plants as far away as Georgia and Texas demanded the kind of high-speed, low-cost transportation only railroads could provide. Acting together, Burlington Northern Santa Fe and Union Pacific built the Orin Line, sometimes known as the Coal Line. This 100-mile extension was the first major rail line construction in the United States since the 1930s. On any given day some sixty-five fully loaded coal trains leave the mines by way of the Orin Line. Weighing anywhere from 19,000 to 23,000 tons, a unit train of 120 to 130 hoppers stretches out a mile and three-quarters from head-end locomotive to rear-end pusher. In a year the Orin Line carries some 23,000 fully loaded trains.

In early 1812 Hunt finally reached the Columbia, the river Thomas Jefferson

believed was the far western part of the fabled Northwest Passage. Jefferson's easy route up the Missouri River, across the mountains, and down the Columbia to the Pacific proved an illusion. But if Hunt stopped today at the Bridge of the Gods on the Oregon side and looked across the river, he might see the daily parade of BNSF trains. Those mile-long freights bear witness to a passage idea that is anything but dead. Along with the ever-present grain trains that rumble through the gorge, there are trains with containers marked APL, K-Line, and Hanjin full of shoes, shirts, and consumer electronics from Asian factories bound for shelves at Target and Wal-Mart. Along the Columbia, the passage is more iron than water, more locomotive than boat.

Robert Stuart, one of Hunt's fellow fur traders, was near present-day North Platte in late March 1813, on his way back to Saint Louis. Were he to visit North Platte today, Stuart would encounter the Union Pacific's Bailey Yard, the world's largest railroad freight facility. North Platte's passenger station is gone, as are the name trains. In its place is the Triple Track Main, the busiest freight line in the world. Standing trackside, Stuart might see endless strings of coal trains, container trains, and grain trains. From the Columbia River gorge and the Powder River Basin by way of North Platte's Bailey Yard, this is the railroad West today.[37]

WHEN ALBRO MARTIN PUBLISHED HIS *RAILROADS Triumphant: The Growth, Rejection, and Rebirth of a Vital American Force* in 1992, the book had more than a catchy title. It reflected the revitalization of railroads as part of a national transportation system. Railroads had once Americanized the West. Historian Maury Klein put it simply: "The one supreme effect of the railroads may have been their role in literally making the United States a nation."[38] Asa Whitney and a dozen other visionaries would have nodded in agreement. Now, at the beginning of the twenty-first century, railroads are part of the global West—one that stretches from Shanghai, Pusan, and Nagoya to Fort Worth, Tulsa, and Bismarck by way of Seattle, Tacoma, Saint Louis, and Chicago.

Railroads were once an ever-present part of daily life in the West. Few westerners were beyond the railroad's reach. Trains, tracks, depots, and roundhouses were in the western foreground. Once upon a time in the West the most important business publication was the *Official Guide of the Railways*, first published the year before Promontory. Traffic managers today spend more time consulting highway maps and maritime shipping schedules. Now, in the first years of the twenty-first century, western superrailroads and smaller regional carriers have moved into the background. Railroads that were once uncommon have become part of the common landscape, so common as to be nearly invisible. If the railroad establishment is no longer at the center of western life, perhaps it is because the Iron Road has become so fully a part of what is today's West.

In creating the railroad West, visionaries, publicity agents, and railroaders of all sorts drew on two powerful dreams. First, the West promised a land of beginning again. This was the place where big dreams might produce grand success. James J. Hill is reputed to have said that every man needs a dream, and that the Great Northern was his. He might have added that the West gave him space enough for such a dream and the possibility of success. Second, if the West was the place to escape the past and embrace the future, it was also the garden of the world. This was a country blessed with fertile soil, plentiful rain, and abundant sunshine. A Santa Fe poster promoting lands in southwest Kansas summed up all the lure of the West in four revealing images. A farm in the woods could only produce a miserable field dotted with rotting tree stumps. But the railroad offered "A Start on the Prairies." From that start might spring bountiful wheat fields and a handsome house to match. Railroads were the most pervasive symbol of a nearly unshakable faith in progress by machine. Locomotives meant power, what Walt Whitman called "the pulse of the continent."[39] The machine in the garden was no remote abstraction. Some Americans believed that the locomotive made the wilderness a garden. This was the real magic of railroad iron. Railroads provided the means to spread the spiritual rewards and material values of what railroad journalist Henry Varnum Poor proudly called "the refinement and intellectual culture of a high civilization."[40]

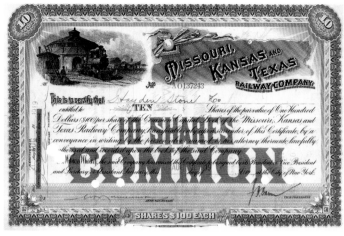

One key feature of a landscape defined by steam railroads was the locomotive roundhouse, depicted here on a stock certificated (reduced in size from the original) issued in 1919 by the Missouri, Kansas, and Texas Railway Company, an integral part of the Union Pacific's modern landscape of the West since 1989. *Courtesy of Barriger Railroad Library of the St. Louis Mercantile Library.*

BUT LIKE ANY OTHER PLACE TOUCHED BY A NEW TECHNOLOGY, the West could not escape Henry George's law of compensation. Historical geographer D. W. Meinig once described railroads as "a radical, transforming instrument."[41] As an instrument of national ambition and corporate power, railroads transformed the West in profound and enduring ways. At the most sweeping level, railroads brought the modern industrial world into the West and in turn shaped the way westerners understood that world. It was as if the metropolitan corridor John Stilgoe describes in the book of the same name expanded beyond the railroad right-of-way to become the railroad West. Railroad lines on a map of the West became the West itself.

Railroads of the West once bragged about every new technological advance. A Milwaukee Road brochure from the mid-1920s showcased the brawny General Electric locomotives used to haul its premier passenger trains over the mountains of Montana, Idaho, and Washington along the way between Chicago and Puget Sound. *Courtesy of Special Collections, Washington State Historical Society.*

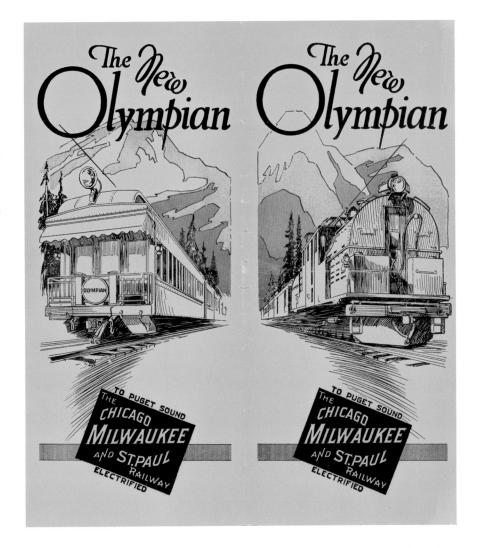

The signs of transformation were everywhere. Prairie country was fenced or plowed to make range land and farm land. Grasslands became coal fields. Mountains were drilled and blasted to become mines. Almost overnight, seemingly empty places became towns like Cheyenne and North Yakima. Relatively small, homogeneous human populations were edged out by large, diverse ones. Work in the West once meant hunting, trapping, and small-scale agriculture. None of that completely disappeared, but work increasingly meant something done for a wage in a shop, mill, or laundry. Railroads brought a new labor force to the West, one that was often disgruntled and sometimes violent. Old plant species were crowded out as railroads brought settlers eager to plant Turkey Red wheat in Kansas or Pacific Bluestem wheat in the Palouse of southeastern Washington State. Animal life in the West changed as bison, wolves, and coyotes made way for cows, sheep, and pet dogs. And wrapped around all of this was a new understanding of time. The old clock of sunrise and sunset was replaced by the mechanical predictability of a clock set to railroad time.

This was the railroad West, the West given a new shape by the locomotive, the market, and the corporate state. But all these transformations—no matter how passionately advanced or eagerly embraced—came at some cost. The price of living in the railroad West included ethnic tensions, as newcomers from Norway, China, and the German states argued—sometimes violently—about their place under the western sky. Racial tensions between newcomers and first-comers exploded as railroads brought a tidal wave of settlers into Indian Country. Little wonder that Frances Palmer's *Across the Continent: Westward the Course of Empire Takes Its Way* depicted Indians enveloped in a plume of smoke from a westbound locomotive. Army General William Tecumseh Sherman made the connection between railroads and Indian dispossession brutally clear when he matter-of-factly reported, "Immigration and the occupation by industrious farmers and miners of land vacated by the aborigines have been largely instrumental [in ending the Indian Wars], but the *railroad* which used to follow in the rear now goes forward with the picket-line in the great battle for civilization with barbarism, and has become the *greater* cause."[42] As part of industrial America, the West could not escape industrial turmoil. Those struggles highlighted an increasingly rancorous debate about railroads and corporate power in public life. Crusading journalists, reform-minded novelists, and Populist Party orators brought to light the seamy realities of political corruption as railroad officials and politicians exchanged bribes and favors for a sympathetic hearing or a vote. The physical world also paid a price. Environments rich in diversity were replaced by monocultures of wheat, corn, and sugar beets—crops more valuable in a global market economy.

Perhaps the highest price came in a sense of helplessness and disillusionment. The inventors and promoters of the railroad West made extravagant promises beyond keeping. This was the garden of the world, they said; a paradise on earth, the best place to begin again. At the heart of those promises was the dream of independence. But all too often promises of independence turned into realities of dependence. Westerners found their lives and futures increasingly in the hands of businessmen and politicians far distant from Montana homesteads, Colorado mines, and the wheat fields of the Palouse. Empty farmhouses, abandoned towns, and boarded-up railroad stations were testimony to overexpansion and overpromising. It was not the land that had failed. The failure came when those who created the railroad West and those who lived in it believed they could control nature and shape it to their own desires. Unbridled arrogance, unpredictable weather, and the "iron hand" of the market place often made the

western
NORTH DAKOTA

Northern Pacific Railway

West a field of shattered dreams and lost fortunes. The famous Milwaukee Road poster showing a farmer slicing his way across Montana as the earth curling off the plow's moldboard turned to gold coins suggests the promise. But, as in western Oklahoma, the Great Plow-up turned dirt to dust.

Plowing coins from the rich soil that supposedly defined the Milwaukee Road's right-of-way across Montana. No agrarian could misunderstand the symbolism. *Courtesy of University of Montana.*

As they stood trackside at opposite ends of the continent, Henry D. Thoreau and Henry George might have cautioned western folk eager to welcome the railroad that every train carried cargoes of progress and poverty, triumph and failure. Writing for the *Railroad Gazette* in 1884, a journalist confidently described railroads west of the Mississippi as "one of the greatest industrial feats in the world's history."[43] What the writer politely ignored was the dispossession, disappointment, and sometimes even death that came with the shriek of the locomotive whistle. The men who famously waved hats and whiskey bottles at Promontory in 1869 could not have known that every mile of track would transform the West in ways both unimagined and unexpected.

Across the continent on the Kansas Pacific. *Courtesy of Barriger Railroad Library of the St. Louis Mercantile Library.*

Notes

Foreword

Thomas Hart Benton, "Lecture on the Progress of the Age," delivered before the St. Louis Mercantile Library Association, November 14, 1850.

Hudson E. Bridge, president of the St. Louis Mercantile Library and the Pacific Railroad Company, address at the annual meeting of the St. Louis Mercantile Library Association, January 1852.

Preface

William H. Maher, The Golden West: "Where Money Grows on Trees," (Toledo, OH: (1911), 51.

Title page

John Herapath, The Railway Magazine and Annals of Science, vol. 1, no.1 (March 1836), 1.

Charles Francis Adams, Jr., and Henry Adams, *Chapters of Erie* (1871; repr., New York: Augustus M. Kelley Publishers, 1967), 338.

Chapter One

Israel E. Dwinnell, *The Higher Reaches of the Great Continental Railway: A Highway for Our God* (Sacramento: H. S. Crocker, 1869), as quoted in William Deverell, *Railroad Crossing: Californians and the Railroad, 1850–1910* (Berkeley: University of California Press, 1994), 1.

1 Henry D. Thoreau, *Walden,* ed. Jeffrey S. Cramer, 2 (New Haven: Yale University Press, 2004).

2 Henry D. Thoreau, "Walking," in *Henry David Thoreau: Collected Essays and Poems,* ed. Elizabeth Hall Witherell, 234 (New York: Library of America, 2001).

3 Thoreau, *Walden,* 90, 186.

4 Ibid., 116.

5 Ibid., 114–15.

6 Ralph Waldo Emerson, "The Young American," in *Ralph Waldo Emerson: Essays and Lectures,* ed. Joel Porte (New York: Library of America, 1983), 213.

7 Henry Adams, *The Education of Henry Adams,* ed. Jean Gooder (New York: Penguin Books, 1995), 11.

8 I. Edwards Clarke, "By Rail to the Rocky Mountains," *The Galaxy* 6 (November 1868): 668.

9 William Wordsworth, as quoted in Michael Robbins, *The Railway Age* (London: Routledge and Kegan Paul, 1962), 62.

10 John M. Niles, *Hunt's Merchants' Magazine* 21 (July 1849), as quoted in Henry Nash Smith, *Virgin Land: The American West as Symbol and Myth* (Cambridge, MA: Harvard University Press, 1950), 11.

11 Asa Whitney, *Address of Mr. A. Whitney before the Legislature of Pennsylvania* (Harrisburg, PA: M'Kinley and Lescure, 1848), 12.

12 Sidney Dillon, "Historic Moments. V. The Last Spike of the Union Pacific," *Scribner's Magazine* 12 (August 1892): 253.

13 [Hezekiah Niles], *Niles' Weekly Register* 48 (April 25, 1835): 129.

14 Henry Varnum Poor, "The Pacific Railroad," *North American Review* 128 (June 1879): 671.

15 "The Pacific Railroad and How It Is to be Built," *Putnam's Monthly Magazine* 2 (November 1853): 500.

16 Asa Whitney, "The Proposed Railroad to the Pacific," *Hunt's Merchants Magazine* 19 (November 1848): 529.

17 Dillon, "Last Spike," 254.

18 J. K. Medbery, "Our Pacific Railroads," *Atlantic Monthly* 20 (December 1867): 715.

19 John Loughborough, *The Pacific Telegraph and Railway* (Saint Louis: Charles and Hammond, 1849), 47.

20 Harold Perkin, as quoted in Michael Freeman, *Railways and the Victorian Imagination* (New Haven: Yale University Press, 1999), 27.

Tracks through Clear Creek Canyon in Colorado. *Courtesy of Barriger Railroad Library of the St. Louis Mercantile Library.*

The Georgetown Loop in the Rocky Mountains west of Denver, Colorado, formed a popular tourist attraction. The engineering marvel surmounted the challenges posed by rugged but scenic terrain. *Courtesy of Barriger Railroad Library of the St. Louis Mercantile Library.*

21 Speech of the Hon. Isaac I. Stevens to the House of Representatives, May 25, 1858, 35th Cong., 1st sess., *Congressional Globe*, 430.

22 Medbery, "Our Pacific Railroads," 715.

23 "The Pace that Kills," *World's Work* 13 (March 1907): 8595–96, as quoted in John R. Stilgoe, *Metropolitan Corridor: Railroads and the American Scene* (New Haven: Yale University Press, 1983), 25.

24 Willa Cather, *A Lost Lady* (New York: Vintage Books, 1990), 45.

25 Guillaume Poussin, as quoted in Leo Marx, *The Machine in the Garden: Technology and the Pastoral Ideal in America* (New York: Oxford University Press, 1964), 208.

26 William C. Redfield, *Sketch of the Geographical Rout of a Great Railway* (New York: 1830), as quoted in Richard V. Francaviglia and Jimmy L. Bryan, Jr., "'Are We Chimerical in this Opinion': Visions of a Pacific Railroad and Westward Expansion before 1845," *Pacific Historical Review* 71 (May 2002): 183. Italics in original.

27 [Hezekiah Niles], *Niles' Weekly Register* 40 (June 18, 1831): 285.

28 Samuel Dexter, *Western Emigrant*, February 6, 1832, as quoted in Margaret Louise Brown, "Asa Whitney: Projector of the Pacific Railroad" (PhD dissertation, University of Michigan, June, 1930), 70.

29 Letter from Reverend Henry Harmon Spalding, Fort Vancouver, September 20, 1836, in *Missionary Herald* 33 (October 1837): 425.

30 Francaviglia and Bryan, "'Are We Chimerical,'" 183n10.

31 Samuel Parker, *Journal of an Exploring Tour beyond the Rocky Mountains* (Ithaca, NY: Mark, Andrus, and Woodruff, 1838), 73.

32 Whitney, *Address*, 8.

33 James J. Hill, as quoted in Claire Strom, *Profiting from the Plains: The Great Northern Railway and Corporate Development of the American West* (Seattle: University of Washington Press, 2003), 42.

34 Asa Whitney, *A Project for a Railroad to the Pacific* (New York: George W. Wood, 1849), 39.

35 Whitney, *Address*, 14.

36 Ibid.

37 Asa Whitney, "A Memorial Praying a grant of public land to enable him to construct a railroad from Lake Michigan to the Pacific Ocean," February 24, 1846, 29th Cong., 1st sess., Senate documents, no. 161, 8.

38 Whitney, *Address*, 9.

39 Ibid., 15.

40 "The Great Pacific Railroad," *American Whig Review* 10 (July 1849): 70.

41 D. W. Meinig, *The Shaping of America*, vol. 3, *Transcontinental America, 1850–1915* (New Haven: Yale University Press, 1998), 8.

42 "The Great Pacific Railroad," 78.

43 Clarke, "By Rail to the Rocky Mountains," 668.

44 Charles Nordhoff, "California," *Harper's New Monthly Magazine* 44 (May 1872): 877.

45 Craig Miner, *West of Wichita: Settling the High Plains of Kansas, 1865–1890* (Lawrence: University Press of Kansas, 1986), 27.

46 J. D. Cox, *Report of the Secretary of the Interior, 1869*, 41st Cong., 2nd sess., House executive document 1, serial 1414, vii.

47 Samuel Bowles, *Our New West* (Hartford: Hartford Publishing Co., 1869), 73.

48 Ibid., v.

49 J. H. Noteware, *The State of Nebraska* (Lincoln: Nebraska State Board of Immigration, 1873), as quoted in David M. Emmons, *Garden in the Grasslands: Boomer Literature of the Southern Plains* (Lincoln: University of Nebraska Press, 1971), 54.

50 Chicago, Rock Island and Pacific Railroad Company, *Western Trails* (January 1887), as quoted in Emmons, *Garden in the Grasslands*, 35–36.

51 Nordhoff, "California," 877.

52 Thoreau, *Walden*, 119.

53 Henry George, "What the Railroad Will Bring Us," *Overland Monthly* 1 (October 1868): 298.

54 Ibid., 303.

55 Ibid., 306.

56 Robert P. Porter, *The West from the Census of 1880* (Chicago: Rand, McNally and Co., 1882), 575.

57 Ibid., 577.

Ernte-Maſchine.

Opposite, above: Shoshone Falls on the Snake River of southern Idaho. Clever railroad publicists advertised it as the Niagara Falls of the West. *Courtesy of Barriger Railroad Library of the St. Louis Mercantile Library.*

Opposite, below: In a world still dominated by agricultural production, railroad publicists used illustrations from farm and ranch life to encourage Europeans to seek new opportunities in the American West. *Courtesy of Barriger Railroad Library of the St. Louis Mercantile Library.*

Chapter Two

Report of the St. Louis Delegation to Omaha and Terminus of the Union Pacific Railroad (Saint Louis: George Knapp and Co., 1869), 84.

1 The first bridge of any type across the Mississippi River was completed in early 1855 to link Saint Anthony and Minneapolis, Minnesota. The wire suspension bridge extended 630 feet.

2 *Missouri Republican*, April 24, 1854.

3 As quoted in James H. Lemly, "The Mississippi River: St. Louis' Friend or Foe?" *Business History Review* 39 (Spring 1965): 9.

4 *The Northern Pacific Railroad: Its Land Grant, Traffic, Resources, and Tributary Country* (New York: Jay Cooke & Co., 1873), 38.

5 *The Illustrated Miners' Hand-Book and Guide to Pike's Peak* (Saint Louis: Parker & Huyett, 1859).

6 Samuel Parker, *Journal of an Exploring Tour beyond the Rocky Mountains* (1838; repr., Minneapolis: Ross & Haines, 1967), 310–11, 343.

7 Nathaniel Philbrick, *Sea of Glory: America's Voyage of Discovery, the U. S. Exploring Expedition, 1838–1842* (New York: Penguin Books, 2003), 18–21.

8 As quoted in Tom Chaffin, *Pathfinder: John Charles Frémont and the Course of American Empire* (New York: Hill and Wang, 2002), 391.

9 Ibid.

10 Karen Meador, "An Unlikely Champion: Jefferson Davis and the Pacific Northwest" *Columbia* (Winter 2004–05): 16.

11 "Guide to the Sceneries of St. Louis County" (Saint Louis: E. and C. Robyn, 1852), 8. Copy in Special Collections, Washington University, Saint Louis.

12 *Address of Thomas Allen of St. Louis to the Board of Directors of the Pacific Railroad Company at their First Meeting, January 31, 1850* (Saint Louis: Printed at the Republican Office, 1850), 3, 4.

13 As quoted in James Neal Primm, *Lion of the Valley: St. Louis, Missouri, 1764–1980*, 3rd ed. (Saint Louis: Missouri Historical Society Press, 1998).

14 Letter from W. Milnor Roberts to Samuel Wilkeson, September 23, 1878, Letter Press, Washington State Historical Society.

15 David P. Billington, *The Tower and the Bridge: The New Art of Structural Engineering* (Princeton: Princeton University Press, 1985), 113.

16 In the 1870 census, the population of Saint Louis was 310,864 to Chicago's 298,877. Historians have suggested that Saint Louis census takers dishonestly inflated the figures. By that date, Chicago was almost certainly ahead in population.

17 Paul F. Sharp, *Whoop-Up Country: The Canadian-American West, 1865–1885* (Minneapolis: University of Minnesota Press, 1955), 157.

AQUEDUCT OF THE PLATTE CANAL, CROSSING PLUM CREEK AT ACEQUIA STATION, NEAR DENVER, COLO.
LENGTH, 1,000 FEET; WIDTH, 36 FEET; DEPTH, 7 FEET.

Railroads promoted irrigation of the American West as a way to transform the "Great American Desert" into a new Garden of Eden. *Courtesy of Barriger Railroad Library of the St. Louis Mercantile Library*

This book is presented with the compliments of the
Western Pacific Railway Company

More Pounds of the

POTATO

are produced than of any other

Food Crop in the World

There are nearly 250,000 Acres
of land in California and Nevada

along the line of the

Western Pacific

that are adapted to the
Potato Culture
Sow the crop from which you reap
the greatest harvest

PLANT POTATOES

The Western Pacific, built in the early twentieth century to link Salt Lake City with San Francisco Bay, promoted potato production along its right-of-way. This carrier was one of several latecomers that received no donation of federal land to support its construction; nonetheless, it had much to gain from promoting settlement and agricultural development. *Courtesy of Special Collections, Washington State Historical Society.*

Chapter Three

Henry George, "What the Railroad Will Bring Us," *Overland Monthly* 1 (October 1868), 392.

1   George, "What the Railroad Will Bring Us," 297–306 passim.

2   Eugene V. Smalley, *Completion of the Cascade Division Northern Pacific R. R.* (St. Paul: Pioneer Press Company, 1887).

3   *The Pacific Northwest* (New York: 1882).

4   Charles Francis Adams, Jr., and Henry Adams, *Chapters of Erie* (1871; repr., New York: Augustus M. Kelly, 1967), 346.

5   Smalley, *Completion of the Cascade Division.*

6   *Wonderland Junior* (Saint Paul: 1888), 21.

7   Northern Pacific Railroad, "Information for Contractors" [1878]. Photocopy in Edward W. Nolan papers, Washington State Historical Society.

8   *Rules Governing Uniforming of Employes and Specifications of Uniforms* ([Saint Paul]: Northern Pacific Railway Company, 1913).

9   "Rules and Regulations," obverse of Oregon Railway & Navigation Company "Schedule No. 10, Railway Division, effective December 11, 1881." Original in Special Collections, Washington State Historical Society.

10 As quoted in Lawrence O. Christensen and Gary R. Kremer, *A History of Missouri, 1875 to 1919* (Columbia: University of Missouri Press, 1997), 28.

11 As quoted in David Prerau, *Seize the Daylight: The Curious and Contentious Story of Daylight Saving Time* (New York: Thunder's Mouth Press, 2005), 47.

12 Charles Shackford, "Asleep at the Switch" (Chicago: E. T. Paull Music Co., 1897). The sheet music is preserved in Special Collections, Washington State Historical Society.

13 Union Pacific, *Seventeenth National Irrigation Congress, Spokane, Washington* (Omaha: 1909). The brochure featured a picture of the Chicago-Portland Special speeding along the Union Pacific track west of Omaha, protected by signals that tell the engineer "Proceed!"

14 Ray Stannard Baker, "Destiny and the Western Railroad," *Century Magazine* 75 (April 1908): 892.

15 Copy of Indian ticket (Saint Paul: 1886). Preserved in Special Collections, Washington State Historical Society.

16 From *Settlers' Guide to Oregon and Washington Territory* (New York: Land Department, Northern Pacific Railroad, 1873), 30.

17 *The Northern Pacific Railroad: Its Land Grant, Traffic Resources, and Tributary Country* (New York: Jay Cooke & Co., 1871), 4.

18 Great Northern Railway, "Opening of Three Indian

Willamette Steam Mills. Scenes of heavy industry as well as sublime spectacles of nature, such as Yellowstone geysers, the Great Salt Lake, or the Grand Canyon, appealed to many tourists who traveled west to view for themselves the wonders of the rapidly developing region. *Courtesy of Barriger Railroad Library of the St. Louis Mercantile Library.*

After lumber companies harvested the timber of the Great Lakes, they found a new source of supply in the "timber billions" of the Pacific Northwest in the early twentieth century. *Washington State Historical Society.*

Reservations" (Seattle: 1909). The broadside is preserved in Special Collections, Washington State Historical Society.

19 Northern Pacific Railway, *Summer Tours to the North Pacific* (Saint Paul: North Pacific Rail Road, 1913), 3.

20 Governor Marshall F. Moore, December 9, 1867, as quoted in Charles M. Gates, ed., *Messages of the Governors of the Territory of Washington to the Legislative Assembly, 1854–1889* (Seattle: University of Washington Press, 1940), 142.

21 Letter from W. Milnor Roberts to Samuel Wilkeson, September 23, 1878. Photocopy in Edward W. Nolan papers, Washington State Historical Society.

22 Lewis Atherton, *Main Street on the Middle Border* (Bloomington: Indiana University Press, 1954), 231.

23 Christensen and Kremer, *A History of Missouri,* 43.

24 Three generations of Casteens worked for the Atlantic Coast Line Railroad in Wilmington, North Carolina. Ruth Casteen, the grandmother of Carlos Schwantes, recalled that one important benefit railroad families enjoyed was free travel by train. She thus felt deprived when my grandfather lost his job as a result of the great shopmen's strike of 1922, thus ending the family connection to railroading.

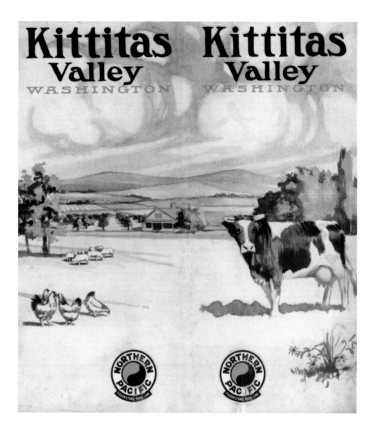

Washington's bucolic Kittitas Valley, as idealized by a Northern Pacific brochure in the early twentieth century. *Courtesy of Special Collections, Washington State Historical Society.*

Chapter Four

   Olin D. Wheeler, *Indianland and Wonderland* (Saint Paul: Northern Pacific Railroad, 1894).

1   Charles F. Adams, Jr., and Henry Adams, *Chapters of Erie* (1871; repr., New York: Augustus M. Kelly, 1967).

2   Northern Pacific Railroad, *Statement of Its Resources and Merits, as Presented to the Pacific Railroad Committee of Congress* (Washington: Intelligencer Printing, 1868).

3   [Northern Pacific Railroad Company], *The Pacific Northwest: Information for Settlers and Others* (New York: John C. Rankin, Jr., 1883)

4   *Descriptive of Yakima County, Washington Territory, for the Benefit of Immigrants* (North Yakima, WA: Yakima Signal, 1887), 23.

5   Ibid.

6   *The Northern Pacific Railroad: Its Land Grant, Traffic Resources, and Tributary Country* (New York: Jay Cooke & Co. 1871).

7   Adams and Adams, *Chapters of Erie*, 346.

8   [Northern Pacific Railroad Company], *The Pacific Northwest*, 30.

9   *Descriptive of Yakima County*, 27, 29.

10   William H. Maher, *The Golden West: "Where Money Grows on Trees"* (Toledo, OH: 1911), 6.

11   *Settlers' Guide to Washington Territory and to the Lands of the Northern Pacific Railroad on the Pacific Slope* (Portland: Land Department, [1880]).

12   John Brent, as quoted in *Empire of the West* (Omaha: Union Pacific Railroad, 1910), 15.

13   Sylvester Mowry to his father, September 16, 1853, Washington State Historical Society.

14   Letter from W. Milnor Roberts to Addie Roberts, July 26 [1869], as quoted in Edward W. Nolan, "Exploring the Northern Pacific Railroad Route: W. Milnor Roberts' Letters from the Expedition of 1869" (master's thesis, University of Oregon, 1971).

15   Letter from W. Milnor Roberts to Samuel Wilkeson, September 23, 1878, Letter Press, Washington State Historical Society.

16   *Descriptive of Yakima County.*

17   From "Guide to the Sceneries of St. Louis County," (Saint Louis: E. and C. Robyn, 1852). Copy in Special Collections, Washington University, Saint Louis.

18   Letter from W. Milnor Roberts to Samuel Wilkeson, September 23, 1878, Letter Press, Washington State Historical Society.

19   Ibid.

20   *Corn Primer* (Portland: Union Pacific System, [1916]).

21   *The Old Timer and the Home Seeker* (Portland: Sunset Magazine Homeseeker's Bureau, 1911), 15.

22   Northern Pacific Railway Company invoice, Office of the General Emigration Agent, 1901, preserved at the Washington State Historical Society.

23   Olin D. Wheeler, *Eastward through the Storied Northwest* (Saint Paul: Northern Pacific [1906]).

24   Wheeler, *Indianland and Wonderland.*

25 Great Northern Railway, "Short Jaunts for Little Money in Glacier National Park" [ca. 1914].

26 Richard Harding Davis, *The West from a Car-Window* (New York: Harper and Brothers, 1892), 225.

27 Northern Pacific Railway, *Summer Tours to the North Pacific* (St. Paul, MN: Northern Pacific Railway, 1913], 3.

Railroad publicists tried to make relocation simple. If such promotions were undertaken today, brochures of this genre might be titled "Immigration for Dummies." Not all railroad publicists assumed that farmers were relocating to the West from another agricultural region. Some brochures were obviously directed to city dwellers, who were presumed to know very little about farming and needed all the good advice that was available. *Courtesy of Special Collections, Washington State Historical Society.*

28 Observations of Richard Goode, 1883, original at Washington State Historical Society.

29 "Guide to the Sceneries," 1. The Pacific Railroad of Missouri issued this early brochure in 1852, when its tracks were still confined to the Saint Louis area.

30 *On the Wings of the Wind* (Saint Paul: Northern Pacific Railway, 1910).

31 Northern Pacific Railway, *Tourist Sleeping Car* (1915), 9.

32 *The New Olympian* (1927).

33 *There is a Happy Land: The Pacific Northwest* (1923)

Like father, like son: advertising farmland in northern Idaho and western Montana in terms of creating an inheritance for your children. *Courtesy of Special Collections, Washington State Historical Society.*

Although railroads devoted tons of paper and rivers of ink to advertising the lightly populated lands of the Great Plains and Rocky Mountains, railroads opened other parts of the trans-Mississippi West as well. When the Kansas City Southern constructed a line south from Kansas City to the Gulf of Mexico, photographers and wordsmiths were ready to work their magic on the landscapes of eastern Texas and western Louisiana. The same was true even for the Florida frontier during the Gilded Age, when oil baron Henry Flagler extended his Florida East Coast Railway as far south as Key West to foster rapid agricultural development, city growth (most notably of Miami), and upscale tourism along the state's Atlantic coast.

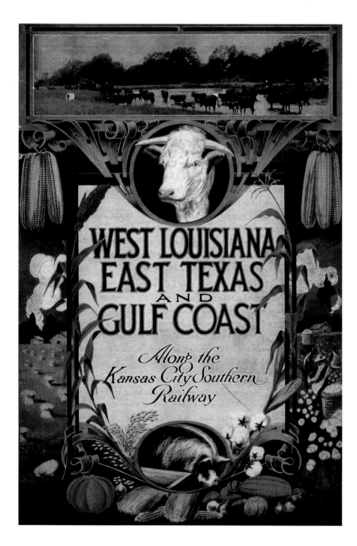

A visually appealing brochure issued in the early twentieth century by the Kansas City Southern Railway. *Courtesy of Barriger Railroad Library of the St. Louis Mercantile Library.*

Chapter Five

Samuel Bowles, *Across the Continent: A Summer's Journey to the Rocky Mountains, the Mormons, and the Pacific States* (Springfield, MA: Samuel Bowles and Co., 1865), 19.

1 W. W. Cox, *History of Seward County, Nebraska* (Lincoln: State Journal Company, 1888), 111.

2 Maury Klein, *Union Pacific: Birth of a Railroad, 1862–1893* (Garden City, NY: Doubleday and Company, 1987), 385.

3 John R. Stilgoe, *Metropolitan Corridor: Railroads and the American Scene* (New Haven: Yale University Press, 1983), 209.

4 William Cronon, *Nature's Metropolis: Chicago and the Great West* (New York: W. W. Norton & Co., 1991), 180–81.

5 Ibid.

6 Sidney Dillon, "Historic Moments. V. The Last Spike of the Union Pacific," *Scribner's Magazine* 12 (August 1892): 254.

7 Frank Norris, *The Pit: A Story of Chicago* (New York: Curtis Publishing Company, 1902), 79–80.

8 E. H. Saltiel and George Barnett, comps., *History and Business Directory of Cheyenne and Guide*

to the Mining Regions of the Rocky Mountains (Omaha: Omaha Republican Printing Office, 1868;New Haven: Yale University Library, 1975), 6, 22, 36.

9   These examples are drawn from Stilgoe, *Metropolitan Corridor*, 199.

10 Samuel Bowles, *The Pacific Railroad—Open. How to Go: What to See. Guide for Travel to and through Western America* (Boston: Fields, Osgood and Company, 1869), 5.

11 The phrase belongs to Craig Miner as the title for chapter three of his *West of Wichita: Settling the High Plains of Kansas, 1865–1890* (Lawrence: University Press of Kansas, 1986)

12 Walter P. Chrysler with Boyden Sparks, *Life of an American Workman* (New York: Dodd, Mead and Company, 1937), 31.

13 This analysis is based on D. W. Meinig, *The Shaping of America*, vol. 3, *Transcontinental America, 1850–1915* (New Haven: Yale University Press, 1998), 253–65.

14 Bowles, *Pacific Railroad*, 5.

15 Robert P. Porter, *The West from the Census of 1880* (Chicago: Rand, McNally and Co., 1882), 558.

16 Henry Varnum Poor, *American Railroad Journal*, January 18, 1851, in James A. Ward, *Railroads and the Character of America, 1820–1887* (Knoxville: University of Tennessee Press, 1986), 29.

17 Northern Pacific Railway Company, *Annual Report for 1883*, in Julius Grodinsky, *Transcontinental Railway Strategy, 1869–1893* (Philadelphia: University of Pennsylvania Press, 1962), 423.

18 *Railroad Gazette*, August 1, 1884, in Grodinsky, *Transcontinental Railway Strategy*, 429.

19 Ibid.

20 Henry C. Adams, "Second Annual Report," Interstate Commerce Commission, 1888, in Meinig, *Shaping of America*, 3:247.

21 E. P. Ripley to Henry B. Stone, November 6, 1888, in Grodinsky, *Transcontinental Railway Strategy*, 331, 334.

22 *Railroad Gazette*, February 26, 1886, in Grodinsky, *Transcontinental Railway Strategy*, 319.

23 Frank Norris, *The Octopus: A Story of California* (1901; repr., New York: Penguin Books, 1994), 538.

Railroad advertising of the West in the early twentieth century emphasized the unparalleled opportunity the region offered newcomers. In those days, the railroad companies did more to promote the West to the world than all state government efforts combined. *Courtesy of Special Collections, Washington State Historical Society.*

24 Woodrow Wilson, "Annual Message to Congress," December 5, 1916, in *The Papers of Woodrow Wilson*, 69 vols., ed. Arthur S. Link et al. (Princeton, NJ: Princeton University Press, 1966–1994), 40:156. My analysis of Wilson's decision is based on K. Austin Kerr, "Decision for Federal Control: Wilson, McAdoo and the Railroads, 1917," *Journal of American History*, 54 (December 1967): 550–60.

25 Chrysler, *Life of an American Workman*, 103–4.

26 Warren G. Harding, April 12, 1921, in James J. Flink, *The Car Culture* (Cambridge, MA: MIT Press, 1975), 140.

27 These statistics are compiled in James J. Flink, *America Adopts the Automobile, 1895–1910* (Cambridge, MA: MIT Press, 1970), 75, table 2.1.

28 James J. Flink, *The Automobile Age* (Cambridge, MA: MIT Press, 1988), 229. See also Reynold M. Wik, *Henry Ford and Grass-roots America* (Ann Arbor: University of Michigan Press, 1972), especially chapters 1–3.

29 The term "automobility" was coined by John C. Burnham in his article "The Gasoline Tax and the Automobile Revolution," *Mississippi Valley Historical Review* 48 (December 1961): 435–59, and has been used widely in the work of James J. Flink.

30 Chrysler, *Life of an American Workman*, 104.

31 David Plowden, *A Time of Trains* (New York: W. W. Norton, 1987), 13.

32 Thomas Harris MacDonald, "The Urgent Necessity for Uniform Traffic Laws and Public Safety Devices," in Tom Lewis, *Divided Highways: Building the Interstate Highways, Transforming American Life* (New York: Penguin Books, 1997), 18.

33 Pierce Lewis, "The Landscapes of Mobility," in *The National Road*, ed. Karl Raitz (Baltimore: Johns Hopkins University Press, 1996), 36

34 Lewis, *Divided Highways*, 155–58, and personal observation.

35 Personal observation, July 2006.

36 Sandra S. Vance and Roy V. Scott, *Wal-Mart: A History of Sam Walton's Retail Phenomenon* (New York: Twayne Publishers, 1994), 51, 71.

37 John McPhee, "Coal Train," *The New Yorker* (October 3 and 10, 2006): 72–83 and 62–71, and conversations with John L. Allen, chair, Department of Geography, University of Wyoming.

38 Maury Klein, *Unfinished Business: The Railroad in American Life* (Hanover: University Press of New England, 1994), 17.

39 Walt Whitman, "To a Locomotive in Winter," *Leaves of Grass and Selected Prose*, ed. John Kouwenhoven (New York: Modern Library, 1950), 367.

Railroads of the West once maintained a sizeable fleet of cars to ship live cattle to market. Cattle traffic by rail is now only a memory, but other commodities of the West, notably coal and grain, remain vital to railroad prosperity. *Courtesy of Barriger Railroad Library of the St. Louis Mercantile Library.*

40 Poor, *American Railroad Journal*, June 28, 1851, in Ward, *Railroads and the Character of America*, 28.

41 Meinig, *Shaping of America*, 3:5.

42 William Tecumseh Sherman, "Report, October 27, 1883," in *Documents of United States Indian Policy*, 2nd ed., ed. Francis Paul Prucha (Lincoln: University of Nebraska Press, 1990), 159.

43 *Railroad Gazette*, August 8, 1884, in Grodinsky, *Transcontinental Railway Strategy*, 429.

Suggestions for Further Reading

Achenbach, Joel. *The Grand Idea: George Washington's Potomac and the Race to the West.* 2004. Reprint, New York: Simon & Schuster, 2005.

Adler, Jeffrey S. *Yankee Merchants and the Making of the Urban West: The Rise and Fall of Antebellum St. Louis.* New York: Cambridge University Press, 1991.

Ambrose, Stephen E. *Nothing Like It in the World: The Men Who Built the Transcontinental Railroad, 1863–1869.* New York: Simon & Schuster, 2000.

Ambruster, Kurt E. *Orphan Road: The Railroad Comes to Seattle, 1853–1911.* Pullman: Washington State University Press, 1999.

Athearn, Robert G. *Union Pacific Country.* Chicago: Rand McNally, 1971.

Bain, David Haward. *Empire Express: Building the First Transcontinental Railroad.* New York: Viking, 1999.

Bartky, Ian R. *Selling the True Time: Nineteenth-Century Timekeeping in America.* Stanford: Stanford University Press, 2000.

Beebe, Lucius, and Charles Clegg. *The Trains We Rode,* 2 vols. Berkeley, CA: Howell-North Books, 1965–66.

Belcher, Wyatt Winton. *The Economic Rivalry Between St. Louis and Chicago, 1850–1880.* New York: Columbia University Press, 1947.

Best, Gerald M. *Snowplow—Clearing Mountain Rails.* Burbank, CA: Howell-North Books, 1966.

Billington, David P. *The Tower and the Bridge: The New Art of Structural Engineering.* Princeton: Princeton University Press, 1985.

Borchgrave, Alexandra Villard de, and John Cullen. *Villard: The Life and Times of an American Titan.* New York: Doubleday, 2001.

Chandler, Alfred D., Jr. *Henry Varnum Poor: Business Editor, Analyst, and Reformer.* Cambridge: Harvard University Press, 1956.

Chittenden, Hiram Martin. *History of Early Steamboat Navigation on the Missouri River: Life and Adventures of Joseph La Barge.* 2 vols. New York: Francis P. Harper, 1903.

Cook, Richard J. *The Beauty of Railroad Bridges in North America—Then and Now.* San Marino, CA: Golden West Books, 1987.

Cotterill, R. S. "The National Railroad Convention in St. Louis, 1849." *Missouri Historical Review* 12 (July 1918): 203–15.

Cronon, William. *Nature's Metropolis: Chicago and the Great West.* New York: W. W. Norton & Company, 1991.

Portland and the Columbia River, as advertised by a Northern Pacific brochure in 1916. *Courtesy of Special Collections, Washington State Historical Society.*

A brochure cover from *Western Trips for Eastern People.* Railroad publicists sought to offer the perfect combination of western wildness and familiar hometown comforts to lure vacationers from the East. *Courtesy of Special Collections, Washington State Historical Society.*

Danley, Susan, and Leo Marx, eds. *The Railroad in American Art: Representations of Technological Change.* Cambridge: MIT Press, 1988.

Davis, Clarence B., and Kenneth E. Wilburn, Jr., eds. *Railway Imperialism.* New York: Greenwood Press, 1991.

Derleth, August. *The Milwaukee Road: Its First Hundred Years.* New York: Creative Age Press, 1948.

Deverell, William. *Railroad Crossing: Californians and the Railroad, 1850–1910.* Berkeley: University of California Press, 1994.

Dorin, Patrick C. *The Domeliners: A Pictorial History of the Penthouse Trains.* Seattle: Superior Publishing Company, 1973.

Douglas, George H. *All Aboard! The Railroad in American Life.* New York: Marlowe & Company, 1995.

Dubin, Arthur D. *More Classic Trains.* Milwaukee: Kalmbach Publishing, 1974.

———. *Some Classic Trains.* Milwaukee: Kalmbach Publishing, 1964.

Emmons, David M. *Garden in the Grassland: Boomer Literature and the Central Great Plains.* Lincoln: University of Nebraska Press, 1971.

Fifer, J. Valerie. *American Progress: The Growth of the Transport, Tourist, and Information Industries in the Nineteenth-Century West.* Chester, CT: The Globe Pequot Press, 1988.

Flink, James J. *America Adopts the Automobile, 1895–1910.* Cambridge: MIT Press, 1970.

——— *The Automobile Age.* Cambridge: MIT Press, 1988.

——— *The Car Culture.* Cambridge: MIT Press, 1975.

Frederick, J. V. *Ben Holladay, The Stagecoach King: A Chapter in the Development of Transcontinental Transportation.* 1940. Reprint, Lincoln: University of Nebraska Press, 1989.

Freeman, Michael. *Railways and the Victorian Imagination*. New Haven: Yale University Press, 1999.

Gordon, Sarah. *Passage to Union: How Railroads Transformed American Life, 1829–1929*. Chicago: Ivan R. Dee, 1997.

Grant, H. Roger. *The North Western: A History of the Chicago & North Western Railway System*. DeKalb: Northern Illinois University Press, 1996.

Grant, H. Roger, Don L. Hofsommer, and Osmund Overby. *St. Louis Union Station: A Place for People, A Place for Trains*. Saint Louis: St. Louis Mercantile Library, 1994.

Greever, William S. "Railway Development in the Southwest." *New Mexico Historical Quarterly* 32 (April 1957): 151–203.

Grodinsky, Julius. *Transcontinental Railway Strategy, 1869–1893*. Philadelphia: University of Pennsylvania Press, 1962.

Hidy, Ralph W., Muriel E. Hidy, and Roy V. Scott, with Don L. Hofsommer. *The Great Northern Railway: A History*. Boston: Harvard Business School Press, 1988.

Hofsommer, Don L. *Minneapolis and the Age of Railways*. Minneapolis: University of Minnesota Press, 2005.

———, ed. *Railroads in the West*. Manhattan, KS: Sunflower University Press, 1978.

——— *The Southern Pacific, 1901–1985*. College Station: Texas A&M University Press, 1986.

Hudson, John C. *Chicago: A Geography of the City and Its Region*. Chicago: University of Chicago Press, 2006.

——— "Railroads and Urbanization in the Northwestern States." In *Centennial West: Essays on the Northern Tier States*, edited by William L. Lang, 169–93. Seattle: University of Washington Press, 1991).

Hunter Louis C. *Steamboats on the Western Rivers: An Economic and Technological History*. Cambridge: MA: Harvard University Press, 1949.

Jackson, W. Turrentine. *Wagon Roads West: A Study of Federal Road Surveys and Construction in the Trans-Mississippi West, 1846–1869*. 1964. Reprint, Lincoln: University of Nebraska Press, 1979.

Keiser, John H. *Building for the Centuries: Illinois, 1865–1898*. Urbana: University of Illinois Press, 1977.

Klein, Maury. *Unfinished Business: The Railroad in*

Enjoying the scenic West from the rear platform of a Northern Pacific observation car. *Courtesy of Special Collections, Washington State Historical Society.*

American Life. Hanover: University Press of New England, 1994.

Lass, William E. *A History of Steamboating on the Upper Missouri*. Lincoln: University of Nebraska Press, 1962.

Lemly, James H. "The Mississippi River: St. Louis's Friend or Foe?" *Business History Review* 39 (Spring 1965): 7–15.

Lubetkin, M. John. *Jay Cooke's Gamble: The Northern Pacific Railroad, the Sioux, and the Panic of 1873*. Norman: University of Oklahoma Press, 2006.

Lyden, Anne M. *Railroad Vision: Photography, Travel, and Perception*. Los Angeles: J. Paul Getty Museum, 2003.

MacKay, Donald. *The Asian Dream: The Pacific Rim and Canada's National Railway*. Vancouver, BC: Douglas & McIntyre, 1986.

Served by the passenger trains of four different railroads, Yellowstone Park was probably advertised more than any other natural feature of the West. *Courtesy of Special Collections, Washington State Historical Society.*

Martin, Albro. *James J. Hill and the Opening of the Northwest*. New York: Oxford University Press, 1976.

———— *Railroads Triumphant: The Growth, Rejection & Rebirth of a Vital American Force*. New York: Oxford University Press, 1992.

McKee, Bill, and Georgeen Klassen. *Trail of Iron: The CPR and the Birth of the West*. Vancouver, BC: Douglas & McIntyre, 1983.

McNichol, Dan. *The Roads that Built America: The Incredible Story of the U. S. Interstate System*. New York: Sterling Publishing, 2005.

Mickelson, Siegfried. "Promotional Activities of the Northern Pacific Railroad's Land and Emigration Departments, 1870 to 1902; A Case Study of Commercial Propaganda in the Nineteenth Century." Master's thesis, University of Minnesota, 1940.

Miller, Donald L. *City of the Century: The Epic of Chicago and the Making of America*. 1996. Reprint, New York: Simon & Schuster, 2003.

Mills, Randall V. *Stern-Wheelers up Columbia: A Century of Steamboating in the Oregon Country*. 1947. Reprint, Lincoln: University of Nebraska Press, 1977.

Nolan, Edward W. *Northern Pacific Views: The Railroad Photography of F. Jay Haynes, 1876–1905*. Helena: Montana Historical Society Press, 1983.

Orsi, Richard J. *Sunset Limited: The Southern Pacific Railroad and the Development of the American West, 1850–1930*. Berkeley: University of California Press, 2005.

Overton, Richard C. *Burlington West: A Colonization History of the Burlington Railroad*. Cambridge, MA: Harvard University Press, 1941.

Pomeroy, Earl. *In Search of the Golden West: The Tourist in Western America*. New York: Alfred A. Knopf, 1957.

Prerau, David. *Seize the Daylight: The Curious and Contentious Story of Daylight Saving Time*. New York: Thunder's Mouth Press, 2005.

Primm, James Neal. "The Economy of Nineteenth-Century St. Louis." In *St. Louis in the Century of Henry Shaw: A View beyond the Garden Wall*, edited by Eric Sandweiss, 103–35 . Columbia: University of Missouri Press, 2003.

Rae, John B. *The Road and the Car in American Life*. Cambridge: MIT Press, 1971.

Rae, W. F. *Westward by Rail: A New Route to the East*. New York: D. Appleton & Company, 1871.

Reed, Robert C. *The Streamliner Era*. San Marino, CA: Golden West Books, 1975.

Richter, Amy G. *Home on the Rails: Women, the Railroad, and the Rise of Public Domesticity*. Chapel Hill: University of North Carolina Press, 2006.

Riegel, Robert Edgar. *The Story of Western Railroads: From 1852 through the Reign of the Giants*. New York: Macmillan, 1926.

Ronda, James P. *Beyond Lewis & Clark: The Army Explores the West*. Tacoma: Washington State Historical Society, 2003.

———— "River Worlds: The Sweep of Cultures on the Columbia." *Columbia* 5 (Fall 1991): 28–33.

Runte, Alfred. *Allies of the Earth: Railroads and the Soul*

Escorted rail tours were once a popular way for tourists to experience the West. *Courtesy of Special Collections, Washington State Historical Society.*

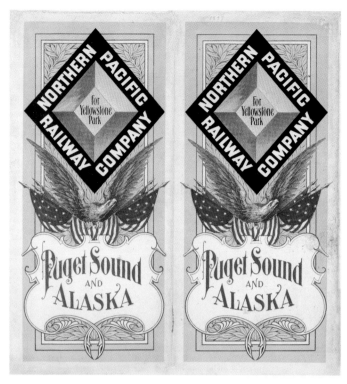

The Northern Pacific apparently used this logo only once, in 1897, when it issued this brochure to attract tourists to Puget Sound, and from there to Alaska by ship. Cruises of the Inside Passage to Alaska date back at least to the early 1880s. *Courtesy of Special Collections, Washington State Historical Society.*

of Preservation. Kirksville, MO: Truman State University Press, 2006.

——— "Promoting the Golden West: Advertising and the Railroad." *California History* 70 (Spring 1991): 62–75.

——— *Trains of Discovery: Western Railroads and the National Parks.* Revised edition. Niwot, CO: Roberts Rinehart, 1990.

Schivelbusch, Wolfgang. *The Railway Journey: Trains and Travel in the 19th Century.* New York: Urizen Books, 1979.

Schnell, J. Christopher. "Chicago Versus St. Louis: A Reassessment of the Great Rivalry." *Missouri Historical Review* 71 (April 1977): 245–65.

Schwantes, Carlos A. *Railroad Signatures across the Pacific Northwest.* Seattle: University of Washington Press, 1993.

Scott, Roy V. *Railroad Development Programs in the Twentieth Century.* Ames: Iowa State University Press, 1985.

Shaffer, Marguerite S. *See America First: Tourism and National Identity, 1880–1940.* Washington: Smithsonian Institution Press, 1991.

Sharp, Paul F. *Whoop-Up Country: The Canadian-American West, 1865–1885.* Minneapolis: University of Minnesota Press, 1955.

Stilgoe, John R. *Metropolitan Corridor: Railroads and the American Scene.* New Haven: Yale University Press, 1983.

Stover, John F. *American Railroads.* 2nd ed. Chicago: University of Chicago Press, 1997.

——— *Iron Road to the West: American Railroads in the 1850s.* New York: Columbia University Press, 1978.

Strom, Claire. *Profiting from the Plains: The Great Northern Railway and Corporate Development of the American West.* Seattle: University of Washington Press, 2003.

Taylor, George Rogers. *The Transportation Revolution, 1815–1860.* New York: Holt, Rinehart and Winston, 1951.

Taylor, George Rogers, and Irene D. Neu. *The American Railroad Network, 1861–1890.* Cambridge: Harvard University Press, 1956.

Vance, James E., Jr. *Capturing the Horizon: The Historical Geography of Transportation since the Sixteenth Century.* 1986. Reprint, Baltimore: Johns Hopkins University Press, 1990.

——— *The North American Railroad: Its Origin, Evolution, and Geography.* Baltimore: Johns Hopkins University Press, 1995.

Wade, Richard C. *The Urban Frontier: The Rise of Western Cities, 1790–1830.* Cambridge: Harvard University Press, 1959.

Ward, James A. *Railroads and the Character of America, 1820–1887.* Knoxville: University of Tennessee Press, 1986.

White, John H. *The Great Yellow Fleet: A History of the American Railroad Refrigerator Cars.* San Marino, CA: Golden West Books, 1986.

White, W. Thomas, ed. "Railroads and the American West." Theme issue of *Journal of the West* 39 (Spring 2000).

Winther, Oscar Osburn. *The Transportation Frontier: Trans-Mississippi West, 1865–1890.* New York: Holt, Rinehart and Winston, 1964.

Wrobel, David M. *Promised Lands: Promotion, Memory, and the Creation of the American West.* Lawrence: University Press of Kansas, 2002.

Wrobel, David M., and Patrick T. Long, eds. *Seeing & Being Seen: Tourism in the American West.* Lawrence: University Press of Kansas, 2001.

Young, David M. *The Iron Horse and the Windy City: How Railroads Shaped Chicago.* Dekalb: Northern Illinois University Press, 2005.

Zega, Michael E., and John E. Gruber. *Travel by Train: The American Railroad Poster, 1870–1950.* Bloomington: Indiana University Press, 2002.

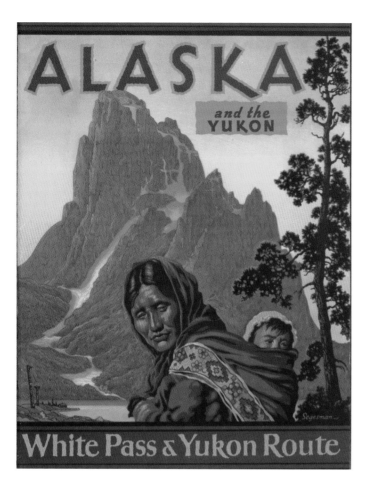

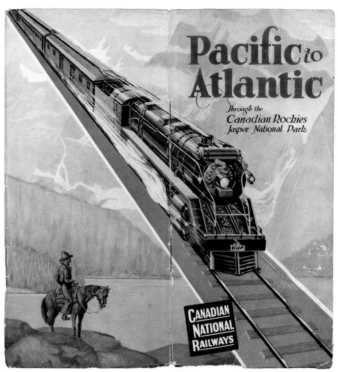

Colorful railroad brochures were by no means limited to the United States. Many different ones appeared during the early twentieth century in such places as Europe, Australia, and Canada. This one from 1925 emphasized the continent-spanning reach of the Canadian National Railways. *Courtesy of Special Collections, Washington State Historical Society.*

The White Pass and Yukon Route linked the port of Skagway, Alaska, with Whitehorse, the capital of Canada's Yukon Territory. Its freight and passenger trains hauled mainly minerals and tourists from the early twentieth century until 1982, the year that through train service ceased. *Courtesy of Special Collections, Washington State Historical Society.*

Opposite: By 1916, Northern Pacific brochures advertising Puget Sound and Alaska had grown much more colorful. That was due in part to turn-of-the-century advances in printing technology pioneered by German postcard manufacturers. *Courtesy of Special Collections, Washington State Historical Society.*

AMERICAN RAILROAD SCENE.
LIGHTNING EXPRESS TRAINS LEAVING THE JUNCTION.

Popular imagery from the post-Civil War era, when railroads were America's "ruling passion."
Courtesy of Library of Congress.

Index

CHOKEMOFF STATION.

SCOOT FOR THE TRAIN WHEN THE GONG SOUNDS.

PUBLISHED BY CURRIER & IVES   COPYRIGHT 1884, BY CURRIER & IVES, N.Y.   115 NASSAU ST. NEW YORK

A WILD CAT TRAIN.
No Stop Overs.

"A Wild Cat Train." *Courtesy of Barriger Railroad Library of the St. Louis Mercantile Library.*

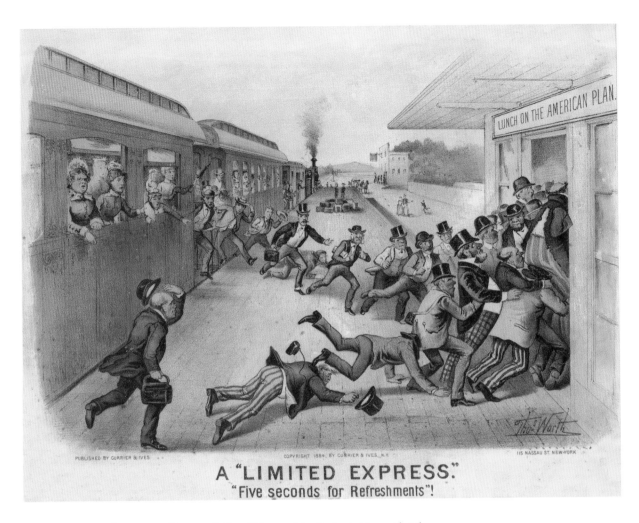

"A Limited Express." Courtesy of Barriger Railroad Library of the St. Louis Mercantile Library.

Railroad iconography was once ubiquitous. This colorful image comes from the cover page for sheet music called "The Midnight Flyer," published in 1903. *Courtesy of Special Collections, Washington State Historical Society.*

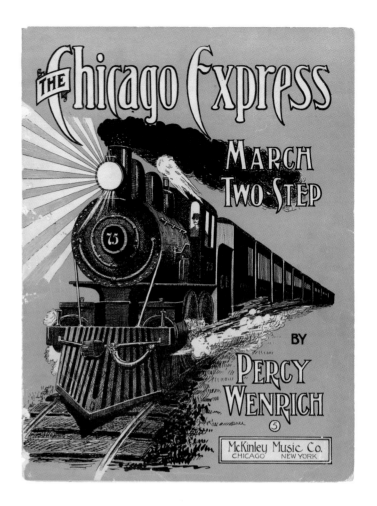

The cover page from sheet music called "The Chicago Express." *Courtesy of Special Collections, Washington State Historical Society.*

The bears and beauties of Glacier National Park. Cute bears with human-like personalities once offered numerous illustrative possibilities for rail promoters on all trunk lines of the West. *Courtesy of Special Collections, Washington State Historical Society.*